Endangered Animals

VOLUME 5

Frog, Green and Golden Bell – **Kestrel,** Lesser

GROLIER EDUCATIONAL

MONMOUTH COUNTY LIBRARY
MARLBORO BRANCH

Published 2002 by Grolier Educational, Danbury, CT 06816

This edition published exclusively for the school and library market

Produced by Andromeda Oxford Limited
11–13 The Vineyard, Abingdon,
Oxon OX14 3PX, U.K.
www.andromeda.co.uk

Copyright © Andromeda Oxford Limited 2002

All rights reserved. No part of this publication may be reproduced, stored in a retrieval system, or transmitted in any form or by any means electronic, mechanical, photocopying, recording, or otherwise, without the permission of the copyright holder.

Principal Contributors: *Amy-Jane Beer, Andrew Campbell, Robert and Valerie Davies, John Dawes, Jonathan Elphick, Tim Halliday, Pat Morris. Further contributions by David Capper and John Woodward*

Project Director: *Graham Bateman*
Managing Editors: *Shaun Barrington, Jo Newson*
Editor: *Penelope Mathias*
Art Editor and Designer: *Steve McCurdy*
Cartographic Editor: *Tim Williams*
Editorial Assistant: *Marian Dreier*
Picture Manager: *Claire Turner*
Production: *Clive Sparling*
Indexers: *Indexing Specialists, Hove, East Sussex*

Reproduction by A. T. Color, Milan
Printing by H & Y Printing Ltd., Hong Kong

Set ISBN 0-7172-5584-0

Library of Congress Cataloging-in-Publication Data

Endangered animals.
      p. cm.
   Contents: v. 1. What is an endangered animal? -- v. 2. Addax - blackbuck -- v. 3. Boa, Jamaican - danio, barred -- v. 4. Darter, Watercress - frog, gastric brooding -- v. 5. Frog, green and golden bell - kestrel, lesser -- v. 6. Kestrel, Mauritius - Mulgara -- v. 7. Murrelet, Japanese - Pupfish, Devil's Hole -- v. 8. Pygmy-possum, mountain - Siskin, red -- v. 9. Skink, pygmy blue-tongued - tragopan, Temminck's -- v. 10. Tree-kangaroo, Goodfellow's - zebra, mountain.
   ISBN 0-7172-5584-0 (set : alk. paper) -- ISBN 0-7172-5585-9 (v. 1 : alk. paper) –
ISBN 0-7172-5586-7 (v. 2 : alk. paper) -- ISBN 0-7172-5587-5 (v. 3 : alk. paper) –
ISBN 0-7172-5588-3 (v. 4 : alk. paper) -- ISBN 0-7172-5589-1 (v. 5 : alk. paper) –
ISBN 0-7172-5590-5 (v. 6 : alk. paper) -- ISBN 0-7172-5591-3 (v. 7 : alk. paper) –
ISBN 0-7172-5592-1 (v. 8 : alk. paper) -- ISBN 0-7172-5593-X (v. 9 : alk. paper) –
ISBN 0-7172-5594-8 (v. 10 : alk. paper)
   1. Endangered species--Juvenile literature. [1. Endangered species.] I. Grolier Educational (Firm)

QL83 .E54 2001
333.95'42--dc21

00-069134

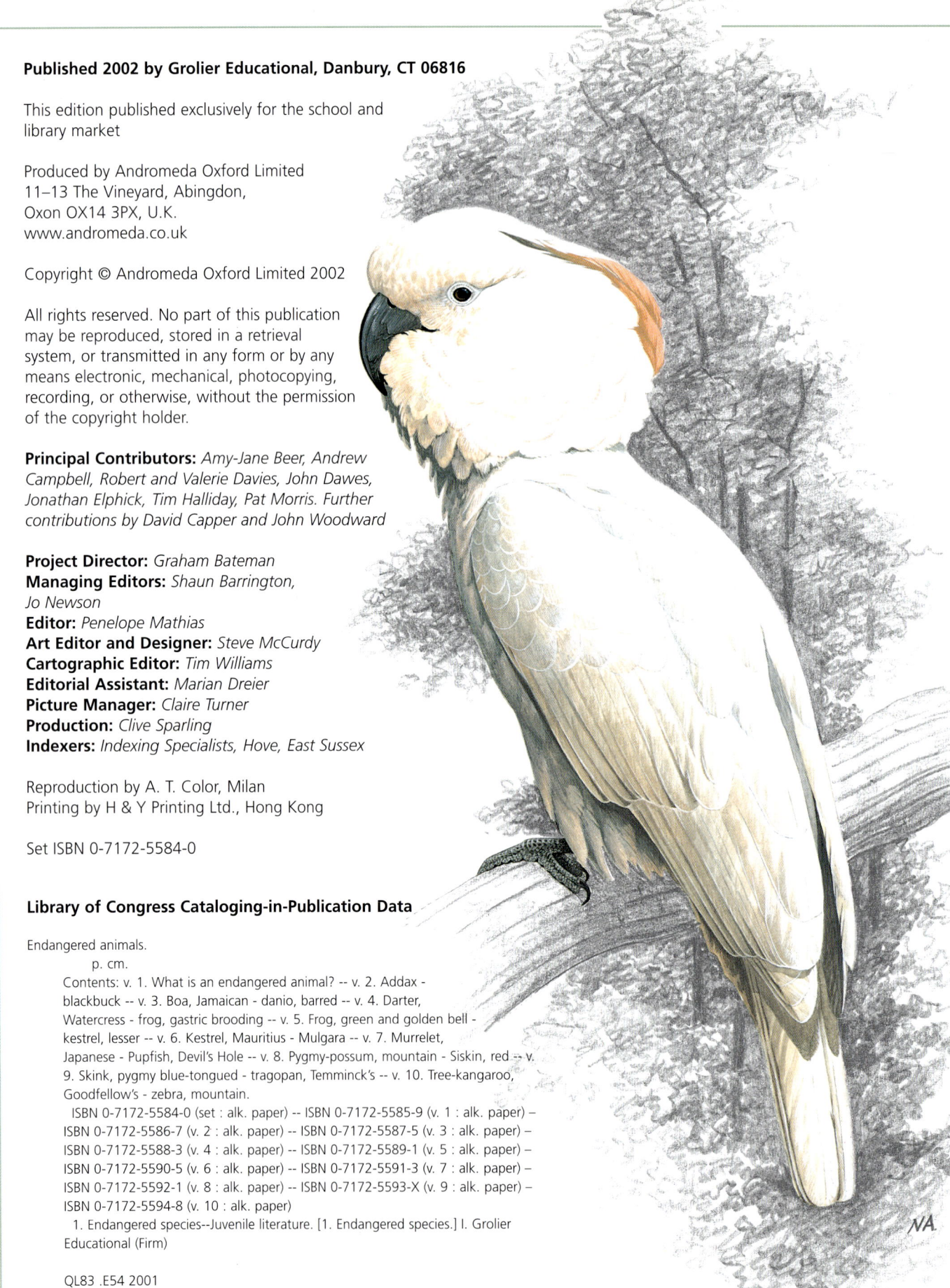

Contents

Frog, Green and Golden Bell	4	**Gorilla,** Mountain	38	**Ibis,** Northern Bald	72
Frog, Hamilton's	6	**Gorilla,** Western Lowland	40	**Iguana,** Fijian Crested	74
Frog, Harlequin	8	**Grebe,** Atitlán	42	**Iguana,** Galápagos Land	76
Frog, Red-Legged	10	**Guan,** Horned	44	**Iguana,** Galápagos Marine	78
Frog, Tinkling	12	**Gull,** Lava	46	**Iguana,** Grand Cayman Blue Rock	80
Frog, Tomato	14	**Gymnure,** Hainan	48	**Ikan Temoleh**	82
Galaxias, Swan	16	**Hare,** Hispid	50	**Indri**	84
Gaur	18	**Hippopotamus,** Pygmy	52	**Jaguar**	86
Gazelle, Dama	20	**Honeyeater,** Regent	54	**Kagu**	88
Gecko, Round Island Day	22	**Hornbill,** Writhed	56	**Kakapo**	90
Gharial	24	**Horse,** Przewalski's Wild	58	**Kea**	92
Gibbon, Black	26	**Huia**	60	**Kestrel,** Lesser	94
Gila Monster	28	**Hummingbird,** Bee	62	Glossary	96
Giraffe, Reticulated	30	**Hutia,** Jamaican	64	Further Reading and Websites	99
Glider, Mahogany	32	**Hyena,** Brown	66	List of Animals by Group	100
Goby, Dwarf Pygmy	34	**Hyena,** Spotted	68	Set Index	102
Goodeid, Gold Sawfin	36	**Ibex,** Nubian	70	Picture Credits and Acknowledgments	112

About This Set

Endangered Animals is a 10-volume set that highlights and explains the threats to animal species across the world. Habitat loss is one major threat; another is the introduction of species into areas where they do not normally live.

Examples of different animals facing a range of problems have been chosen to include all the major animal groups. Fish, reptiles, amphibians, and insects and invertebrates are included as well as mammals and birds. Some species may have very large populations, but they nevertheless face problems. Some are already extinct.

Volume 1—What Is an Endangered Animal?—explains how scientists classify animals, the reasons why they are endangered, and what conservationists are doing about it. Cross-references in the text (volume number followed by page number) show relevant pages in the set.

Volumes 2 to 10 contain individual species entries arranged in alphabetical order. Each entry is a double-page spread with a data panel summarizing key facts and a locator map showing its range.

Look for a particular species by its common name, listed in alphabetical order on the Contents page of each book. (Page references for both common and scientific names are in the full set index at the back of each book.) When you have found the species that interests you, you can find related entries by looking first in the data panel. If an animal listed under Related endangered species has an asterisk (*) next to its name, it has its own separate entry. You can also check the cross-references at the bottom of the left-hand page, which refer to entries in other volumes. (For example, "Finch, Gouldian **4:** 74" means that the two-page entry about the Gouldian finch starts on page 74 of Volume 4.) The cross-reference is usually made to an animal that is in the same genus or family as the species you are reading about; but a species may appear here because it is from the same part of the world or faces the same threats.

Each book ends with a glossary of terms, lists of useful publications and websites, and a full set index.

Frog, Green and Golden Bell

Litoria aurea

One of Australia's most attractive frogs, the green and golden bell frog has vanished from much of its previous range. The reasons for its decline are not fully understood.

The strikingly colored green and golden bell frog is one of the most extrovert of Australia's frogs. A voracious predator, it will readily eat smaller frogs as well as insects. The frogs tend to be active in and around ponds by day. At night they climb into pondside vegetation in search of prey.

The green and golden bell frog breeds in open, shallow ponds, preferring those with emergent vegetation (plants that have most of their growth above the water, such as bullrushes) around the edges. It chooses short-lived or "ephemeral" ponds that dry out during the winter months. Such ponds are ideal breeding sites because they do not support fish that would prey on the frog's spawn and tadpoles. Breeding takes place in the summer, following rain that fills breeding ponds and floods swamps. The breeding season usually lasts from October to March, but is known to begin as early as August in some places.

During breeding males call from open water, producing a deep, growling sound, described as being like "a distant motorbike changing gear." Females produce a clutch of between 3,000 and 10,000 eggs in a floating, gelatinous mass, which sinks to the bottom of the pond after six to 12 hours. The fertilized eggs hatch after two days, and the larvae grow quite large before metamorphosing (changing their physical form) from tadpoles to frogs about two months later.

Dramatic Decline

An abundant species in the 1950s, the green and golden bell frog's current distribution covers only a small part of its original range. The frogs were previously found at altitudes up to 2,300 feet (700 m), but they are now found only at altitudes below 490 feet (150 m). Consequently, it is confined to a few areas close to the coast of New South Wales, where it is categorized as a Threatened species, and Victoria, where it is Vulnerable.

DATA PANEL

Green and golden bell frog (green and golden swamp frog)

Litoria aurea

Family: Hylidae

World population: Unknown

Distribution: Coastal areas in southeastern Australia

Habitat: Large and small ponds with marginal vegetation

Size: Length: male 2.2–2.7 in (5.7–6.9 cm); female 2.5–4.2 in (6.5–10.8 cm)

Form: Body flattened and slender. Coloration green above with irregular bronze patches; flanks brown with cream spots; belly white; groin bright turquoise-blue; long legs brown or bronze. Prominent fold of pale skin runs from behind each eye to the groin; irregular white stripe runs from the corner of the mouth to each armpit. Skin is smooth on the back, granular on the belly. Adhesive disks at the tips of fingers and toes; webbed feet. In the breeding season males develop large nuptial pads on their thumbs

Diet: Invertebrates and other frogs

Breeding: Summer (August–March)

Related endangered species: Several *Litoria* species, notably New England swamp frog *(Litoria castanea)* LRnt

Status: IUCN LRnt; not listed by CITES

See also: Categories of Threat **1:** 14; Introductions **1:** 54; Frog, Hamilton's **5:** 6; Frog, Tinkling **5:** 12

The reason why the species has declined so dramatically is unknown. Much of its habitat has been lost, largely as a result of swamp drainage, but this does not explain why the green and golden bell frog has disappeared so quickly from higher altitudes. It is known that its tadpoles are defenseless against predatory fish. One theory is that the decline is due to the introduction of the North American mosquito fish to control mosquitoes. The evidence is not strong however: There are sites with no mosquito fish where the frogs have also disappeared and others where the fish and frogs coexist. There is also no evidence that the green and golden bell frog has fallen victim to the chytrid fungus that has so seriously affected other frog species farther north, in Queensland.

Population declines were most marked in the 1990s. Of 137 sites where the frogs were reported before this period, they have disappeared from 113. One site that contained an adult population of 138 in 1968 contained only three in 1993. Since 1990 the frog has been reported in only 38 locations, some supporting only five to 15 adult frogs. The largest known population was threatened by the building of a tennis facility for the Sydney 2000 Olympic Games, but the facility was put elsewhere.

The green and golden bell frog is one of a group of species that has suffered population declines. The New England swamp frog, for example, has not been seen since the mid-1970s, although it has been successfully bred in captivity. Captive breeding is also an option for the future conservation of the green and golden bell frog. From a small number of adults a large number of young can be reared for release into the wild. Where the species has been introduced outside Australia, for example, in New Zealand and on some Pacific islands, it has built up large populations.

The green and golden bell frog *gets its name from the coloration on its back: bright green with irregular spots or blotches of gold or bronze.*

Frog, Hamilton's

Leiopelma hamiltoni

Precariously confined to a single protected locality, Hamilton's frog is one of the rarest and most primitive frog species in the world.

New Zealand is the natural home of only four species of frog, all belonging to the Leiopelmatidae family. Three fossil species belonging to the same family have been found in New Zealand, suggesting that it was once a diverse and widespread group of frogs. While some frog species introduced from Australia have thrived and spread in New Zealand, the endemic leiopelmatids have vanished from most of the country and are now confined to tiny areas of protected habitat. The rarest of them, Hamilton's frog, is confined to Stephens Island, in Cook Strait, where it is found in an area of boulder-strewn ground no more than 656 square yards (600 sq. m) in size.

The leiopelmatids share a number of primitive features with the tailed frog of the Pacific Northwest region of North America. They have nine vertebrae in the backbone (most frogs and toads have eight or fewer) and retain into adulthood the muscles that wag the tail in the tadpole stage. Most remarkably, while most frogs swim by kicking their hindlegs simultaneously, leiopelmatids and the tailed frog kick their legs alternately. This suggests that the two kinds of frog, now living in restricted ranges and separated by thousands of miles of ocean, are the direct descendants of a group of frogs that were the ancestors of all other frogs and toads.

Unusual Breeding Strategy

Hamilton's frog lives in cool, humid habitats in coastal forests. A compact and secretive creature, it is brown in color with dark markings on its flanks. It lacks the tympanum (eardrum) that is visible in most frogs, but has large glands just behind its eyes. Unlike many frogs and toads, it does not require standing water for breeding, instead depositing its eggs on land in damp places under rocks and logs. The eggs are large and contain a lot of water. When they hatch, the larvae remain within the egg capsule and complete their development there, emerging after about 40 days as miniature adults, still with tails. The male remains close to the eggs while they develop; when the froglets emerge, they climb onto his back, where they complete their development.

DATA PANEL

Hamilton's frog
Leiopelma hamiltoni
Family: Leiopelmatidae
World population: Fewer than 200
Distribution: Stephens Island, New Zealand
Habitat: Cool, humid areas in coastal forests

Size: Length: 1.5–2 in (3.5–5 cm)
Form: Light to dark brown with darker markings on the flanks; no tympanum (eardrum); eyes have horizontal pupils
Diet: Small invertebrates
Breeding: Eggs laid on land; larval phase completed in the eggs, which hatch into tiny tailed froglets after about 5 weeks

Related endangered species: Archey's frog *(Leiopelma archeyi)* LRnt; Maud Island frog *(L. pakeka)* VU
Status: IUCN VU; not listed by CITES

See also: Introductions 1: 54; Saving the Habitats 1: 88; Frog, Green and Golden Bell 5: 4; Frog, Tinkling 5: 12

FROG, HAMILTON'S

Driven into Marginal Habitats

Isolated for centuries, New Zealand has become home to a unique endemic fauna (animals found only in one place), none of which are mammals. As a result, when mammals such as rats, cats, goats, and pigs were introduced from other parts of the world, many of the native species, most notably several bird species, were defenseless against the new predators. Several of New Zealand's endemic species are now confined to remote habitats such as high mountain ranges and offshore islands that introduced mammals have not been able to colonize. Probably unable to coexist with introduced rodents, New Zealand's native frogs have retreated to similar remote areas. In addition, much of the damp coastal forest that provides their natural habitat has been destroyed and replaced by farmland.

There are three surviving species of New Zealand frogs in addition to Hamilton's frog. Hochstetter's frog is confined to a few patches of forest on North Island, while Archey's frog occurs only in North Island's Coromandel Mountains. The third surviving species—the Maud Island frog— was thought to be Hamilton's frog until fairly recently, but has been found to be genetically distinct. It is confined to Maud Island in Cook Strait, where it is comparatively common.

Hamilton's frog is threatened by further risks common to many rare species. First, there is the danger that a single environmental catastrophe, such as severe weather or a major pollution event, could wipe out the entire population. Second, there is the problem of inbreeding. In small populations genetic variation is reduced because matings between closely related individuals happen more frequently. Reduced genetic variation limits the capacity of a species to adapt to any changes that may occur in its environment. Consequently, the conservation action plan instituted for the endangered Hamilton's frog not only involves continued protection of its remaining habitat, but also the possibility of establishing additional populations elsewhere if suitable localities can be found.

Hamilton's frog inhabits a tiny range some 660 square yards (600 sq. m) in size in a cool, humid area of coastal forest in Cook Strait, New Zealand.

Frog, Harlequin

Atelopus varius

The brightly colored and highly aggressive harlequin frogs have suffered severe declines in recent years, probably because of the combined effects of climate change and disease.

The group of species known as harlequin frogs belong to the genus *Atelopus*. All are noted for their startlingly bright coloration. At present 55 species have been described, but the number is likely to increase as more is learned about this poorly known group.

Harlequin frogs are found in Central and South America, where several species occupy tiny geographic ranges. The frogs live in both dry and wet forest, and are found close to flowing streams at altitudes between sea level and 6,600 feet (2,000 m). They rarely enter the water, but are found on wet rock faces by the side of streams. Both sexes are aggressive, especially when defending a small territory; some individuals have been seen in the same territory for two years.

A harlequin frog's skin secretes powerful toxins, protecting it against predators; its bright coloration is a warning to potential attackers that it is poisonous. Harlequins are unusual among frogs in being conspicuously active during the day.

Extended Breeding Season

The breeding season begins with the start of the rainy season. Males become more aggressive and call to attract females. Pairing occurs from mid-August to December and is prolonged; one pair of harlequin frogs was observed in amplexus (where the male clasps the female for mating) for 32 days. Eggs are laid in flooded pools from October to December, where they hatch quickly. The resulting tadpoles must metamorphose before their pool dries out.

Fighting among harlequin frogs of both sexes is more elaborate and more frequent than in other frogs; most aggressive interactions are about territories. Individuals display to one another, waving forelimbs and feet. If this does not resolve the dispute, they will chase, pounce, and wrestle. The winner is generally the owner of a territory, regardless of who is the larger. Fights between females tend to be shorter than those between males and do not involve wrestling.

A Natural Enemy

Harlequin frogs have a natural enemy that is unaffected by their toxins: a fly that lays its eggs on

---

DATA PANEL

Harlequin frog (clown frog)

Atelopus varius

Family: Bufonidae

World population: Unknown

Distribution: Costa Rica and Panama

Habitat: Close to streams in wet and dry tropical forests

Size: Length: male 1–1.6 in (2.5–4.1 cm); female 1.3–2.3 in (3.3–6 cm)

Form: Highly variable in color; usually yellow or red with black markings. Pointed snout, slender body, and long limbs

Diet: Small invertebrates

Breeding: Occurs during the wet season of May–December. Eggs are laid in pools October–December; tadpoles hatch and develop quickly, metamorphosing before the pool dries out

Related endangered species: Most of the 55 species of *Atelopus* are threatened

Status: Not listed by IUCN; not listed by CITES

See also: Disease 1: 55; Natural Disasters 1: 57; Toad, Golden 9: 70; Toad, Natterjack 9: 74; Toad, Western 9: 76

The harlequin frog's *vivid coloration warns off most predators. However, it is no protection against an invasive fungus or the maggots of a fly that can burrow through the skin.*

their skin. The eggs hatch into maggots that burrow into the frog, eventually killing it. It is possible that the fly is partly responsible for the recent decline that has occurred among harlequin frogs. Periods of drought force frogs to congregate together in whatever damp places they can find, increasing the risk that parasitic flies can get from one frog to another.

Population Declines

Harlequin frogs were abundant in the forests of Costa Rica and Panama up until the late 1980s, but by 1992 they had disappeared from many areas, including Monteverde in Costa Rica. That was a time of marked climate change that was associated with an unusual sequence of climatic events known as El Niño. The result has been a general drying out of the habitat, with longer dry periods and fewer wet days. Climate change is probably not by itself accountable for the dramatic disappearance of harlequin frogs and other frogs in the region, since many parts of the habitat have remained wet. However, dry conditions force frogs of all species to congregate in the remaining wet places, and overcrowding during dry periods has probably increased the spread not only of parasitic flies but of other diseases as well. During the last 10 years Central America has been subject to a major epidemic of the frog disease chytridiomycosis, caused by a parasitic fungus that invades the skin of adult frogs. It is thought that the fungus interferes with the passage of water and oxygen across a frog's skin, or that it produces a substance that is toxic to the frog.

Frog, Red-Legged

Rana aurora

Once one of the most common frogs in western regions of North America, the red-legged frog has vanished from much of its range. It has been badly affected by the direct and indirect impact of humans on its habitat.

The red-legged frog is one of a group of five similar species all belonging to the "true frogs" that have declined dramatically in western North America in the last 20 to 30 years. All have long, muscular legs, smooth skin, and webbing between their hind toes; and all are athletic jumpers. The red-legged frog is the largest and most widely distributed of this group.

Coloration can be brown, gray, olive-green, or red and covered in irregular dark blotches. A dark "mask" on the sides of its head is bordered by a white stripe along the upper jaw. Its eyes point outward, and it has folds of skin running down its back from behind the eyes. The male has larger forelimbs than the female, a greater degree of webbing between the toes, and in the breeding season nuptial pads on his thumbs.

A Variable and Wide-Ranging Frog

Across its range the red-legged frog shows marked variation. Frogs from the north and south are assigned to different subspecies; the southern subspecies has shorter limbs, smaller eyes, rougher skin, and more dark spots, which have pale centers.

The red-legged frog lives in a variety of habitats such as humid forests, woodland, grassland, and along streams. All provide good cover. It occurs from sea level to altitudes of 8,000 feet (2,400 m). For breeding it requires permanent water bodies. Breeding begins in January in the southern part of its range, but in the north it starts as late as April. Males gather at breeding sites and start to call, producing a series of guttural notes. Compared with many frogs, its call is not loud and is often produced underwater. Females lay between 500 and 1,100 eggs in clumps attached to submerged vegetation. The eggs hatch after between one and seven weeks (depending on the water temperature), and the tadpoles metamorphose into frogs 11 to 20 weeks later. Young frogs reach sexual maturity at two years.

Red-legged frogs are generally found only in damp places. They are inactive when it is very cold or very hot, and at such times they disappear underground, either digging themselves into loose soil or making use of the burrows of other animals, such as ground squirrels.

Casualty of Development

The main reason the red-legged frog has disappeared from much of its former range is the

---

DATA PANEL

Red-legged frog

Rana aurora

Family: Ranidae

World population: Unknown

Distribution: Western North America, from British Columbia to Mexico; from sea level to 8,000 ft (2,440 m)

Habitat: Humid forests, woodland, grassland, streamsides with good cover

Size: Length: 1.8–5.3 in (4.4–13.1 cm)

Form: Long legs; eyes point outward; prominent skin folds; red on lower abdomen and underside of hind legs; dark "mask" through eye bordered by white stripe on jaw

Diet: Invertebrates, especially beetles and caterpillars

Breeding: Breeds in permanent water bodies: marshes, streams, lakes, and ponds. Short season 1 or 2 weeks in spring (January–April)

Related endangered species: Vegas Valley leopard frog *(Rana fisheri)* EX; Cascades frog *(R. cascadae)* VU; relict leopard frog *(R. onca)* VU; mountain yellow-legged frog *(R. muscosa)* VU

Status: Not listed by IUCN; not listed by CITES

See also: Pollution 1: 50; Introductions 1: 54; Mantella, Golden 6: 70

destruction of its habitat to make way for housing, industry, and agriculture as the west of the United States and Canada has been developed, and the population has expanded. Although it was the most common frog in San Diego County in the 1960s, the red-legged frog is now extinct in that part of southern California. It has also declined markedly through most of its natural habitat. There are several reasons why.

In the late 1800s and early 1900s the red-legged frog was still abundant. At that time it was collected and its legs sold as food. While this probably affected its numbers in some places, more subtle influences are responsible for its general decline. Western parts of the United States, especially California, have been invaded by a number of alien species that have been introduced—trout, for example. These fish are voracious predators of amphibian tadpoles and have contributed to the demise of red-legged and many other frog species.

In addition, the North American bullfrog (native to eastern and central parts of North America) was

The red-legged frog, *as its name implies, has a distinctive flush of red on the legs, especially on the inside of the thighs, and on the lower abdomen.*

introduced. It does not occur naturally west of the Sierra Nevada and Rocky Mountains. It has thrived to the detriment of native species. Adult bullfrogs grow very large and readily eat smaller native frogs. More importantly, they are very fecund, and their larvae are more competitive in obtaining food than the tadpoles of native frogs.

Another factor that has adversely affected the red-legged frog, as well as other native amphibians, is nitrate pollution. Nitrates wash into the water bodies that frogs use for breeding from nearby agricultural areas where they have been applied as fertilizer.

The decline of the red-legged frog is part of a much larger problem that has affected the wildlife of the American west. Urbanization represents a threat for 188 species of the 286 species in the region that are protected.

Frog, Tinkling

Taudactylus rheophilus

Never a common species, the tinkling frog is one of several frog species that have disappeared from high-altitude forest habitat in Queensland's wet tropics. The cause of the declines is not known, but a fungal disease is strongly suspected.

The tinkling frog was last seen in the wild in 1991. Belonging to the family Myobatrachidae—species that are found in Australia, Tasmania, and New Guinea—it is known to have lived in and around fast-flowing streams in Queensland's wet tropical region. It was confined to a small area of mountains only at altitudes of between 305 and 423 feet (940 and 1,300 m). Little is known about the natural history of this species. However, it is one of a group of similar frogs in the region that have suffered population declines or disappeared.

A smooth-skinned frog, the tinkling frog had no webbing between its fingers or toes. However, it had well-developed adhesive disks at the end of its digits, which enabled it to cling to rock faces. It had a rounded snout, and its ears were hidden beneath the skin. It was red-brown or brown with darker markings on the back, its flanks were dark gray or black, and the belly was yellowish. The pale legs were marked with dark bars.

The mating patterns of the tinkling frog have never been described. It is known that the males called to attract females, producing a soft, metallic call, consisting of a single short note repeated four or five times in quick succession. This "tink-tink" sound gave the species its common name. Its eggs and tadpoles have not been found in nature, although dissected females were found to contain between 35 and 50 large eggs.

Mysterious Disappearance

It is thought that, like other frogs in the region, the tinkling frog declined dramatically in numbers between 1989 and 1991. It is likely that, as in the other species, mortality occurred among adults but not among tadpoles. There is a strong indication that the cause of their decline was the highly virulent chytrid fungus that has affected many frog species, not only in Australia but also in Central America, South America, and Europe.

The chytrid fungus causes a disease called chytridiomycosis. The fungus invades the skin of adult frogs, where it reproduces repeatedly, feeding on keratin—a tough protein found in the skin of most vertebrates. It is not yet known precisely how it kills frogs. It may be that the fungus interferes with the mechanism of respiration across the skin, causing the frog to suffocate; or the fungus may produce a toxin that poisons its host.

DATA PANEL

Tinkling frog (northern tinker frog; northern timber frog)

Taudactylus rheophilus

Family: Myobatrachidae

World population: Probably extinct

Distribution: Northeastern Queensland, Australia

Habitat: Fast-flowing streams in upland rain forest at altitudes between 3,080 and 4,265 ft (940 and 1,300 m)

Size: Length: male 1–1.1 in (2.4–2.7 cm); female 1–1.3 in (2.4–3.1 cm)

Form: Small frog with rounded snout, disks on fingers and toes. Back red-brown or brown with darker markings; flanks dark gray or black; underside yellowish

Diet: Small invertebrates

Breeding: Not observed

Related endangered species: Sharp-snouted day frog (*Taudactylus acutirostris*) CR

Status: IUCN CR; not listed by CITES

See also: Populations **1:** 20; Disease **1:** 55; Frog, Gastric Brooding **4:** 94; Mantella, Golden **6:** 70

Frog tadpoles do not have keratin in their skin, which is why they are apparently not affected by the fungus. They do, however, have keratin in the horny beak that surrounds their mouth. So while they appear unaffected, when a tadpole metamorphoses into a frog, it is probably already infected by the fungus. As the new adult frogs disperse, they probably carry the fungus along the streams, thereby spreading it to other populations.

Vulnerability to Extinction

It is typical of the major population declines that have occurred in the last 20 years among amphibians around the world that while some species have declined, others living in the same areas have been unaffected. This suggests that some species of amphibian have some kind of natural vulnerability to whatever process is adversely affecting amphibians.

The tinkling frog was one of several species that have declined or disappeared in the wet tropics region of Australia, and all have a number of features in common. They all have very specific habitat requirements and thus a restricted range; they all breed in streams and lay only a small number of eggs. These factors may provide a clue to their population declines. The fact that they breed in streams is consistent with their being attacked by the chytrid fungus, a waterborne pathogen. It is likely that the tinkling frog's low reproductive rate also reduced its capacity to recover numbers again following population crashes.

The tinkling frog *had adhesive disks at the end of its digits that enabled it to cling to rock faces.*

Frog, Tomato

Dyscophus antongilii

The red or orange-colored tomato frog of Madagascar has been threatened by habitat destruction, pollution, and overcollection for the pet trade. It is now protected and responding well to captive-breeding programs.

The tomato frog gets its name from the rounded shape of the female and her red coloration, which makes her resemble a ripe tomato. Not all tomato frogs are red; some are orange, others dark brown, and males are generally less vividly colored than females. The frog has a flat head, a rounded body, and white underside; females are considerably larger than males. Their striking coloration, combined with the fact that they thrive in captivity, have made them popular animals in the international pet trade.

Found only in Madagascar, the tomato frog has a small range. It occurs in two main areas on the coastal plain in the northeast of the island. Its preferred habitat is soft soil, where standing water for it to breed in accumulates during the rainy season. A secretive, nocturnal animal, it hides during the day, emerging at night to hunt ground-dwelling invertebrates. The frog's round shape and lack of adhesive disks on its fingers and toes mean that it is unable to climb. Nor is it particularly well adapted for swimming, having only partial webbing between its toes and none between its fingers. During the dry season it burrows deep into sandy soil, using horny protuberances on its hind feet.

Sticky Defense

In many amphibians bright coloration is associated with skin toxins that make them unpalatable or poisonous to potential predators. The tomato frog's bright color serves to warn predators that it is not good to eat. When attacked or handled, it secretes copious amounts of sticky mucus from its skin; any animal trying to eat it is likely to find its jaws glued together. A number of amphibians have this kind of defense, but the tomato frog produces mucus with stronger sticking power than that of any other frog. It is also mildly toxic, often causing an allergic reaction in humans.

Breeding after Rain

With the first indication of rain male tomato frogs emerge from underground and head for ditches, ponds, and pools as they fill with water. It is thought that the sound of rain falling on the ground is a sufficient stimulus to bring males out of hiding. Males call to attract females

DATA PANEL

Tomato frog
Dyscophus antongilii
Family: Microhylidae
World population: Unknown
Distribution: Eastern coastal plains of Madagascar
Habitat: Lowland habitats with soft soil; some agricultural areas
Size: Length: male 2.5 in (6.5 cm); female 3.3–4.8 in (8–12 cm)
Form: Flat head, plump body, partial webbing between toes. Female bright red, occasionally orange or dark brown on the back; belly white. Male has duller, yellow-orange coloration
Diet: Small invertebrates
Breeding: 1,000–1,500 black-and-white eggs laid on water surface; tadpoles hatch within 36 hours; metamorphosis complete at 6.5 weeks; fully mature at 12 months. Life span 10 years
Related endangered species: Neither of the 2 other known species of *Dyscophus* is threatened
Status: IUCN VU; CITES I

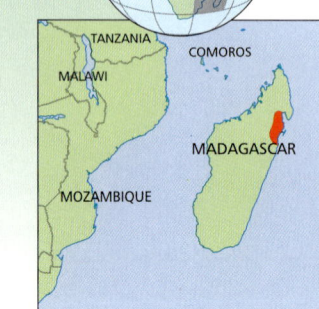

See also: Exploitation of Live Animals 1: 49; Captive Breeding 1: 87; Frog, Gastric-Brooding 4: 94; frog species 4: 94–95 and 5: 4–13

from the edge of the water, inflating a single vocal patch under the chin. Females lay between 1,000 and 1,500 eggs that float on the surface of the water. Filter-feeding tadpoles hatch from the eggs within two days and take a further six weeks to metamorphose into juvenile froglets. The young frogs are about 0.4 inches (1 cm) long by this stage and black or brown with a tan stripe down the back. They develop the characteristic adult colors at about three months and are fully mature by one year.

Threats and Conservation

The tomato frog has a restricted range in Madagascar, and much of its natural habitat has been destroyed to make way for building and agricultural land. This has not been as disastrous for the tomato frog as for other species, since they thrive alongside human activities and habitations. Large breeding populations form in man-made drainage ditches, rice fields, and flooded meadows, but these habitats are susceptible to pollution from pesticides, herbicides, and detergents.

The main threat to the tomato frog comes from the worldwide trade in amphibians. Large numbers used to be exported from Madagascar to Europe and the United States. Although it is nocturnal, the frog's distinctive nighttime call made it possible for poachers to identify and capture it in the dark.

The trade in tomato frogs for pets has now been stopped. The species is fully protected under CITES and breeding successfully in captivity, although lack of genetic diversity is a problem. To help increase diversity, attempts will be made to crossbreed frogs from European and American collections. The aim is also to build up captive populations in Madagascar for export to foreign breeding programs. The pet-trade market could then be met by captive-bred, rather than wild-caught frogs, and captive-bred animals could be used to reestablish populations in the wild.

The female tomato frog's *vivid red color has made it a target of poachers in its native Madagascar. CITES legislation has now outlawed this practice.*

Galaxias, Swan

Galaxias fontanus

In Australia galaxiids and their relatives fill the niche occupied by salmon and trout elsewhere. It is somewhat ironic, therefore, that the Australian salmonlike fish are under threat of extinction partly because of the unnatural presence of their northern cousins in their waters.

The family Galaxiidae, commonly referred to as Galaxias or native minnows, is represented by about 40 species, of which about half occur in Australia. Tasmania is particularly rich in galaxiids, with 15 of the Australian species found there. Some look remarkably like small trout. In fact, one species is so like a trout that it is known as the spotted mountain trout or trout minnow.

Characteristics

Despite overall superficial similarity with their Northern Hemisphere counterparts, galaxiids have a number of features that set them apart. In addition to their small size they have a scaleless body. Perhaps most noticeably, the members of the subfamily Galaxiinae lack an adipose fin—a small, fleshy "second" dorsal (back) fin. The dorsal fin in galaxiids is set so far back on the body that it is more or less in the same spot as the salmon and trout adipose fin. In galaxiids the body is also characteristically "tubular" in cross section—it is rounder than in salmon and trout—while the snout is generally blunt and the head flattened to a greater or lesser extent.

Poorly Known Species

The Swan galaxias, so called because it is known to occur, possibly exclusively, in the upper reaches of the Swan River in eastern Tasmania, is a typical galaxiid.

It is a small species that, like most of the other members of the family, lives its whole life in fresh water. Only a few species, among them the remarkable climbing galaxias, spend any part of their life in the sea, and this only amounts to the first five or six months of their post-hatching development.

The Swan galaxias is believed to have evolved from a landlocked population of ancestral climbing galaxias stock with which it shares the same overall physical characteristics (except size). However, while the biology of climbing galaxias (which can climb waterfalls and rocks) is reasonably well documented, that of the Swan galaxias is very poorly understood.

It is known to feed primarily on aquatic insects, as well as aerial ones that fall into the water, small crustaceans, and algae. It is also known to occur in shoals,

DATA PANEL

Swan galaxias

Galaxias fontanus

Family: Galaxiidae

World population: Unknown; once near extinction, but now expanding

Distribution: At most, several headwater streams of the Swan and Macquarie Rivers in eastern Tasmania; several populations from translocated stocks now established

Habitat: Cool, flowing waters; primarily pools and shallow-water stretches of stream edges associated with submerged logs

Size: Length: up to maximum of 5.3 in (13.5 cm)

Form: Tubular body; dorsal (back) and anal (belly) fins set well back; no adipose (second dorsal) fin. Head flattened with large eyes and blunt snout. Brown to olive-colored body with irregular mottling and a light-colored belly. The fins have little color

Diet: Aquatic and terrestrial insects; some aquatic invertebrates and algae

Breeding: No spawning migrations occur. Spawning is restricted to the spring months, but exact spawning sites, or their nature, are unknown

Related endangered species: Barred galaxias *(Galaxias fuscus)* CR; clarence galaxias *(G. johnstoni)* CR; pedder galaxias *(G. pedderensis)* CR

Status: IUCN CR; not listed by CITES

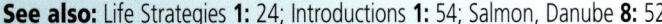

See also: Life Strategies 1: 24; Introductions 1: 54; Salmon, Danube 8: 52

Swan galaxias

populations are thought to be expanding. However, they are still at risk from predation by introduced species.

rather than as solitary individuals, and seems to prefer flowing open water, a trait that places it under risk from predators. Some reports, however, say that the species may also be found "along shallow stream margins around log debris."

Spawning was believed to occur during the Australian spring or early summer, this conclusion being based on the presence of small juveniles during January. More recently, however, the consensus is that spawning occurs only in spring, with the post-hatching to juvenile phase lasting about five weeks. During this time the young fish are said to prefer shallow, slow-flowing water. No spawning migration of adults is believed to be undertaken by this species.

Decline and Recovery

At some stage in the past—probably up to the mid- to late 1800s—the Swan galaxias may have occurred throughout the Swan and Macquarie river basins in eastern Tasmania. In 1862, however, the European perch—known in Australia as the redfin perch—was introduced into Tasmania, followed, two years later, by the arrival in Australia of the brown trout.

Together the two predators decimated the local Swan galaxias population, which from the outset presented an easy target because of its tendency (especially seen in juveniles) to gather in open-water pools. The end result of this constant pressure, exerted over more than 100 years, has been a progressive reduction in both total numbers of Swan galaxias, as well as its range. It is likely that their continued presence in the small, headwater streams of the Swan and Macquarie river tributaries is the direct result of natural barriers such as waterfalls, which prevent the brown trout and redfin perch from gaining access to these water stretches. It is this same "inaccessibility factor" that has been put to work to rescue the species from impending extinction.

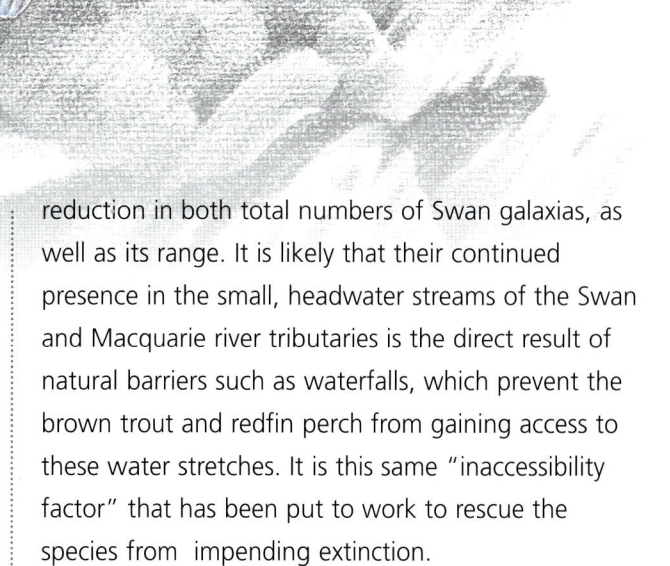

In 1989 the Australian Inland Fisheries Commission initiated a relocation program that transferred Swan galaxias stocks from existing populations to suitable alternative locations out of reach of the predators. The results are proving encouraging, and there are now 12 large and expanding populations.

This seems to bode well for the future of the species. However, a promising future could be thrown away if any of the predatory exotic species are released into any of the new Swan galaxias strongholds. If this happens, it would undoubtedly spell disaster for the species, with the added factor that next time around it might not prove possible to mount another successful rescue mission.

Gaur

Bos frontalis

Pressures of habitat loss and hunting have brought the gaur to crisis point. Scientists have now succeeded in producing a baby gaur—the first endangered animal ever to have been cloned.

The enormous gaur is a tropical equivalent of the yak or bison. Its massive, muscular body is accentuated in males by a large shoulder hump. The thickness of the bull gaur's neck is enhanced by a large flap of skin, called a dewlap, dangling from the throat between the chin and the chest. A shaggy mane like that of a bull yak would be impractical for a gaur, since it needs to keep cool in the tropical heat and spends much of its time pushing through dense vegetation that would snag long hair.

Both male and female gaurs are armed with large, upcurved horns, joined across the top of the head by a prominent brow ridge. The horns look fearsome, but gaurs rarely use them for fighting. Disputes over females occur between rival males, but most of the time they are settled by displays. They give the rivals a chance to size each other up, and the inferior male usually backs off. Females are even less aggressive, and the average gaur mother loses at least half her offspring to the species' main predator, the tiger.

Gaurs sometimes live in herds of up to 40 animals, though groups of 10 to 15 are more usual. Most herds consist of females and young with one mature male. Immature males roam in bachelor groups, awaiting the opportunity to take over a herd of their own. Most births occur between December and June, and young gaurs are integrated into the herd soon afterward. Being part of a herd is a gaur's best defense against predators—there is safety in numbers. At the first sign of danger a gaur will alert the herd by giving a snorting alarm, while standing still and facing the direction of the threat. If the attack continues, the gaur begins to run, sending out further warnings in the form of vibrations as it pounds the ground.

Competition

Predation by tigers is a significant factor in the gaur's decline, but it is difficult to

DATA PANEL	
Gaur *Bos frontalis* **Family:** Bovidae **World population:** Unknown, perhaps upward of 1,000 **Distribution:** India, Indochina, and Malay Peninsula **Habitat:** Tropical thickets and forests **Size:** Length: 8.2–11 ft (2.5–3.3 m); height at shoulder: 5.5–7.2 ft (1.7–2.2 m). Weight: 1,540–2,200 lb (700–1,000 kg)	**Form:** Massive, powerfully built ox with short, dark brown hair and curved horns linked by prominent brow ridge **Diet:** Grasses, bamboo, other shoots, and fruit **Breeding:** One, occasionally 2 calves born at any time of year. Life span up to 30 years **Related endangered species:** Wild yak *(Bos grunniens)** VU; banteng *(B. javanicus)** EN; kouprey *(B. sauveli)** CR; mountain anoa *(Bubalus quarlesi)** EN **Status:** IUCN VU; CITES I

See also: Special Techniques **1:** 88; Banteng **2:** 50; Tiger **9:** 68

know how to tackle the problem without harming the tigers, which are also endangered. It makes better sense to address the other main problem facing the gaur: the expansion of human settlement and livestock farming. Gaurs and domestic cattle compete for the same food; and when domestic herds move in, the gaurs retreat. Where their daily routine is disturbed by people, gaurs become virtually nocturnal.

First Clone

There is no doubt that the gaur is facing a crisis. Several zoos are participating in a species-recovery program, but at the start of the 21st century captive stocks were so low that scientists in Iowa took the drastic step of cloning a gaur. Genetic material—DNA—taken from the skin of a dead gaur was inserted into a cow's egg from which the cow DNA had been removed. The egg was then implanted into the womb of an ordinary cow, where it developed into a normal gaur calf. The calf, named Noah, is the first endangered animal ever to have been cloned.

The arrival of Noah has stirred up a lot of debate. Because clones can be made from dead animals, some people believe that the same techniques could be used to resurrect extinct species. Others say that cloning is unethical and that populations of clones lack the genetic diversity needed to make them stable; the genetic diversity of captive gaur herds already has to be closely monitored to prevent inbreeding.

The gaur *has never been particularly common largely due to the patchy nature of its habitat and its apparent vulnerability to predation.*

Gazelle, Dama

Gazella dama

Elegant desert dwellers, dama gazelles are victims of climate change. As the largest of the gazelles, they make attractive prey to a number of hunters, including humans.

Until relatively recently there were five subspecies of dama gazelle living across much of northern Africa. Sadly, only three remain, mostly in the northwest, and all are in serious decline. Dama gazelles are very much herd animals, usually living in groups of between 15 and 20 animals. They are active by day, braving the desert heat to wander widely in search of food—typically leaves and shoots from scrubby shrubs and trees, especially acacia. In order to browse well above their normal head height, dama gazelles have perfected the art of standing on their two back legs while they stretch up and pluck leaves with their lips and teeth.

Living in herds is a distinct advantage for an animal that is a popular prey. As well as human hunters, dama gazelles are constantly on the alert for lions, hyenas, cheetahs, leopards, and hunting dogs. Even pythons are known to capture smaller specimens and swallow them whole.

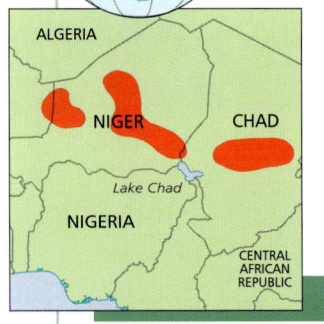

Defense Tactics

Dama gazelles are nervous and alert, with huge, constantly swiveling ears. Their eyes are large and placed toward the side of the head so that the gazelle can see in front, to the sides, and almost behind itself, all without having to turn its head. At the slightest sign of danger a gazelle will raise the alarm by bouncing rapidly up and down on straight legs. This vigorous and conspicuous behavior is known as "pronking" and serves as a warning signal to the rest of the herd; within a fraction of a second they are all on the move. The defense tactics work well enough to preserve most gazelles from predators such as big cats and wild dogs, but they are no match for a human with a rifle.

Herds contain adults of both sexes for much of the year, but between March and June the males detach themselves and set up territories of their own. Normally shy and docile animals, the males become quite fiercely territorial at this time, diligently scent-marking their patch and displaying to females and rival males alike. Having mated, females give birth to a

DATA PANEL

Dama gazelle

Gazella dama

Family: Bovidae

World population: Unknown

Distribution: Mauritania, Mali, Chad, Niger, and part of northern Sudan

Habitat: Semidesert, moving out of desert during dry season

Size: Length: 4.5–5.4 ft (1.4–1.7 m); height at shoulder: 36–48 in (90–120 cm). Weight: 88–165 lb (40–75 kg)

Form: Large, slender gazelle with a white coat marked with variable amounts of reddish brown on the head, neck, back, and legs, depending on subspecies. There is a distinctive white patch on the throat. Both sexes have S-shaped horns

Diet: Grazes grass and herbs; browses leaves and shoots from shrubs and trees

Breeding: Single young born October–January after 6.5-month gestation. Life span up to 12 years

Related endangered species: Several other gazelles, including Arabian gazelle (*Gazella arabica*) EX; sand gazelle (*G. leptoceros*) EN; Cuvier's gazelle (*G. cuvieri*) EN; various other bovids, including Nilgiri tahr (*Hemitragus hylocrius*)* EN and Jentink's duiker (*Cephalophus jentinki*)* VU

Status: IUCN EN; CITES I

See also: Pasture 1: 38; Climate Change 1: 53; Ibex, Nubian 5: 70

single calf, and the youngster is able to get to its feet within an hour or so. After just a week the young gazelles are as swift and nimble as their parents.

Most desert wildlife is nocturnal, but dama gazelles remain active during the day. Not surprisingly, they need more water than most other desert dwellers. Even so, they can still go for days on end without drinking and manage to thrive in conditions that would defeat most of their close relatives. They venture into the Sahara during the rainy season, retreating south to the semidesert of the Sahel when the rains dry up. During the migrations the usually small groups of gazelles form large traveling herds numbering up to 600 animals in the past.

Competition for Food

There has always been intense competition for food in the Sahel, but in most years there was enough to go around. However, the desert and the semiarid Sahel are changing: Global warming and competition with people and livestock for land and food are enemies from which the dama gazelle cannot run. As global temperatures rise, the Sahara is expanding. Once-habitable land on the margins of the desert has lost its scrubby vegetation and is now parched and barren.

The problem is made much worse by the clearance of land for agriculture. The loss of even sparse vegetation to livestock grazing not only deprives the gazelles of food and cover, it allows the desert to gradually engulf what little habitat remains in a merciless sea of baking sand.

Dama gazelles *are distinctive-looking animals. They search the deserts and scrubland of northern Africa for food, migrating from the Sahara to the semiarid Sahel.*

Gecko, Round Island Day

Phelsuma guentheri

The Round Island day gecko is found only on Round Island off the coast of Mauritius. Introduced animals have drastically overgrazed the vegetation, and cyclones have caused severe soil erosion. The island's unique gecko populations have been severely depleted as a result.

Before 1969 several studies of Round Island's wildlife and vegetation had been made. A study in 1975 estimated that the total gecko population was 1,800. In the same year Cyclone Gervaise hit the island, causing widespread destruction. Further investigation revealed that gecko numbers had dropped to between 200 and 300.

Round Island is dome shaped and covers an area of about 370 acres (150 ha). Its steep slopes make it unsuitable for human habitation, but goats and rabbits were introduced many years ago. Expanding populations have grazed much of the vegetation, leaving a thin soil prone to erosion by wind and rain.

The Round Island day gecko is one of about 26 species of day gecko. Day geckos are like lizards in appearance, and most are brightly colored. They are known as day geckos because, unlike most geckos, they are diurnal (active during the day). Most species are found in Madagascar; in recent years some of them have become popular pets, but collecting from Round Island has never been a problem because of its remoteness. Compared to the often brilliant colors of other day gecko species, the Round Island form is quite drab. However, its hatchlings have the ability to change color in response to certain conditions of light, temperature, and mood.

The Round Island form is possibly the largest of all the day geckos. Although mainly active in the mornings and evenings, they have been seen on the ground at night hunting insects. By day they normally hunt on the trunks of palm trees. They eat mainly insects, but captive specimens readily eat ground-up fruit and vegetables. Other day geckos are known to have a "sweet tooth" and eagerly accept soft fruits, honey, and nectar mixtures.

Rescue Remedy

Plans to save the Round Island gecko began in the aftermath of Cyclone Gervaise. Gerald Durrell, the wildlife author and founder of the Jersey Wildlife

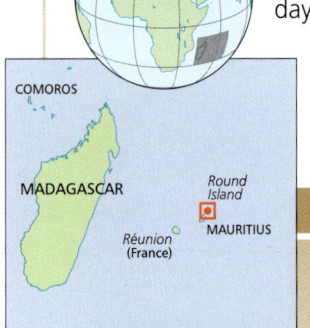

DATA PANEL

Round Island day gecko

Phelsuma guentheri

Family: Gekkonidae

World population: Probably fewer than 2,000

Distribution: Round Island, Mauritius

Habitat: Mainly trees; often found on trunks of palms; also on weathered volcanic rock

Size: Length: males up to 9 in (24 cm); females up to 8 in (22 cm). Males larger and more heavily built than females

Form: Uniformly brown with darker blotches; when basking in strong light, color changes to olive green. Belly white with yellow on underside of feet. Hatchlings paler; ventral surface bright yellow with darker bars

Diet: Insects and invertebrates

Breeding: One or 2 eggs per clutch; up to 5 clutches per year

Related endangered species: Rodrigues day gecko *(Phelsuma gigas)* EX; Namaqua day gecko *(P. ocellata)* LRnt; Standing's day gecko *(P. standingi)* VU

Status: IUCN EN; CITES II

See also: Natural Disasters 1: 57; The Role of Zoos 1: 86; Chameleon, South Central Lesser 3: 36; Iguana, Grand Cayman Blue Rock 5: 80

Preservation Trust (based at Jersey Zoo in the Channel Islands, off Britain) arranged to remove a number of geckos to Jersey for captive breeding. By 1976, 20 geckos were installed at Jersey. At first their care in captivity was experimental. The daylight period and temperature ranges were designed to mimic those in the wild. A supply of ultraviolet light was important since basking is essential for the making of a vitamin (D3) in diurnal lizards. The vitamin helps the gecko make use of calcium in its diet. The light was provided by full-spectrum fluorescent tubes (now widely used by keepers of diurnal lizards). One problem was social interaction: Many lizards fight when placed together, especially in a confined space. The geckos' reluctance to feed was overcome by offering waxmoth larvae and ground liquid baby food; they were then weaned onto crickets and locusts.

The use of a one-way glass panel allowed observation without disturbing the geckos. Breeding began in 1977; clutches consisting of one egg (or two joined together) were found stuck to the side of the vivarium (transparent enclosure). While some day geckos are "egg stickers," others simply deposit the eggs in a crevice or a concealed spot. Once mated, the females produce their season's eggs even if the males are removed. The eggs are fertilized at the same time, but laying is staggered over several weeks.

The sex of many reptiles is determined by the incubation temperature of the eggs. At Jersey it was difficult to vary the temperatures since the eggs were stuck to the vivarium wall: Most of the offspring turned out to be female. Although the breeding program was successful, the imbalance of sexes led the zoo to discontinue the project. All specimens were returned to Mauritius, where they were placed in an outdoor enclosure that allowed for further behavioral studies. The rabbits and goats had been removed from the island, and the vegetation was allowed to recover, so preventing soil erosion and providing cover from predators and storms. However, in such a restricted territory natural disasters are an ever-present threat.

The day gecko *has digits with adhesive pads that enable it to climb on smooth surfaces. It is often found gripping the trunks of palm trees as it goes in search of food.*

Gharial

Gavialis gangeticus

One of the largest crocodilian species, the gharial (or gavial) came close to extinction in the 1970s. Traditionally, gharials were not threatened by humans since they were regarded as sacred. Today they have disappeared from much of their original range. Conservation programs have increased numbers, but the gharial's future is still uncertain.

An unusual crocodilian, the gharial's common name comes from the Indian word "ghara," a pot, and refers to the bulbous growth on the male's snout. The growth is thought to act as a resonator when the male calls, or it may be used for recognition of males by females.

The gharial's distinctive narrow, tooth-lined snout, which seems at odds with the heavy body, is an adaptation to a diet of fish. The snout can be quickly slashed sideways, and the razor-sharp, slightly angled teeth are able to gain a firm grip on the slippery fish. Large specimens sometimes seize larger prey such as mammals, but youngsters feed on aquatic invertebrates and small creatures such as frogs.

Gharials spend much of their time in water, crawling onto land to bask or nest. Once out of water, their legs cannot raise the body off the ground, but they are capable of rapid movement by slithering on the belly. Unlike most crocodilians, gharials do not transport hatchlings from the nest to water, possibly because of their jaw structure, but the mothers do guard their young once they have hatched and reached water.

Population Decline

The gharial was once found in the major rivers and their tributaries in the northern parts of the Indian subcontinent, namely the Brahmaputra (India, Bhutan, Bangladesh); the Indus (Pakistan); the Ganges (Nepal and India); the Mahandi (India); and the Narayoni River and

DATA PANEL

Gharial (gavial)

Gavialis gangeticus

Family: Gavialidae

World population: Fewer than 2,500

Distribution: Northern Indian subcontinent

Habitat: Largely aquatic; calmer areas of deep rivers with sandbanks for nesting

Size: Length: male 19–22 ft (6–7 m); female about 16 ft (5 m)

Form: Typical crocodilian shape. Elongated, narrow snout with many interlocking, sharp teeth. Males have a bulbous growth on the end of the snout.

Adult color: uniform olive gray, sometimes with brownish blotches or bands, especially on the tail. Juveniles have dark spots and crossbands on a yellow-brown background

Diet: Fish; sometimes small mammals

Breeding: Clutch of 30–50 eggs buried in loose sand; eggs take 12–13 weeks to hatch

Related endangered species: None

Status: IUCN EN; CITES I

See also: What Is a Reptile? **1**: 72; Alligator, Chinese **2**: 12; Crocodile, American **3**: 80

its tributaries (Nepal), with smaller populations in the Kaladan and Irrawaddy Rivers in Myanmar (Burma). Today the remaining populations are in India and Nepal, with perhaps a few specimens in isolated areas.

The gharial's decline has been due to human activity. Settlements set up along the rivers have destroyed or disturbed breeding areas. Fishermen regard the gharials as direct competitors and destroyers of fishing nets. Furthermore, gharials are reputed to be man-eaters. While they do not attack people, they are thought to scavenge on human remains in the river (traditionally corpses are placed in the Ganges during funeral ceremonies). In some areas people hunt gharials for meat, and the eggs and body parts are also used in traditional medicine.

Chances of Survival

The gharial has benefited from a recovery plan set up in India in the 1970s to prevent poaching losses. Nine protected areas were established along the Ganges and its tributaries, and six captive-breeding and ranching centers were started, where eggs were taken from the wild to be hatched and raised in captivity. Several thousand young gharials have been released into the wild, which has steadied the decline in some areas. At smaller sites, however, numbers have not increased since youngsters do not always remain in the release area. In Nepal captive breeding and releases have produced only a small improvement in gharial numbers.

The gharial is still rare in India and Nepal and remains at risk from habitat degradation, fishing, and hunting. There is a shortage of suitable release sites in the protected areas, and the high cost of captive breeding and protection is also a problem. Ideally, youngsters should not be released until they are about five years old. However, the cost of feeding and caring for them means that some have been prematurely released, which reduces their chances of survival in the wild.

The gharial *is distinguished by its long, slender snout and sharp-toothed jaws.*

Gibbon, Black

Hylobates concolor

Black gibbons are distinctive and social creatures that bring benefits to their forest habitats. If they are allowed to become extinct, there could be severe consequences for an entire ecosystem.

There are nine species of gibbon in Southeast Asia, all of which look fairly similar and have a similar way of life. They spend most of their time high in the forest canopy, where they feed on leaves and fruit. They have amazingly long, strong arms, powerful shoulders, and hook-shaped hands, which enable them to swing from branch to branch or simply dangle for hours at a time.

Most gibbon species are monogamous, which means that a single male and female form a bond that lasts until one of them dies. Black gibbons, however, are polygynous: A single male black gibbon may have a harem of up to four females, and they all live with their offspring of various ages.

Gibbons are famed for their haunting songs and loud hooting calls; they produce whooping sounds that carry for huge distances through the forest. The sounds are usually performed by a bonded pair, but often the whole family joins in. Other important group activities include grooming and play—the youngsters are full of fun, and sometimes the whole group participates in their antics. The gibbons seem to delight in their acrobatic skill, and no one watching them could fail to be entertained. This means, however, that many baby gibbons are taken from the wild to be kept as pets.

Young gibbons normally stay with their mothers for several years, only leaving to seek mates of their own when they are seven or eight years old. Without their mother they cannot learn many of the skills they need to survive in the wild. In captivity most end up serving a lonely and miserable life sentence and develop abnormally limited behavior patterns.

Illegal Hunting

Most of the black gibbons' problems are, in fact, relatively recent. They do not suffer unduly from predation and have lived harmoniously with humans for many thousands of years. It seems that early forest people respected the gibbons and left them in peace; hunting (by humans) is a recent threat.

In China black gibbons are legally protected, and many live in reserves. However, people break the law to obtain black gibbon meat, which is considered a delicacy; gibbon bones also fetch a good price for use in eastern medicines that are supposed to help relieve rheumatism. The booming Chinese economy is

DATA PANEL

Black gibbon (concolor gibbon, crested gibbon)

Hylobates concolor

Family: Hylobatidae

World population: Thought to be about 5,000 in China; populations elsewhere much smaller; all declining

Distribution: Cambodia, Vietnam, Laos, and southern China

Habitat: Closed canopy evergreen forests

Size: Height: 18–25 in (46–68 cm); males and females similar size. Weight: 11–17 lb (5–8 kg)

Form: Slender ape with long arms and hook-shaped hands; fur dense and silky. Mature males black with white cheeks; breeding females pale buff

Diet: Ripe fruit, tender young leaves, and buds, some invertebrates

Breeding: Single young born every 2–3 years after gestation of 7–8 months; weaned at about 2 years; mature at about 8 years. Life span up to 25 years

Related endangered species: Silvery gibbon (*Hylobates moloch*) CR; other gibbons also face similar threats

Status: IUCN EN; CITES I

See also: Hunting 1: 42; Exploitation of Live Animals 1: 49; Monkey, Douc 6: 86

making more money available for purchasing these products, regardless of the law, and illegal hunting is undoubtedly a growing problem. The main cause of the black gibbon's decline, however, is another all too familiar one: Local human populations have increased by about 50 percent in less than 25 years. The resulting expansion of human communities into the gibbons' habitat has caused a disastrous drop in gibbon numbers.

Added Value

Black gibbons eat mostly fruit, and in doing so they provide a valuable service to the forest trees. Most fruits have seeds that will pass through a gibbon's digestive system unharmed; in fact, some appear not to germinate unless they have been eaten and then deposited in the gibbon's dung. In the few million years since gibbons first appeared in the region, the trees of Southeast Asia have evolved to bear fruit at different times of the year. Consequently, there is always a good chance of the fruit being eaten and the seeds dispersed far and wide, along with a helping of manure fertilizer, which gets the seedling off to a good start. To allow the black gibbon to become extinct would not only be a tragic loss to humankind; their disappearance could have drastic consequences for an entire ecosystem.

On a note of optimism, however, it seems that the gibbons can return to areas of previously felled forest that have been allowed to regenerate. With careful management and goodwill it should be possible to restore black gibbon populations to at least some of the areas from which they have disappeared.

The black gibbon *probably evolved as a separate species about a million years ago. It differs from other gibbons in its coat markings and social behavior. Mature males are black with white cheeks, while breeding females are pale buff.*

Gila Monster

Heloderma suspectum

In spite of its sluggish, awkward movement, the Gila monster can turn quickly if attacked. Its powerful venomous bite has made it the subject of many myths.

Venomous bites are usually associated with snakes, but the Gila monster and its close relative, the Mexican beaded lizard, are the only two venomous lizards in the world. The Gila monster, sometimes referred to as the Aztec lizard because it featured in paintings by the Aztec people of the ancient Mexican-Indian empire, has been the subject of many myths. They are supposed to be unable to pass out body waste and so to have poisonous breath. They are also reputed to spit venom, have a venomous tongue, and to be impossible to kill. Their venomous bite is real; the remainder untrue.

The Gila monster's bite is surprisingly quick and powerful, considering the animal generally moves in a sluggish, awkward way. Once it has its prey in its jaws, the Gila will then hang onto it, using a chewing motion to introduce venom into the prey's wounds. The venom is contained in glands in either side of the lower jaw from where it flows along grooves in some of the teeth. These pink glands contrast with the dark mouth lining, possibly acting as a visible warning when the mouth is open in a threat display. There is some debate over whether the venom is mainly for defense or for subduing prey. Gila venom is not highly toxic to humans, though bites have been described as extremely painful: Symptoms can include severe localized pain, sweating, breathing difficulty, blurred vision, swelling, vomiting, and reduced blood pressure. However, the Gila monster only uses venom in about a third of all bites.

Desert Destruction

Much of the Gila monster's habitat has been reduced by human encroachment into desert areas. Like many other creatures, it has been affected by urban development, agriculture, and industry. Construction

DATA PANEL

Gila monster (Aztec lizard)

Heloderma suspectum

Family: Helodermatidae

World population: Unknown

Distribution: Southwestern U.S. (Sonoran, Chihuahan, and Mojave Deserts)

Habitat: Desert and semiarid regions among sand, gravel, rocks, and vegetation such as saguaro, cholla, and prickly pear; often shelters in burrows of other animals

Size: Length: 18–24 in (45–60 cm)

Form: Heavy-bodied; short, fat tail used to store fat; short, powerful limbs for digging; black face; scales small and beadlike; coloration and pattern vary: mixture of black, orange, yellow, and pink markings in irregular bars, spots, or blotches

Diet: Eggs, small mammals, and birds

Breeding: One clutch of up to 12 eggs

Related endangered species: Mexican beaded lizard *(Heloderma horridum)* VU

Status: IUCN VU; CITES II

See also: Superstition 1: 47; Komodo Dragon 6: 12; Lizard, Blunt-Nosed Leopard 6: 36

work, use of offroad vehicles, and other human activities destroy the burrows where the Gila monster spends much of its time, particularly during the cold winter months. One study estimates that the Gila spends 90 percent of the year in burrows. The Gila's slow metabolism means that it does not need to feed as often as smaller, more active lizards. Its prey consists of eggs, small mammals, and young birds, usually swallowed whole, which provide moisture as well as sustenance. Once fed, the Gila rests until another meal is needed or it wants to bask in the sun.

Deliberate killing of the Gila has taken its toll on the species. Gilas are often killed out of fear, bravado, or simply ignorance. However, not all people fear Gila monsters. There has been a huge interest in reptile-keeping in the past few decades, and Gilas are now kept by many hobbyists. Many have been taken from the wild, even though it is now illegal to do so.

Protection

Some towns have municipal ordinances against keeping Gilas. In Arizona state legislation protecting Gilas was enacted as far back as 1952 but was not always enforced. The species is listed on CITES Appendix II, which means that only Gilas bred in captivity can be exported, and they require appropriate licenses. There has recently been pressure to upgrade Gilas to CITES Appendix I to legislate against any trade in the species.

In some areas only authorized people can handle "nuisance" Gilas that turn up on people's property. There are guidelines on where they can then be released so that they are not left in unsuitable habitats or too far away from their home range.

Some areas of habitat are now reserves, and many zoos have groups, although not all are able to breed. Since captive-breeding is possible, numbers can be increased, but habitat loss remains a problem. Recent scientific research has shown that the Gila monster's venom contains a substance useful in the treatment of diabetes. It is likely that it will be synthesized in the laboratory for use with patients.

The Gila monster's *differently colored scales and black face can be effective camouflage. The colors may also act as a warning to other animals.*

Giraffe, Reticulated

Giraffa camelopardalis reticulata

There are many races of giraffe living in Africa, but the northern ones are distinctively marked and more seriously threatened by natural and man-made dangers.

There is only one species of giraffe, but it is divided into many local races, each of which has a different coat pattern. The most distinctive form is the reticulated giraffe, found in northern Kenya and southern Somalia, with a similar race farther north in Eritrea and Ethiopia. Reticulated giraffes have a neatly patterned coat of chocolate-brown patches separated by narrow white lines; other giraffes tend to have irregularly shaped blotches on a sand-colored background. The reticulated giraffe is sufficiently distinct that it is sometimes considered to be a separate species.

Giraffes are very selective feeders, choosing the best quality leaves from the tops of more than 100 plant species. The main food source is acacia and other common savanna trees. The animals feed only on leaves, not grass (which they cannot easily reach or digest). For this reason they need to live where green foliage is available throughout the year. Giraffes can go for long periods without drinking—and are often seen far from water—but they do not thrive in areas that have desert conditions in the dry season. During hot, dry periods giraffes tend to congregate in lower, wetter areas where the vegetation remains green all year round. Populations disperse widely after the rains, when there is plenty of nourishing food available.

Giraffes browse the tops of bushes and trees up to heights of 17 feet (5.5 m) and rarely feed below 6 feet (2 m). Persistent browsing from the same trees results in dense, flat-topped foliage or vigorously trimmed branches. In this way giraffes shape the scenery! The animal uses its very long tongue, which is up to 18 inches (45 cm) long, to grasp small branches and strip off the leaves along the length. The giraffe also has a complex and efficient stomach, with a greater area for digesting food than any other cud-chewing animal.

The giraffe's long legs and unusual stride make it appear to run in slow motion, yet it can travel at more than 35 miles per hour (60 km/h), easily

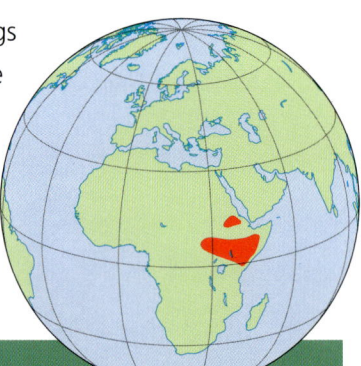

DATA PANEL

Reticulated giraffe

Giraffa camelopardalis reticulata

Family: Giraffidae

World population: Thousands, but spread over a wide area and divided into local and distinct populations

Distribution: Sub-Saharan Africa

Habitat: Savanna

Size: Length: 10.5–15 ft (3.4–4.8 m); height at shoulder: 12 ft (3.5 m), total height: up to 16 ft (5.2 m). Weight: 1,100–8,800 lb (500–4,000 kg); female smaller and more lightly built than male

Form: The tallest mammal, with very long legs and neck. Colored in brown patches separated by narrow white lines. Males have 4 hairy horns on the top of the head

Diet: Leaves browsed from the tops of trees and bushes

Breeding: A single calf is born (rarely twins) at 2–3 year intervals; mature at 3–4 years. Life span up to 20 years

Related endangered species: Okapi *(Okapia johnstoni)** LRnt

Status: IUCN LRcd; not listed by CITES

See also: Speciation 1: 26; Pasture 1: 38; Okapi 7: 22

GIRAFFE, RETICULATED

outpacing predators; small giraffes can be caught by lions, but the main predators have been humans.

Diminishing Habitat

Through the years giraffes have been shot and trapped for food, and caught in wire snares meant for small antelope. They are now protected by law, but enforcement is ineffective, except in national parks and other protected areas. However, the main problem facing giraffes is competition from other herbivorous mammals, including domestic livestock. This may seem odd, as giraffes feed where few other species can reach, but grazing by gazelles, sheep, goats, and cattle prevents the growth of new trees. When large old trees die off, there are no new trees to replace them. Impala, monkeys, and rodents eat the seeds of the trees too, also preventing regeneration. As a result, open grassland is maintained and extended, so giraffes have to find new feeding grounds. This can be difficult, particularly in drier areas where natural vegetation is scarce. In addition, the giraffe cannot make use of thickly forested areas.

Most giraffes are now only found in protected conservation areas where few humans live. Their range continues to contract over the whole of Africa. The giraffe is not seriously endangered, but local races are vulnerable. This is particularly true of the reticulated giraffe. This subspecies is especially at risk from many natural and human threats, including diminishing habitat, civil wars, and illegal hunting.

Giraffes, the tallest of all mammals, are unmistakable creatures, and the many subspecies are distinguished by their different coat patterns. They have keen senses of sight, smell, and hearing, and can defend themselves by kicking with their hooves.

Glider, Mahogany

Petaurus gracilis

The story of the rediscovery of the mahogany glider is the stuff of a field biologist's dreams. However, this gliding marsupial mammal is now restricted to a small strip of coast in northern Queensland and is threatened by habitat loss and fragmentation.

The mahogany glider was first discovered and described in 1883. Only four specimens were recorded, and it was concluded over the following six years that the animal was, in fact, just a large example of another species: the common squirrel glider. This was the accepted view for about 100 years, during which time the original specimens lay undisturbed in natural history museum collections in Australia. It was not until 1986 that three of the skins—by now in fairly poor condition—were reexamined. Researchers decided that the mahogany glider was, after all, a species in its own right. This revelation immediately prompted the question of whether any examples could still be found in the wild.

Bad Timing

The original specimens of mahogany glider had supposedly been trapped near Cardwell in Queensland, but a thorough search of that area did not yield any further examples. Then, in 1989 another old specimen was found during the reorganization of a museum; it had been misidentified and stored under the wrong name. However, what was exciting was the fact that it had been collected as recently as 1974 at Barrett's Lagoon, near Tully on the Queensland coast.

When a team of researchers went out to the site, they found a living population. However, in a tragic twist of bad timing, the site had been earmarked for clearance; within a month of the rediscovery the glider's forest habitat had been felled and replanted with banana and pineapple trees.

Endangered Species

Fortunately, in the following years further populations of mahogany glider were found nearby, but with each new discovery came the growing realization that the species was in real trouble. The entire known world population was found to be restricted to a single 80-mile (130-km) strip of coast within which over 80 percent of the suitable habitat had already been destroyed and the remaining habitat carved into hundreds of fragments. Most of the patches of forest were privately owned and in

DATA PANEL

Mahogany glider

Petaurus gracilis

Family: Petauridae

World population: 2,000–3,000 (estimated 1989), but probably fewer

Distribution: Northern Queensland coast, Australia

Habitat: Coastal tropical forest, no higher than 400 ft (120 m) above sea level

Size: Length head/body: 8–10.5 in (21.5–26.5 cm); tail: 12–15 in (30–38 cm); male about 10% bigger than female. Weight: 9–15 oz (250–400 g)

Form: Gray, cat-sized marsupial with long, furry tail. Flaps of skin between front and back legs become sails when limbs are extended in gliding

Diet: Nectar, sap, and gum; some invertebrates and lichens

Breeding: Litters of 1 or 2 young; little else is known about its breeding biology

Related endangered species: Leadbeater's possum *(Gymnobelideus leadbeateri)** EN; Tate's triok *(Dactilopsila tatei)* EN

Status: IUCN EN; not listed by CITES

See also: What Is a Species? **1:** 26; Research **1:** 84; Possum, Leadbeater's **7:** 88

GLIDER, MAHOGANY

The mahogany glider *has a long tail to form a counterbalance when scrambling around in the trees. Large flaps of skin between its front and back legs enable it to glide through the air from tree to tree.*

danger of being cleared for agriculture or having their trees felled for timber.

The mahogany glider was declared an endangered species in 1994, and millions of dollars of local and national government money were set aside for buying as much glider habitat as possible. Landowners who did not want to sell the land were asked instead to guarantee the security of their forests in order to conserve the gliders.

Footprints in the Dust

After a decade of intensive study we know a lot more about the mahogany glider. It feeds largely on insects and the secretions of coastal forest trees.

The gliders show a good deal of foresight in their feeding behavior, particularly in the way they exploit the sap from shoots of the so-called "grass" tree. The glider uses its teeth to cut a growing spear, which gradually exudes a gooey sap. Having made the cut, the glider goes away, returning the next night when the blob of congealed, jellylike sap is big enough to make a decent meal.

The footprints the mahogany glider leaves on the dusty older spears of the grass tree are one of the few distinctive signs that the species is still living in an area. More research into the habits of the animal will help ensure that the best protection can be planned.

Goby, Dwarf Pygmy

Pandaka pygmaea

Dwarf pygmy gobies are the smallest-known freshwater fish in the world. The species inhabits rivers and mangrove swamps in parts of Southeast Asia, where it is increasingly at risk from human disturbance, including the felling of mangrove trees for charcoal.

The family Gobiidae includes about 1,900 species. In both their freshwater and marine habitats gobies are often the most numerous fish. Among the gobies there are a few "giants." One is the violet goby from the western Atlantic and Carribean, which can grow to 20 inches (50 cm). Most species, however, are smaller than 4 inches (10 cm).

Unusual Lifestyles

With so many species in the family and with such an extensive geographical range—gobies are found in most tropical, subtropical, and temperate regions—it is not surprising to find that some have evolved specific, and sometimes unusual, lifestyles. Some species, such as the neon goby, have become "cleaner" fish—like the better-known cleaner wrasse that feeds almost exclusively on ectoparasites (external parasites) carried by other fish.

In another interesting association several types of goby live in a burrow shared with a shrimp. The shrimp keeps the tunnels in good order, while the gobies stand guard at the entrance, protecting the communal burrow against intruders and warning the shrimp of the approach of any predators. Other goby species live virtually confined to a single coral, sponge, or giant clam; they have even been found in the spaces between the spines of sea urchins.

Perhaps the most unusual adaptations are exhibited by the mudskippers of the genera *Boleophthalmus* and *Periophthalmus* that also inhabit mangrove swamps. These mudskippers live in mud burrows; as the tide goes out, exposing the mangrove flats, they emerge. A layer of thick mucus helps keep the skin moist, while a rich blood supply to the skin facilitates oxygen extraction from the air. Oxygen—also obtained from huge gulps of water from pools on the flats—enables mudskippers to remain exposed for long periods, feeding, courting, and defending territories. Once the tide comes in, they retreat to their burrows, where they await the next low tide.

Despite their diversity of shape, habits, and size, gobies share a number

---

DATA PANEL

Dwarf pygmy goby

Pandaka pygmaea

Family: Gobiidae

World population: Unknown, but believed to be about 80% lower than in the mid-1980s

Distribution: The Philippines and Indonesia; now reported from Bali, Singapore, and Sulawesi

Habitat: Freshwater/brackish (slightly salty) rivers and mangroves, usually close to shady banks. Also reported to be found in genuinely marine conditions

Size: Length: male up to 0.4 in (1.1 cm); female up to 0.6 in (1.5 cm)

Form: Typical "goby" shape of blunt, large head and large eye; body tapers toward the caudal (tail) fin. Pelvic (hip) fins fused into a powerful sucker. Two dorsal (back) fins. Prominent black spots along lower edge of posterior half of body, between anal (belly) fin and caudal peduncle (base of the caudal fin)

Diet: Minute invertebrates

Breeding: No comprehensive details are available, but known to include protection of eggs by at least 1 parent

Related endangered species: Nearly 60 species of goby are officially regarded as under some degree of threat, with 5 believed to be Critically Endangered, including Edgbaston goby (*Chlamydogobius squamigenus*)

Status: IUCN CR; not listed by CITES

See also: Specialization 1: 28; Rocky, Eastern Province 8: 40; Sunfish, Spring Pygmy 9: 40

GOBY, DWARF PYGMY

The dwarf pygmy goby *has the blunt head and large eyes that typify gobies. It is tiny and depicted here at about seven times its actual size.*

of basic characteristics that, until recently, have set them aside from other families. The most distinctive is the fused pair of pelvic (hip) fins that form a powerful sucker in the vast majority of goby species. Recently, however, some authorities have included the variably fused or separated pelvic fin arrangement of the sleeper gobies in the range of characteristics shared by the family Gobiidae: If the interpretation becomes universally accepted, the sleeper gobies would be brought into the family Gobiidae.

Threats to Survival

Mangrove areas—one of the main homes of the dwarf pygmy goby—are dangerous places to live in. The naturally fluctuating environmental conditions are often compounded by human intervention, including drainage, dredging, and pollution. The construction of aquaculture facilities for prawn farming, for example, is one activity that severely disrupts the dwarf pygmy goby's habitat. Another is denudation (the removal of trees and other plant cover).

Some of the brackish (slightly salty) areas where the dwarf pygmy goby occurs have also been degraded. The fish's freshwater habitats may not have been subjected to the same levels of pollution or denudation, but parts of the Malabon River in the Philippines, for example, are known to have been reclaimed for human use, resulting in drainage.

The dwarf pygmy goby is of no interest to commercial fisheries because of its exceptionally small size; nor, for the same reason, has it ever been popular with aquarists. Consequently, overcollection at least can be discounted as a threat to the ongoing survival of the species.

However, the other factors mentioned are most certainly key contributors. The combined effects of a decline in the size of the "area of occupancy" (the area over which the species occurs, or its range), along with a degradation of environmental conditions, have resulted in population levels falling to about 20 percent of numbers recorded in the mid-1980s. As a result, the tiny, irreplaceable dwarf pigmy goby is now listed by the IUCN as Critically Endangered.

Goodeid, Gold Sawfin

Skiffia francesae

The gold sawfin goodeid was first described in 1978. Within just a decade it was believed to be extinct in the wild. Few fish can have "arisen" and disappeared with such alarming rapidity.

The story of the gold sawfin goodeid—a remarkable little fish—is one that shows two sharply contrasting sides of human nature, the destructive and the protective.

In 1976 some fish were collected in the Río Teuchitlán in Jalisco, Mexico. Among them were specimens of an as yet undescribed species of goodeid fish. Aquarium-bred populations were established from the specimens by dedicated fishkeepers in several countries, most notably the United States, Britain, and Germany.

The new fish was described and named *Skiffia francesae* in 1978. Shortly afterward people began to voice fears for the continued survival of the species in its restricted natural habitat. The cause of concern was the detection of increasing numbers of another small fish, the red platy—a popular aquarium fish the world over—which had been introduced into the river. Like the gold sawfin goodeid, the red platy is a livebearing fish (it gives birth to living young).

Numerical Inferiority

Quite simply, the red platy overwhelmed the gold sawfin. The red platy had a number of features that gave it a tremendous advantage over the native species. Perhaps the most notable (beside being able to survive and breed perfectly well in its newfound home) was the fact that, being a member of the family Poeciliidae, the female platies can store sperm. As a result, they only need to mate once to be able to inseminate a series of egg batches as and when they hatch—usually every four to six weeks. They are prolific breeders: As many as 80 fry (hatchlings) are produced on each occasion.

Goodeids, on the other hand, cannot store sperm. Each brood of young produced is therefore the result of a separate mating. With about 35 fry (although usually fewer) in each brood and a longer gestation period than that of the red platy (about eight weeks), the total number of offspring that the gold sawfin produces in each full season is far outstripped by its exotic competitor.

DATA PANEL

Gold sawfin goodeid

Skiffia francesae

Family: Goodeidae

World population: None in the wild; several hundred in aquaria

Distribution: Río Teuchitlán, Jalisco, Mexico

Habitat: Slow-flowing waters

Size: Length: male up to 1.8 in (4.5 cm); female up to 2 in (5 cm)

Form: Males have a relatively tall dorsal (back) fin with distinctive notch (sawfin); they also have a notch on the anal (belly) fin. Top half of the body is metallic blue, and caudal (tail) fin has pale-orange tinge. Females are drab by comparison and have dark body spots

Diet: Small vertebrates. In aquaria, commercial preparations

Breeding: A short but intensive courtship display is followed by mating (lasting only a few seconds). Subsequently, fertilized eggs are released by the inseminated female into the ovarian cavity, where the embryos develop for a period of about 8 weeks. They obtain nourishment via trophotaeniae (specialized tapelike structures attached to the abdominal vent), which are discarded after birth

Related endangered species: Opal goodeid (*Allotoca maculata*) EN; butterfly goodeid (*Ameca splendens*) EN; blue-tailed goodeid (*Goodea Ataeniobius toweri*) EN; blackfin goodeid (*G. gracilis*) VU; black prince or bold characodon (*Characodon audax*) VU; rainbow goodeid (*C. lateralis*) VU; striped goodeid (*Girardinichthys multiradiatus*) EN; amarillo or maxclapique (*G. viviparus*) EN; *Hubbsina turneri* (no common name) EN; captivus or solo goodeid (*Xenoophorus captivus*) EN

Status: IUCN EW; not listed by CITES

See also: Introductions 1: 54; Platy, Cuatro Ciénegas 7: 80; Sucker, Razorback 9: 38

However, one advantage that sawfins have over the invading platies is that sawfin females actually ovulate after mating and fertilization of their eggs, with the embryos undergoing subsequent development inside the ovarian cavity (the equivalent of a womb, or uterus, in female mammals), rather than inside the egg follicles or sacs, as happens in the platy. As the embryos begin to grow, they develop specialized tapelike feeding structures—known as trophotaeniae—from their abdominal aperture. They are able to absorb so much nourishment through these structures during their period of gestation that by the time they are born, they are extremely well developed. They also weigh many thousands of times more than the fertilized egg. However, cannibalism inside the ovarian cavity is common among some goodeid species, which reduces numbers of fry still further. In platies the newborn fry weigh the same, or less, than a fertilized egg. Nevertheless, the platies are still sufficiently well developed and are produced in such numbers that they can, overall, outcompete gold sawfin fry.

Captive Success

The situation in Río Teuchitlán has now deteriorated to the extent that repeated visits to the river carried out in recent years have failed to locate any gold sawfins. Fortunately for the species the aquarium populations are still thriving; and although the species is not among the easiest of fish to breed in captivity, the ongoing survival of the captive-bred stocks seems to be assured. However, in captivity—where numbers are smaller than they would be in the wild—the risk of inbreeding is always present. Another problem is the possibility of the gold sawfin producing hybrids (crossbreeds) by mating with some of its closest relatives, notably the piebald sawfin goodeid. This destroys the genetic purity of the species, which is already in a precarious state.

The gold sawfin goodeid *has lost out to the red platy in the wild. An adult pair of gold sawfins are shown here (female above male).*

Gorilla, Mountain

Gorilla gorilla beringei

After years of intensive conservation efforts Africa's mountain gorilla population seemed to be overcoming the threat of extinction. However, civil war in the region has since undone much of the progress that had been made.

Mountain gorillas are particularly vulnerable to environmental pressures, both natural and man-made, because of their slow breeding rate, which makes it difficult for them to replenish their numbers. Usually only one baby is born at a time; but on the rare occasions when twins occur, one almost always dies.

Most female gorillas do not breed until they are at least 10. A female can bear young every four years; but because many infants die before they are two, the rate for successful reproduction is closer to one every eight years. Even a female living in exceptionally favorable conditions is unlikely to rear more than six offspring in her 40-year lifetime. It is more likely that she will raise between two and four young. The young are not fully weaned until the age of three and remain with their mothers for several more years.

Major Threats

The major problems facing the mountain gorilla in the mid-20th century were poaching, kidnapping, and habitat loss. Such problems can be prevented by setting aside areas of gorilla habitat and patrolling them to prevent hunting. Such refuges did exist, but the protection provided in the past was nowhere near adequate. Many hundreds were still illegally caught in snares, their flesh sold as bush meat, and their heads, hands, and feet made into trophies and tourist souvenirs. There was also a thriving market in live baby gorillas, a trade made all the more abhorrent by the fact that poachers usually killed the mother, or the entire family, to kidnap one baby. Mountain gorillas do not cope well with captivity—those seen in zoos are of the lowland variety—and few kidnapped youngsters survive. Huge areas of mountain gorilla habitat were lost to cultivation in the 1950s and 1960s. The matter came to a head in 1968 when a single refuge, representing 40 percent of the gorillas' remaining habitat, was turned over to agriculture.

Changing Fortunes

By the late 1960s it was clear that if mountain gorillas were to escape extinction, both the animals and their shrinking habitat needed proper protection. For two decades this was provided, and at the end of the 1980s the mountain gorilla's prospects were looking much brighter. The Rwandan gorilla population had increased by over 20 percent; special reserves gave them a secure habitat, and an intensive education program helped local people realize the value of their great ape neighbors. The gorillas became a national treasure and the focus of a lucrative ecotourism industry, which in 1990 ranked as Rwanda's third highest source of income. Similar projects were also reaping benefits in neighboring Uganda and the Democratic Republic of Congo (formerly Zaire). Ecotourism brings in money, and the presence of visitors makes it more difficult for poachers to operate unseen, but the visitors also bring disease. Gorillas are susceptible to human infections, and there is a risk of passing on flu viruses and other germs to the animals when tourists visit the forests.

In the early 1990s civil war in Rwanda claimed the lives of half a million people and left 750,000 homeless. Not surprisingly the conservation of Rwanda's mountain gorillas slipped down the list of

See also: War **1:** 47; Ecotourism **1:** 90; Chimpanzee, Pygmy **3:** 44; Gorilla, Western Lowland **5:** 40

GORILLA, MOUNTAIN

DATA PANEL

Mountain gorilla

Gorilla gorilla beringei

Family: Pongidae

World population: Fewer than 600

Distribution: Mountains linking the Democratic Republic of Congo, Rwanda, and Uganda, eastern Africa

Habitat: Cloud forests on volcanic slopes at 5,450–12,500 ft (1,650–3,800 m)

Size: Height: 5–9 ft (1.5–1.8 m); male up to twice the size of female. Weight: 154–440 lb (70–200 kg)

Form: Large, powerful ape. Dark brown-black hair, longer than that of lowland gorilla. Walks on all fours using soles of feet and knuckles of hands; arms shorter than those of lowland gorilla. Dominant males very large with silvery hair on back

Diet: Leaves, roots, and shoots; some bark, flowers, fruit, fungi; occasionally invertebrates and even dung

Breeding: Single young born at any time of year after 8-month gestation; births at intervals of at least 4 years; young weaned at 3 years; mature at 10 years (female) or 15 years (male). Life span up to 40 years in wild

Related endangered species: Western lowland gorilla *(Gorilla gorilla gorilla)** EN; eastern lowland gorilla *(G. g. graueri)* EN; chimpanzee *(Pan troglodytes)** EN; pygmy chimpanzee *(P. paniscus)** EN; orang-utan *(Pongo pygmaeus)** VU

Status: IUCN EN; CITES I

---

national priorities. Conservationists stayed to protect the gorillas but were eventually evacuated. The refugee crisis caused by the war has put huge pressure on the land, and the protected status of the gorilla's habitat is again under threat; there simply is not enough room to accommodate both the gorillas and the thousands of people in need of land.

The mountain gorilla *is the world's largest primate, but despite its huge size and obvious strength, it is also one of the gentlest.*

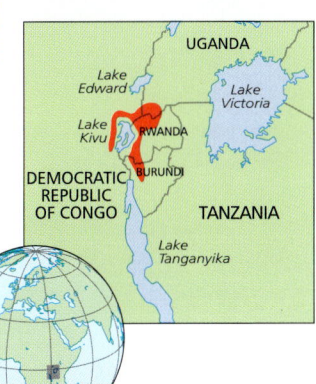

Gorilla, Western Lowland

Gorilla gorilla gorilla

The forest-dwelling western lowland gorilla is a gentle giant. It has suffered from generations of hunting, kidnapping, and habitat destruction, and its numbers are still in decline.

There are three subspecies of gorilla: the mountain gorilla and the eastern and western lowland gorillas. The mountain gorilla lives in eastern Africa; the western lowland form lives in the lowland tropical rain forests of West Africa from Cameroon to the Congo River, and the eastern form lives in the lowland tropical rain forests of what is now the Democratic Republic of Congo (formerly Zaire). All three populations face similar problems.

It is impossible to estimate how many western lowland gorillas are left in the wild. Their dense rain forest habitats are some of the least explored areas of the world, and the terrain makes surveying difficult.

Gorillas live in groups of adult males, females, juveniles, and infants. They are predominantly fruit-eaters and need vast tracts of forest in order to find food. The western lowland gorillas are constantly on the move, looking for trees with a ripe crop. An average troop needs a home range of between 10 and 15 square miles (25 and 40 sq. km) to ensure that they can always find food. The western lowland gorillas live in much smaller groups than their cousins in the east, where fruit is more abundant; a group of five to seven gorillas is less likely to exhaust the fruit supply of any tree than a group of 12 or 15.

Like all great apes, lowland gorillas breed very slowly. A healthy female will produce between three and six babies in her lifetime. The young are so well cared for that they stand a good chance of surviving as long as the troop has plenty of space to forage for food and is not targeted by poachers.

Despite their bulk and power, gorillas are peaceful creatures. Although people who have killed them often claim that they did so in self-defense, the animals are generally not agressive if left unprovoked. Even the intimidating chest-beating display of a dominant male is usually little more than a bluff.

Dwindling Habitat

Although the forests of central Africa are still vast, in the past few decades a dramatic increase in logging and clearing of trees for agriculture has greatly reduced and fragmented their extent, threatening the habitat needed by lowland gorillas. Humans have been farming in Africa for thousands of years, but this used to be

---

DATA PANEL

Western lowland gorilla

Gorilla gorilla gorilla

Family: Pongidae

World population: Unknown; estimates vary from 10,000 to 50,000

Distribution: West Africa, including parts of Cameroon, Central African Republic, Gabon, Congo, Equatorial Guinea, and the Democratic Republic of Congo

Habitat: Lowland tropical rain forests

Size: Height: up to 7 ft (2.1 m). Weight: 300–600 lb (135–275 kg)

Form: Brownish-black fur; long, powerful arms; legs less powerful; broad chest; large head (wider than that of mountain gorilla); heavy brow ridge

Diet: Fruit, shoots, leaves, bark, roots, and bulbs

Breeding: Single young born after gestation of 7–8 months; dependent on mother until fully weaned at 3–4 years; mature at 7–9 years (females) and 9–12 years (males). Life span up to 37 years

Related endangered species: Eastern lowland gorilla (*Gorilla gorilla graveri*) EN; mountain gorilla (*G. g. beringei*)* CR; chimpanzee (*Pan troglodytes*)* EN; pygmy chimpanzee (*P. paniscus*)* EN; orang-utan (*Pongo pygmaeus*)* VU

Status: IUCN EN; CITES I

See also: Hunting 1: 42; War 1: 47; Chimpanzee 3: 42; Gorilla, Mountain 5: 38

done on a relatively small scale. The rapid rise in human populations over the last century has meant that more land is being used for settlement and agriculture than ever before.

The devastation is worse in some countries than in others. For example, the western lowland gorilla had disappeared from Nigeria by 1984, while the relatively untouched forests of Gabon to the south still harbor around half the world's gorilla population. Gabon is a small country, about the size of Ohio, but around 70 percent of it is still forested, providing ideal gorilla habitat. The Gabonese hunt more gorillas than anyone else; but as far as they are concerned, this great ape is still a reasonably abundant animal.

Illegal Trade

Gorillas are killed for several reasons. They are widely eaten as bush meat, and gorilla body parts are traded as souvenirs. Hundreds, possibly even thousands of gorilla babies have been taken from the wild to supply zoos and the pet trade. They are usually kept and transported in atrocious conditions, and at least two-thirds of them do not survive the journey. It is now illegal to export wild-caught gorillas, and today most zoos refuse to take them. Nevertheless, there is still a healthy black market in the young animals.

Civil wars and political instability, especially in the Democratic Republic of Congo and parts of West Africa, have reduced the effectiveness of international legal protection. Such factors have also made it impossible to carry out surveys to find out how many western lowland gorillas remain in the wild. Even in "protected" areas the gorillas are not completely safe.

It is thought that the Kahuzi-Biega National Park in the Democratic Republic of Congo has recently lost half its gorillas as a result of poaching.

The western lowland gorilla, *in common with other gorillas, shares 98 percent of its genes with humans. Most people now realize that gorillas are peaceful creatures. Despite their huge size, they rarely act aggressively toward people.*

Grebe, Atitlán

Podilymbus gigas

A number of factors—including the introduction of nonnative fish, tourist development, and the aftereffects of an earthquake—conspired to drive the flightless Atitlán grebe to extinction in its only home, Guatemala's Lake Atitlán.

The first specimen of the Atitlán grebe was collected in 1862 and scientifically described as merely a geographical race (subspecies) of the similar pied-billed grebe, a widespread and common species that occurs from southern Canada and the United States down to South America. It was reclassified as a distinct species in 1929.

The Atitlán grebe was distinguishable from most of its relatives in that it was unable to fly. It is thought to have evolved from the pied-billed grebe after a population arrived at the high-altitude lake and, without the power of flight, became isolated there.

Compared with other grebes, it had a heavy, powerful bill and well-developed muscles in the jaws and neck. The adaptations enabled the bird to catch and crush the large freshwater crabs that thrived among the aquatic vegetation along the edge of Lake Atitlán. They formed over 50 percent of its diet.

Lake Home

Lake Atitlán is set in dramatic surroundings in the mountains of Guatemala. Ringed by volcanoes, it has a shoreline of 78 miles (125 km) and depths of over 1,100 feet (340 m). Until about 20 years ago the forests that clothed the mountain slopes extended to the lake shore. Great beds of reeds and cattails grew along the southern shore, sheltered from the storms that often blow across the lake.

The grebes would anchor their floating nests to the tall stems of such plants. Local people (descendants of the ancient Maya) also used the reeds, cutting a harvest of stems that they wove to make chairs and other articles to use or sell. Although some grebe nests were destroyed, the reed harvest was sustainable, allowing birds and people to coexist. The lake also supplied the local people with food, water, and a means of transportation for generations.

Setbacks

The Atitlán grebe may never have been particularly numerous: The highest population estimate was of about 400 birds. In 1929 and 1936 there were thought to be about

DATA PANEL

Atitlán grebe (giant pied-billed grebe)

Podilymbus gigas

Family: Podicipedidae

World population: 0 (Extinct)

Distribution: Lived only on Lake Atitlán, southwestern Guatemala

Habitat: Areas of lake with reed-fringed shoreline

Size: Length: 13–16 in (33–40.5 cm)

Form: Big-headed, thick-necked, dumpy-bodied, tailless waterbird; stout whitish or pale-grayish bill with black vertical band; upperparts dark brownish, darker on head and neck; narrow whitish ring around eye; underparts dull creamy-buff; juveniles similar, with pale stripes on side of head and neck

Diet: Mainly *Potamocarcinus* crabs, but after introduction of large-mouthed bass to Lake Atitlán, primarily fish up to 5 in (13 cm) long; also insects and snails

Breeding: Began March with egg-laying peak in April; sometimes nested all year round. Solitary breeders; nest a floating platform of aquatic vegetation anchored to submerged plants; 1–5 whitish eggs stained by vegetation. Chicks independent at 10–12 weeks

Related endangered species: Alaotra grebe (*Tachybaptus rufolavatus*) CR; Madagascar grebe (*T. pelzelnii*) VU; New Zealand dabchick (*Poliocephalus rufopectus*) VU; Junín grebe (*Podiceps taczanowskii*) CR; hooded grebe (*P. gallardoi*) LRnt; Colombian grebe (*P. andinus*) EX

Status: IUCN EX; CITES I

See also: War 1: 47; Natural Disasters 1: 57; Duck, Labrador 4: 42; Guan, Horned 5: 44

100 pairs left. In 1958, and again in 1960, came the first of a whole series of setbacks for the birds, since various nonnative species of fish were introduced to Lake Atitlán to attract tourist anglers. At the time of the second influx grebe numbers stood at about 200. One of the fish species—the large-mouthed bass that could grow to a weight of 26 pounds (12 kg)—thrived in its new home and bred profusely. The bass competed with the grebes, eating many of the smaller fish, invertebrates, and the crabs that formed the bird's main food, and it preyed on the grebe's young.

Rescue Attempts

By 1965 the grebe population had dwindled to an estimated 80 birds. A conservation initiative named Operation Poc—from the local name for the bird—was set up. Involving the Guatemalan government and various international conservation organizations, it focused on dissuading people from cutting reeds during the grebes' nesting season, creating a reserve, and employing guards to protect the birds and their eggs from illegal poaching. It also succeeded in halting a major hydroelectric project planned for the lake.

Thanks these measures, and especially because the numbers of introduced bass fell dramatically, the birds underwent a revival; by 1975 there was a total of 232. However, the recovery was short-lived, since the grebes faced new threats.

The Final Blows

Land around the shore where the grebes lived was sold to city dwellers to build vacation and weekend homes, hotels, and shops. Reed cutting accelerated as the newcomers improved the view of the lake from their properties or created moorings for their boats. Sport fishing, waterskiing, and scuba diving disturbed the birds, and an increase in sewage polluted the water. An additional threat came from the gill nets set to catch fish, which could also drown the birds.

Then, in 1976 an earthquake created new outlets for the lake water. The level of water fell by over 13 feet (4 m) in five and a half years. By 1980, 60 percent of the reeds and cattails had disappeared, removing a major part of the grebes' nesting and sheltering sites.

In 1982, amid political unrest and guerrilla warfare, the government game warden appointed to protect the grebes was killed. By 1983 the population of Atitlán grebes was down to just 30 birds.

A detailed survey of the lake in 1987 failed to find any Atitlán grebes, and the species was pronounced extinct. Grebes were seen there, but they were of the pied-billed species. Perhaps they had competed with their flightless, lake-locked relative or, as its numbers dropped, interbred with it, swamping their genetic difference and thereby contributing to the disappearance of the special bird.

The Atitlán grebe coexisted with people for centuries, until introduced fish, increased development, and natural events conspired to destroy its habitat.

Guan, Horned

Oreophasis derbianus

A distinctive-looking gamebird, the horned guan suffers from destruction of its cloud-forest habitat and is now restricted to relatively small areas of its former range.

The horned guan is a member of a family of gamebirds known as cracids that is restricted to the warmer parts of the New World. The 24 species of guan, along with the other members of the family—namely the mostly larger curassows and smaller chachalachas—are generally regarded as the most primitive of all gamebirds and are the most arboreal, spending a good deal of their lives in the trees, and in most cases nesting in them.

An unmistakable bird, the horned guan also has an unusual voice. During the courtship season the male utters a strange song consisting of three or four soft, deep notes like the mooing of a cow, which it repeats several times a minute, and which has a ventriloquial quality so that it is impossible to tell where the bird is situated.

The song is quite unlike any of the sounds made by other guan species, but instead resembles the songs of curassows. The horned guan's odd appearance, larger size than other guans, and other atypical features have led some ornithologists to suggest that it represents a link between the guans and the curassows. It has sometimes been placed in a subfamily of its own.

Marked Decline

The horned guan is endemic to evergreen cloud forests in the Sierra Madre de Chiapas mountain range that extends from southernmost Mexico into western Guatemala. Although it probably always had a limited range, it was reported to be fairly common toward the end of the 19th century. However, its numbers decreased sharply during the 20th century; as early as the 1930s birds had disappeared from many places in Guatemala where they had previously occurred.

The decline accelerated from the 1960s, as the horned guan's humid subtropical montane forest habitat became increasingly exploited by loggers, local people collecting firewood, and the process of conversion to agriculture. As areas of forest were cleared for planting crops, especially coffee, growing numbers of plantation workers killed more horned guans for their tasty

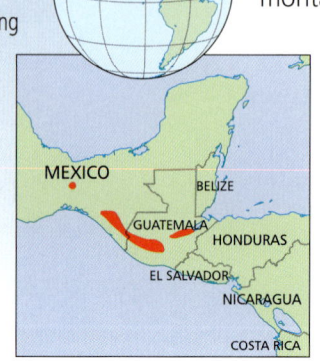

DATA PANEL

Horned guan

Oreophasis derbianus

Family: Cracidae

World population: Estimated at 1,000–2,500 birds

Distribution: Fragmented populations in Sierra Madre de Chiapas in southern Mexico and southern Guatemala

Habitat: Cloud forest, at altitudes of 5,250–8,850 ft (1,600–2,700 m) in Mexico and 3,900–11,500 ft (1,200–3,500 m) in Guatemala

Size: Length: 29.5–33.5 in (75–85 cm)

Form: Large, pheasantlike gamebird, with small head, long neck, stout body, long, broad tail, and strong legs; distinctive black-and-white plumage; tail black with broad white band near base; strong yellow bill, small area of bare red skin on throat, red horn of skin on top of head; juveniles have much smaller horn that grows in their first year; dark-brown wings and tail, the latter with fine cream markings

Diet: Mainly fruit and green leaves of a great variety of plants

Breeding: Mainly January–June; males may mate with more than 1 female in a season; flimsy nest of dry leaves and roots high in tree; 2 large white eggs incubated for about 5 weeks; females may take 12–14 months to reach maturity, males 4 years

Related endangered species: Fourteen other species in family Cracidae, including white-winged guan (*Penelope albipennis*) CR; chestnut-bellied guan (*P. ochrogaster*) EN; Trinidad piping guan (*Pipile pipile*) CR; black-fronted piping guan (*P. jacutinga*) VU

Status: IUCN EN; CITES I

See also: Hunting 1: 42; National Parks 1: 92; Tragopan, Temminck's 9: 94

The horned guan *has boldly marked black-and-white plumage and an extraordinary red "horn" of naked skin that projects from its head.*

meat. Such subsistence hunting continues today, and horned guans are also taken alive for private aviaries and the cage-bird trade.

By the end of the 1970s the total population was thought to be fewer than 1,000 birds, although this may have been too low an estimate. Some populations seem to be fairly secure in the immediate future. But judging by the species' fragmented distribution and the continuing threats it faces, it is almost certain that its population is still in decline.

Hope for the Future

The urgent need to stop the decline of the horned guan led to the creation of the El Triunfo Biosphere Reserve in the state of Chiapas in southern Mexico. As well as halting the forest destruction, conservationists initiated an international program to save the bird. A long-term study of the species was begun in 1987 to learn more of the bird's biology and ecology. That has made it the best known of all threatened members of its family. Other conservation efforts have included successful breeding in captivity and a program of environmental education at El Triunfo. However, much more needs to be done to take the horned guan out of danger.

It is not known for certain whether or not the horned guan undertakes altitudinal migrations; the lack of records between the months of June and August from the El Triunfo reserve suggests that at least some birds may do so. If this proves to be the case, the transformation of the forests at lower altitudes into coffee plantations will have caused additional and serious reductions in the species' range and numbers.

The horned guan is presently known from two other protected areas apart from El Triunfo: the Sierra de las Minas Biosphere Reserve and Atitlán National Park in Guatemala. An international reserve at Volcán Tacaná on the Mexico/Guatemala border is also planned. Also, existing laws protecting the bird from hunting and trapping need to be enforced.

Gull, Lava

Larus fuliginosus

The unusually plumaged lava gull is found only on the Galápagos Islands. Although numbers are assumed to be stable, the small size of the population gives cause for concern.

The world's rarest gull, the lava gull is widely but sparsely distributed on many of the islands that make up the Galápagos archipelago (group of islands) in the Pacific Ocean. It was not until 1960 that ornithologists found the first nest of a lava gull, and by 1970 only six nests had been observed.

The lava gull nests on sheltered sandy beaches or low outcrops, especially near calm water. Unlike almost every other species of gull, lava gulls are solitary breeders and vigorously defend their territory against rival pairs. Once the young have survived the hazardous period before they can fly and find food, their scavenging habits help them survive periods of shortage, including those caused by the abnormal weather conditions and the influx of a warm ocean current known as El Niño. Extreme El Niño events (most recently in 1982 and 1997) have badly hit colonies of other Galápagos seabirds that rely on living fish or other marine creatures for food.

As well as scavenging a variety of dead animals that they find along the shoreline, lava gulls eat offal discarded from fishing boats and scraps of food thrown away by islanders and tourists; they also steal eggs from other seabirds and snatch crabs caught by lava herons. Sometimes they kill and eat small lizards, hatchling marine iguanas, and turtles; and they swoop down to the sea to catch fish or crustaceans.

Relatives

Although several other species of gull in different parts of the world have dark plumage, none seems to be closely related to the lava gull. The lava gull's closest relative is thought to be the laughing gull, which is an abundant and widespread species on the coasts of North America and the Caribbean (and winters in South America). The laughing gull has an immature and

DATA PANEL

Lava gull (dusky gull)

Larus fuliginosus

Family: Laridae

World population: 300–400 pairs

Distribution: Galápagos Islands, Ecuador

Habitat: Sheltered sandy beaches and rocky outcrops near calm water

Size: Length: 20–21.5 in (51–55 cm)

Form: Large gull with dark ash-gray plumage, darker on wings; paler on belly and tail. Head blackish brown with variable white crescents above and below each eye; legs and bill blackish. Juveniles mainly sooty brown

Diet: Dead animals; offal from fishing boats and other waste food; small fish, crustaceans, baby marine iguanas, and seabird eggs

Breeding: Two heavily blotched olive eggs laid in shallow nest scraped in sand; female incubates eggs for about 33 days; fledging period about 9 weeks; parental care extends for further 14–18 days

Related endangered species: Five other species of gull are threatened: Olrog's gull (*Larus atlanticus*) VU; black-billed gull (*L. bulleri*) VU; Saunder's gull (*L. saundersi*) VU; relict gull (*L. relictus*) VU; red-legged kittiwake (*Rissa breviostris*) VU

Status: IUCN VU; not listed by CITES

See also: Life Strategies 1: 24; Introductions 1: 54; Sandpiper, Spoon-Billed 8: 54; Stilt, Black 9: 32

GULL, LAVA

adult plumage that is similar to the lava gull's and a similar long, loud, cackling call. In fact, it is likely that a group of laughing gulls colonized the Galápagos and in isolation gradually evolved into the different species that we recognize today as the lava gull. This may have happened fairly recently in evolutionary terms—perhaps only a few tens of thousands of years ago.

Interference

The greatest threat to the future of the lava gull—and the many other seabirds that help make the Galápagos such a special place—is posed by predators introduced by humans during 300 years of settlement of the islands, especially in the last 50 years. Rats, cats, dogs, and pigs all take their toll on seabird eggs, chicks, and even adults.

Adding to the problem is the fact that the lava gulls—endemic animals that evolved in isolation on the islands—have no instinctive fear of introduced predators. Nesting pairs of lava gulls are wary of humans and will fly off when an intruder is still more than half a mile (about 1 km) away. However, because they nest on the ground and not on cliffs, lava gulls are especially vulnerable to nest robbers.

Programs of research and elimination of the gull's predators have been carried out by conservationists, but attempts are undermined by the fact that animals are still being introduced accidentally or deliberately by boat.

Although over 96 percent of the land area of the Galápagos archipelago is protected as a national park, this excludes harbors that are major feeding grounds for the gulls. About 60,000 people visit the Galápagos Islands every year, and the number of people living in the Galápagos has grown from about 2,000 in the early 1960s to about 18,000 today. Even conservative estimates predict populations of 50,000 by 2020.

The lava gull *is unusual in being dark all over; most of the world's 51 gull species have a plumage pattern of gray or black upperparts and white underparts.*

Human pressure on habitats and wildlife is therefore set to increase substantially. Although numbers of lava gulls are now constant, they are also low; successful breeding may be compromised in the future.

Gymnure, Hainan

Hylomys hainanensis

The Hainan gymnure is found only on Hainan Island in the South China Sea. If forest clearance continues at the current rate, the species may disappear completely during the next 50 years.

Gymnures are often called moonrats, even though they have no connection with rats or the moon. They might be better described as furry hedgehogs, since their basic anatomy resembles that of a typical hedgehog. However, instead of the familiar coat of spines, they have a dense fur that is sometimes overlain with long, shaggy hairs. Although gymnures have a ratlike tail, their teeth are unlike those of rats, being sharp and pointed for catching the small invertebrates on which they feed.

Gymnures have changed little since they first evolved tens of millions of years ago. They are now few in number and scattered widely over the Far East. Two species occur from Thailand into Malaysia, and two are found in the Philippines. A close relative of the Hainan gymnure lives on the Chinese mainland. All are considered Endangered, as is the dwarf gymnure of Indonesia.

Like hedgehogs, gymnures are flat-footed, but they can apparently climb reasonably well and have been observed in trees. They may take to the branches in an effort to escape from predators, although such behavior also gives them access to birds' nests and other food sources that would otherwise be out of their reach. Hainan gymnures are thought to use burrows for some of the time. It is believed that they venture into the open in search of food, but only within a relatively restricted area, perhaps no more than about 150 feet (50 m) from their nest.

Although gymnures are solitary creatures, they need to find mates in the breeding season. To this end they produce a characteristic strong odor from special scent glands. Scent in fact plays an important part in the animals' ecology. It helps them recognize individuals, especially in darkness or in dense undergrowth, and also serves to mark nest sites and territorial boundaries.

Elusive Animals

The exact status of the Hainan gymnure is difficult to determine because the animals are so elusive; the species was only officially discovered in 1959, having

DATA PANEL

Hainan gymnure (Hainan moonrat)

Hylomys hainanensis

Family: Erinaceidae

World population: Unknown

Distribution: Hainan Island, China

Habitat: Dense forests

Size: Length head/body: 4.8–5.8 in (12–15 cm); tail: 1.5–1.8 in (3.5–4.5 cm). Weight: 1.8–2.5 oz (50–70 g)

Form: Rat-sized animal with pointed snout and bare, scaly tail; brown body with black stripe down the back

Diet: Insects, worms, and other invertebrates

Breeding: Poorly known; probably 2–5 young born once or twice per year. Life span probably about 5 years

Related endangered species: Dwarf gymnure (*Hylomys parvus*) CR; Dinagat moonrat (*Podogymnura aureospinula*) EN; Mindanao gymnure (*P. truei*) EN

Status: IUCN EN; not listed by CITES

See also: Island Biogeography 1: 30; Desman, Russian 4: 14; Solenodon, Cuban 9: 16

GYMNURE, HAINAN

escaped notice up until then.

Like all gymnures, the Hainan gymnure lives in dense tropical forests, often on steep mountainsides where it is hard to find; it is difficult to catch more than one or two during a brief study visit. As a result, it is impossible to assess overall numbers or decide if populations are increasing or decreasing.

Individual animals are occasionally trapped for museum collections, at least proving that gymnures are present in a given area. Such specimens are sometimes dissected to reveal details of their diet, but little else can be learned about the animals' ecology or conservation status from dead specimens.

A Crowded Homeland

There can be little doubt that the Hainan gymnure is seriously threatened, if only because of its restricted distribution. The species is found solely on Hainan, which is only 150 miles (240 km) in diameter, so the land area available to it is limited. The island is also overcrowded; it is home to a population of more than 7 million humans, which translates into about 500 people per square mile (200 per sq. km). To accommodate such high densities, about 85 percent of the island's forest cover has been removed in the past 30 years, and the rest is under constant threat of

Little-known relatives of the hedgehog, *the seven gymnure species live in China and Southeast Asia. In place of the hedgehogs' spines they have dense hair. They are not hunted, but are threatened by the loss of the forest habitat on which they depend.*

destruction to make way for farms, housing, roads, and domestic animals.

Within the forest the dense tree canopy stays green all year round, casting shade and maintaining a moist environment at ground level. Once trees are removed or thinned, however, the wind and sun soon dry the soil, reducing the number of invertebrates on which the gymnures can feed. Opening up the habitat also exposes gymnures and other small animals to predators such as dogs and birds of prey that were previously not a threat in the dense forests. Wildlife reserves have been established, but they are difficult to protect, and the distribution of gymnures within them is unknown.

The Hainan gymnure has been known for fewer than 50 years. As is the case with many other obscure and threatened species, it is easy to imagine that it might disappear altogether within the next 50 years.

Hare, Hispid

Caprolagus hispidus

In the southern foothills of the Himalaya Mountains the hispid hare is struggling to eke out an existence in the ever-decreasing areas of natural grassland. Without urgent action both the hare and its habitat could soon disappear for good.

The hispid hare has been on the brink of extinction for much of the last century. More than once it seemed to have disappeared completely, only to be rediscovered a few years later. The population today is restricted to southern Nepal, northern Bangladesh, and northern parts of India, including Assam—hence the species' alternative name of Assam rabbit.

The hispid hare lives in the savanna grasslands of the southern Himalayan foothills, where it depends on the shoots and roots of the tall local grasses for much of its diet. Unfortunately for the hare, the grasses also provide a valuable resource for humans and other wildlife. They are harvested for roofing materials, earning the region the local name of "thatchlands."

Once the grass has been cut down, large areas are burned off to encourage regrowth. The grasses respond well to this kind of management and soon grow again to provide a new harvest. There are other species of vegetation that do not fare so well. Regular burning is not a part of the thatchlands' natural cycle, and those plants that do not have fire-resistant roots or seeds are soon replaced by others that can tolerate the conditions.

Ordeal by Fire

Altering the thatchlands by burning is in itself a serious conservation issue. For the hispid hare, however, it is catastrophic. Not only do many animals die in the flames; those that survive return to find the food sources on which they rely for their survival reduced to ashes. The hares cannot afford to wait for the grass to grow back, and with the natural cover destroyed, they are vulnerable to predation by humans and their dogs. They must find an alternative home, which usually means retreating into the scrub, away from human disturbance.

As agriculture and human settlement expand over the landscape, however, the areas of unused land on which the hares can take refuge are being steadily reduced. More and more pristine habitat is either being reclaimed for thatch or given over to farmland. Herds of domestic animals compete with the hares for the remaining food.

Farming often means making changes to the thatchlands' natural drainage system, either

---

DATA PANEL

Hispid hare (bristly hare, harsh-furred hare, Assam rabbit)

Caprolagus hispidus

Family: Leporidae

World population: Unknown, but almost certainly declining

Distribution: Himalayas in northern India, Nepal, and parts of Bangladesh

Habitat: Tall grassland on flat, well-drained plains; sparse forest

Size: Length head/body: 12–23 in (30–58 cm); tail: 1–1.5 in (2.5–3.8 cm). Weight: 5.5 lb (2.5 kg)

Form: Medium-sized rabbit with coarse, extrathick fur. Ears and hind legs short compared to those of ordinary rabbits

Diet: Shoots and roots of various grass species; bark; some crops

Breeding: Little known, but the young are born from December to March

Related endangered species: Volcano rabbit *(Romerolagus diazi)** EN; Amami rabbit *(Pentalagus furnessi)** EN. Several other species of rabbit and hare are also at risk

Status: IUCN EN; CITES I

See also: Communities and Ecosystems **1:** 22; Rabbit, Volcano **8:** 14

The hispid hare *needs plenty of space in order to survive because it does not live in colonies. In fact, it seems to be almost completely solitary. Males have bigger home ranges than females, but they overlap; so pairs can meet for breeding.*

by diverting water to irrigate crops or by installing dams to control monsoon floods. Seasonal flooding has traditionally been an important part of the thatchlands' ecology because it stops trees and shrubs from encroaching and replacing the grasses. The hares cope with the floods by moving to higher ground in the forested Himalayan foothills during the monsoons. Once flood-control measures are put in place, the grasslands turn into scrub, leaving the hares with nowhere to feed.

A Case of Mistaken Identity

The hispid hare is not a true hare. With its small ears, coarse brown outer fur, and short hind legs, it actually looks more like a rabbit. It has few distinguishing features and is easily mistaken for another species—the Indian hare—that lives in the same areas in the Himalayan foothills. The Indian hare is relatively common and can be hunted without restriction. Unfortunately, most hunters cannot tell the difference between the Indian hare and the hispid hare, so the latter often gets killed in error.

Survival Hopes

Attempts to keep hispid hares in captivity have so far not met with much success. Captured animals die within a few days, presumably as a result of the stress of living in captivity.

The best hope for the hispid hare is that it can be conserved in the wild, which will mean protecting its habitat from further destruction. Other wildlife also suffers from the destruction of the grasslands, in particular the pygmy hog, which occupies much the same range as the hispid hare and has also become endangered. Both the hog and the hare are now protected from deliberate killing, although some hunting still occurs, and the hares also occasionally fall victim to domestic dogs.

Hippopotamus, Pygmy

Hexaprotodon liberiensis

Decades of environmental exploitation and political turmoil have put the future of the pygmy hippopotamus in severe doubt. The key to its survival may lie in the reintroduction of captive-bred individuals into the wild.

Unlike its much larger cousin—the common hippopotamus—the pygmy hippopotamus spends much of its time on land, where it prefers to remain hidden deep in the shelter of thick vegetation. The pygmy hippo is almost completely bald, and the outermost layer of its skin is very thin. As a result, the hippo loses water by evaporation at about five times the rate of a human being. In order to avoid dehydration, pygmy hippos tend to restrict their movements to the humid environment of dense waterside forests. They do not feed in the water, but will often take a dip in order to cool off or to escape from potential danger.

Hunting, Habitat Loss, and War

The main threats to the pygmy hippopotamus are hunting and habitat destruction. Their meat, which is said to taste like pork, is much sought after. Since the pygmy hippo is much less aggressive than the larger and more dangerous common hippo, pursuing them poses little risk to human hunters, who capture and kill them with relative ease.

Pygmy hippos do not gather in large groups. While common hippos are large enough to live in conspicuous herds without fear of predation, living alone is an effective way for the pygmy hippo to avoid the attention of predators. A single animal finds it much easier than a whole herd to melt into the forest or to slip away to hide in the river. However, this low-density, self-sufficient strategy requires plenty of space; and as commercial logging destroys huge areas of the forests, the number of areas capable of supporting viable populations of pygmy hippos has seriously declined. The pygmy hippopotamus is now found only in a few scattered areas of West Africa and is rare wherever it occurs. For example, in 1980 there were thought to be fewer than 100 pygmy hippos living in war ravaged Sierra Leone. Whether the animals can survive the war in that country will not be known for some time. In any event, it will be years before conservation issues receive political attention in Sierra Leone, and by then it may be too late.

It is a similar story in Liberia—home to another vulnerable pygmy hippo population—where there have been severe political problems associated with war. It is feared that an isolated population of pygmy hippos in the Niger delta may already be extinct since they have not been seen for many years.

Conservation Measures

The one glimmer of hope for the pygmy hippo is that there are currently well over 300 individuals living in zoos and conservation institutions around the world. The species takes easily to life in captivity, and a large proportion of the captive population has been born in zoos. The existence of healthy groups of captive animals is no substitute for stable populations of pygmy hippos in the wild. However, it does provide the potential for their reintroduction to areas of secure habitat if and when the environmental and political conditions in their native range improve.

The glossy sheen *of the pygmy hippo's skin is due to a pinkish, oily substance that is secreted from special pores. The secretion helps reduce water loss and protects the hippo from sunburn.*

See also: War **1:** 47; The Role of Zoos **1:** 86; Babirusa **2:** 44

HIPPOPOTAMUS, PYGMY

DATA PANEL

Pygmy hippopotamus

Hexaprotodon liberiensis (formerly *Choeropsis liberiensis*)

Family: Hippopotamidae

World population: A few thousand

Distribution: Liberia, Sierra Leone, Nigeria, Ivory Coast, and Guinea

Habitat: Swamps and lowland forest

Size: Length: 5–5.6 ft (1.5–1.7 m); height at shoulder: 30–40 in (75–100 cm). Weight: 355–600 lb (160–270 kg)

Form: Similar to common hippopotamus but about one tenth the size. Skin hairless and shiny, greenish brown to dark slate gray

Diet: Leaves, shoots, roots, and fruit

Breeding: Single young (very occasionally twins) born at any time of year after 7-month gestation; weaned at 6–8 months; mature at 4–5 years. Life span up to 35 years

Related endangered species: Common hippopotamus subspecies (*Hippopotamus amphibius tschadensis*) of Chad and Niger VU

Status: IUCN VU; CITES II

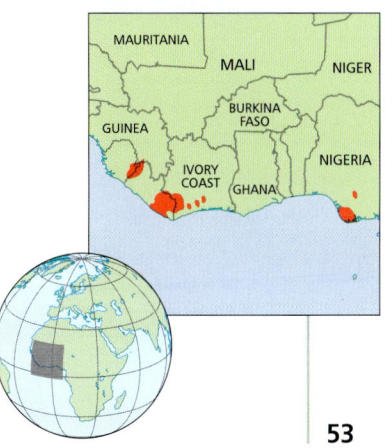

Honeyeater, Regent

Xanthomyza phrygia

The strikingly patterned regent honeyeater has suffered serious declines in range and numbers as a result of the destruction and fragmentation of its forest habitat, and probably also because it has lost out in competition with more adaptable rivals.

The honeyeater family is one of the major groups of Australian birds. Almost 40 percent of the 170 species in the world occur in Australia; the family evolved there and in New Guinea. At least one species occurs in every different land habitat in Australia, and 10 or more species may occur in a single area: Honeyeaters may account for over half of all the birds in a locality.

Brush Tongues

The most distinctive adaptation of the regent honeyeater is its brush-tipped tongue. When the bird pushes its beak into a flower and extends its tongue beyond the beak's tip, the tongue laps up nectar or other sugary fluids the way a paint-brush collects paint. Most honeyeaters can lap up all the nectar from a flower in less than a second. This adaptation is a major factor in the group's success.

Nevertheless, some species of honeyeater are not thriving. One of the most threatened is the regent honeyeater. This attractive and characterful bird feeds on nectar mainly from the flowers of trees—red ironbark, yellow gum and other eucalypts, and yellow box. The bird also eats manna (a sugary sap produced on tree bark in response to injury, especially by insects) and lerps (or honeydew), as well as fruit. All the foods are rich in energy but low in nutrients, so the birds have to spend a lot of time feeding; they live a partly nomadic life, moving around to find the best feeding

DATA PANEL

Regent honeyeater

Xanthomyza phrygia

Family: Meliphagidae

World population: About 1,500 birds

Distribution: Southeastern Australia; mainly at a few sites in northeastern Victoria, along the western slopes of the Great Dividing Range and central coast of New South Wales, with only small numbers elsewhere; now extinct in South Australia

Habitat: Dry, open forests and woodlands, especially those dominated by yellow box, red ironbark, and yellow gum trees; also riverside forests of river she-oaks in New South Wales

Size: Length: 8–9.5 in (20–24 cm)

Form: Slim-bodied, thrush-sized bird with downcurved, sharp-tipped bill; long tail. Male has black head, neck, upper back, and upper breast; patch of bare, pink or yellow skin around each eye; rest of upperparts black with pale-yellow scaly pattern; wings black with broad white fringes to some coverts; 3 broad yellow panels in each folded wing; lower breast, upper belly, and flanks creamy with black chevrons, rest of underparts white; tail black above with yellow edges and tip, bright yellow below. Female smaller and duller. Juvenile browner with yellow bill

Diet: Nectar from various flowers; also insects, manna (sugary sap produced by trees in response to injury), lerps (or honeydew—sugary secretions of aphids and plant-eating insects), and fruit, including mistletoe berries

Breeding: Mainly August–January (may not nest some years); nest of bark and grass strips lined with plant down and hair, built in tree 6.5–33 ft (2–10 m) tall, in an upright fork or among mistletoe; 2–3 salmon-buff eggs with red-brown spots; incubation about 15 days; fledging period about 14 days

Related endangered species: Crow honeyeater (*Gymnomyza aubryana*) EN; black-eared miner (*Manorina melanotis*) EN; stitchbird (*Notiomystis cincta*) VU; dusky friarbird (*Philemon fuscicapillus*) VU; long-bearded melidectes (*Melidectes princeps*) VU; painted honeyeater (*Grantiella picta*) LRnt; white-chinned myzomela (*Myzomela albigula*) DD; Chatham Island bellbird (*Anthornis melanocephala*) EX

Status: IUCN EN; not listed by CITES

See also: Habitat Loss 1: 38; Research 1: 84; Finch, Gouldian 4: 74; Scrub-Bird, Noisy 8: 56

HONEYEATER, REGENT

sites. When breeding, they need more protein, and they include insects in their diet in order to satisfy this requirement. They take them from the trunks, branches, or foliage of trees, but sometimes catch them in flight.

Honeyeaters are quarrelsome birds, often chasing away rivals of their own and other species from flowering trees and other plants. It has been discovered that regent honeyeaters mimic the calls of larger species of honeyeater, such as friarbirds, wattlebirds, and the spiny-cheeked honeyeater, in an attempt to prevent these more dominant relatives from driving them away from sources of nectar.

Fragmented Forests

Despite the skilled mimicry, fragmentation of the regent honeyeater's habitat seems to be favoring more aggressive species, such as the noisy miner, which may be replacing the regent honeyeater in parts of its range. The habitat loss may be affecting the less adaptable regent honeyeater to such an extent that it is unable to gather in sufficient numbers at breeding sites to share the effort of driving rivals away from good nectar sources. Today only about a quarter of its habitat remains, the rest having been cleared for agriculture, timber, and other developments. What remains is often of inferior quality, with larger trees removed and an increasing number of unhealthy trees.

In many places the regent honeyeater appears only sporadically. When breeding, the birds are concentrated at relatively few sites, but numbers fluctuate greatly between sites and from one year to the next. In places where they have been scarce or absent for years they may suddenly return in large numbers. Years when few or no birds breed at a site may be a result of their failure to nest or because they have moved elsewhere to breed. Little is known about the birds' movements outside the breeding season.

The regent honeyeater, *an attractive, brightly plumaged bird, lives, feeds and breeds in dry, open forests.*

Conservationists carry out annual surveys of the species' range and abundance. A captive colony has now been established. Logging and grazing have been restricted at some major sites, and many of the trees favored by the honeyeaters have been planted to replace those destroyed or in poor health.

Plans to build on this work include studying the movements and population dynamics of the species, measuring the degree of isolation between different breeding populations, assessing the effect of noisy miners, and surveying and monitoring the birds' habitat to ensure that it is not degraded.

Hornbill, Writhed

Aceros leucocephalus

The large, impressive writhed hornbill needs extensive areas of lowland rain forest with large nesting trees—a habitat that is increasingly threatened by clearance for logging, plantations, and local agriculture.

Hornbills are the most conspicuous large birds of Asian rain forests. Pairs and flocks wander, often seminomadically, over large home ranges of up to 154 square miles (400 sq. km) in search of ripe forest fruit. Alighting in the forest canopy, they shuffle and hop to within easy reach of selected fruit. The most distinctive and conspicuous feature of the hornbill is the massive bill that it uses dexterously to pluck and chew fruit. The bill and the bony casque above it are bright red in this species and may function as a communication signal. The bony structure may also function as a resonance chamber for the writhed hornbill's deep, loud calls, as does the extendable throat pouch.

Female hornbills stay in a nest hole for the entire incubation and nestling period. Installed inside the chosen hole in a large tree, she seals all but a small slit with a mixture of feces, mud, and pulped plant material, which soon hardens into a cement. The male passes food through the hole, ensuring that the female and brood are protected from many potential predators. Inside the chamber the female molts all her flight feathers simultaneously; if the male were to die or if she broke free, she would be unable to forage for herself. After four months of confinement the female pecks away the cement and returns to a free-flying life, followed by the fledglings.

Shared Forest Home

Writhed hornbills share the Mindanao forests with the larger rufous hornbill and the small Mindanao tarictic hornbill. Writhed hornbills are the rarest species on Mindanao and have the smallest geographical range of the three species. Writhed hornbills on the nearby islands of Negros and Panay differ somewhat in their head coloring, tail pattern, and calls, and have recently been recognized as a separate species, the Visayan (or Walden's) writhed hornbill.

DATA PANEL

Writhed hornbill (Mindanao wrinkled hornbill)

Aceros leucocephalus

Family: Bucerotidae

World population: 10,000–20,000 birds

Distribution: Mindanao and adjacent islands of Camiguin Sur and Dinagat, Philippines

Habitat: Lowland and midaltitude rain forest

Size: Length: 30 in (76 cm). Weight: 28–46 oz (800–1,300 g)

Form: Large, rakish bird with long bill, neck, and tail. Glossy black plumage with black-tipped white tail. Male has pale-buff head, neck, and upper breast. Red bill and skin around eye and throat. Long, broad wings

Diet: Mainly fruit; also large insects, reptiles, birds' eggs, and nestlings

Breeding: Female seals herself into tree hole. One to 3 eggs laid. Male feeds female during incubation and nestling; female breaks seal at about 3 months, and chicks fledge

Related endangered species: Mindoro tarictic (*Penelopides mindorensis*) EN; Visayan tarictic (*P. panini*) EN; Narcondam hornbill (*Aceros narcondami*) VU; plain-pouched hornbill (*A. subruficollis*) VU; Sumba hornbill (*A. everetti*) VU; rufous-necked hornbill (*A. nipalensis*) VU; Visayan writhed (or Walden's) hornbill (*A. waldeni*) CR; Sulu hornbill (*Anthracoceros montani*) CR; Palawan hornbill (*A. marchei*) VU

Status: IUCN LRnt; CITES II

See also: Hunting 1: 42; Saving the Habitats 1: 88; Eagle, Philippine 4: 54

As with other species in lowland rain forest in the Philippines, the birds are threatened by deforestation. Forests have been cleared for logging since colonial times; and although commercial logging is now largely prohibited, there is increasing pressure for agricultural land from a burgeoning human population. Hornbills are particularly susceptible to logging since it destroys the largest trees on which they depend for nesting holes.

Moreover, the species is sometimes hunted for meat. In the course of studying the Visayan writhed hornbill on Panay, researchers learned that 40 hornbills were shot on a single day in 1997. Hunters target the hornbills as flocks gather daily at favored trees with ripe fruit. Small numbers are also taken from the wild as pets. Of 54 species of hornbill in the world, nine are classified as Threatened, including five in the Philippines. The Visayan writhed hornbill is perhaps the most threatened hornbill in the world after the Sulu hornbill—so little of its forest habitat remains on the islands that its population may be fewer than 50 pairs.

The writhed hornbill's *red casque grows continuously, developing more ridges with time. It provides an approximate way of telling a bird's age.*

Conservation Measures

The long-term survival of writhed hornbills depends on conservation of extensive tracts of lowland or hill forest, combined with community education and awareness about sustainable hunting. The last survey of Mindanao in 1988 found that 29 percent of the island was taken up by forest. Today much of the forest has been cleared or degraded, and a large percentage is montane (mountainous) forest, which is unsuitable for writhed hornbills. Protected areas exist on paper, but few have any proper protection. It is hoped that the key forests will receive conservation resources under the National Integrated Protected Areas System. The future of writhed hornbills may be assured if steps are taken to conserve the Philippine eagle, Mindanao's national bird.

Horse, Przewalski's Wild

Equus przewalskii

Excessive hunting, competition with domestic stock, and interbreeding with domestic horses have effectively caused the extinction of purebred herds of Przewalski's horse in the wild.

Przewalski's wild horse is named after the Russian general who discovered it while exploring Central Asia in 1879. It is, or was, the only species of true wild horse, but it is now extinct in its natural range. The horses used to live in large herds, each led by a dominant stallion, wandering the great grassy plains of Central Asia in considerable numbers. The animals would be on the move, feeding almost constantly, and always alert for danger. Although they were occasionally hunted for meat and hides, capture was not a significant threat while human populations remained low, and probably relatively few were killed. However, by the early 1900s hunting pressure had increased substantially, and the horse population began a steady decline in numbers.

The Przewalski's wild horse was given full legal protection in Mongolia in 1926. The legislation did not save the dwindling herds because the growing human population began to fence land for cultivation, excluding the horses from traditional feeding areas and vital places to drink. At the same time, the wild horses began to interbreed with domestic horses that were wandering freely in the same areas. The result was hybrid types and the steady dilution of the genetic integrity and typical features of the purebred wild horse herds. The last true Przewalski's wild horse was reported in 1968.

There now appear to be no Przewalski's horses surviving in the wild, but fortunately there are some in captivity. The horses were never domesticated but kept as a rarity in zoos. From a low point of just 13 animals numbers have been steadily increasing, and over 1,000 have been born in zoos. As a result of the small number of horses involved early on, inbreeding was a problem, leading to poor breeding success and low survival rates. However, zoos in Europe, North America, and the former Soviet Union collaborated constructively to manage a cooperative breeding program that aimed to share animals and to avoid matings between close relatives. About 200 horses are covered by this program, and purebred Przewalski's horses are now well established in captivity.

Reintroduction into the Wild

Many generations of captive breeding, artificial food, confinement in small enclosures, and living in mild climates away from Central Asia may all combine to

See also: Captive Breeding **1:** 87; Ass, African Wild **2:** 34; Ass, Asiatic Wild **2:** 36; Oryx, Scimitar-Horned **7:** 30

HORSE, PRZEWALSKI'S WILD

DATA PANEL

Przewalski's wild horse

Equus przewalskii

Family: Equidae

World population: Several hundred

Distribution: Altai Mountains of Mongolia and (formerly) adjacent parts of China

Habitat: Dry, semidesert plain; steppe grassland

Size: Length head/body: 7 ft (2–2.1 m); tail: 36 in (90 cm); height at shoulder: 4 ft (1.2 m). Weight: 450–650 lb (200–300 kg)

Form: A stockily built pony with short neck and legs. The head is relatively heavy. The fur is sandy brown, much longer in winter, with a white area around the muzzle. Stiff, blackish hairs form an erect mane on the neck

Diet: Mainly grass, but also other small plants; shrubs and bark where they are available

Breeding: One foal born in April or May after 12-month gestation. Life span may exceed 25 years in captivity

Related endangered species: African wild ass *(Equus africanus)** CR; Asiatic wild ass *(E. hemionus)** VU; Grevy's zebra *(E. grevyi)** EN; mountain zebra *(E. zebra)** EN; quagga *(E. quagga)** EX

Status: IUCN EW; CITES I

Przewalski's is the only living species of truly wild horse. It recently became extinct in the wild but is being reintroduced to its former range (see map) using animals bred in captivity.

reduce the ability of the animals to survive in the extreme conditions of their native home. In 1989 an experiment was started at the Bukhara Breeding Center in Uzbekistan to find out whether horses bred for generations in zoos could actually survive the challenge of living wild in the semidesert conditions of Central Asia. A stallion and four mares were released into a huge fenced area and studied. The horses seemed to manage well; they bred successfully and did not suffer ill-effects from mixing with wild asses also present in the area. Efforts are now being made to restore Przewalski's horse to the wild in Mongolia, where they have begun to breed successfully in a protected reserve. It is also planned to reintroduce the Przewalski's wild horse to China.

Huia

Heteralocha acutirostris

The huia was a unique bird: sacred to the Maori peoples of New Zealand and zoologically fascinating to collectors. However, it became extinct mainly through loss of habitat.

The huia is famous for being the only species of bird in which the male and female had a completely different type of bill. The male had a thick, chisellike bill, operated by powerful head muscles and ideal for breaking open rotting wood. Females had a much longer, slender, curved bill capable of probing deeply into nooks and crannies that could not be reached by the male. The birds always fed together, helping each other.

Maori Marriage Symbol

The huia was revered by the local Maori people as the most sacred creature of the forests. The bird's habits made it a symbol of a happy marriage. The distinctive white-tipped tail feathers were collected and used as important gifts among the Maori and were often kept in special boxes among family treasures and worn only by the most senior people. The Maori were careful not to take large numbers of the birds, and powerful taboos restrained them from killing too many.

However, Maori traditions meant little to the European colonizers who began to settle in New Zealand in the late 18th century. Many of the new settlers found it hard to make a living, yet it soon became clear that museums and private collectors in Europe and America would pay good money for specimens of the unique birds of New Zealand. Foremost among the birds sent away was the huia because of its unique anatomy. Records show that collectors obtained over 600 skins from the hills east of Wellington in 1874. In total several thousand skins were exported, leaving few birds alive until protective legislation banned such trading.

Basic Instinct

The birds were easy to hunt: By imitating their call, a hunter could get them within easy range of a gun, although this was not always necessary. Huias did not fly much since they had short wings. Instead, they hopped between logs and branches on the forest floor, where they could be killed even with sticks. They were also tame: One story tells of a female huia that allowed herself to be lifted off her nest during

DATA PANEL

Huia

Heteralocha acutirostris

Family: Callaeidae

World population: 0 (Extinct)

Distribution: Formerly North Island, New Zealand

Habitat: Lowland forests

Size: Length head/body: 10–12 in (25–30 cm); tail: 7–9 in (18–23 cm)

Form: A black, long-legged, slender, crowlike bird with orange wattles (loose folds of skin hanging from bill base). Differently curved beak on male and female. White tip to tail

Diet: Insects, grubs, and worms found on forest floor and among rotting wood

Breeding: Little known; 2–4 gray, brown, and purplish-spotted eggs laid October–November in a large cup-shaped nest of sticks and twigs lined with finer material

Related endangered species: Kokako (*Callaeas cinerea*) EN; saddleback (*Philesturnus carunculatus*) LRnt

Status: IUCN EX; not listed by CITES

See also: Specialization 1: 28; Introductions 1: 54; Crow, Hawaiian 3: 82; Dodo 4: 20

incubation. Another describes how a chick was taken into camp and fed by hand, with its parents bringing in food from the forest.

Huias had evolved for millions of years in the absence of land mammals, which is why they were not afraid of people. The first people (Polynesians) did not arrive until the 12th century, but they brought with them dogs and also rats. From about 1800 onward large numbers of domestic animals were imported, including cats. In addition, stoats and ferrets were used to control rats and rabbits.

In a short time introduced mammals became a serious threat to many tame native birds, especially those that nested on the ground or in easily accessible places, such as the low tree branches favored by huias. Other birds posed a threat too; Indian mynah birds, brought in as pets, carried ticks and disease. This may have affected huias, although there is no direct evidence of it.

Vanishing Habitat

Heavy collection and predation would have been enough to bring about the extinction of the huia sooner or later, but the bird's main problem was loss of forest habitat. Even if left alone, the birds could not survive once their trees were cut down for timber and fuel. The forests were also removed to make way for grazing land for domestic livestock, and land clearance created areas where the huias could not feed. The huia's habitat—moist, warm forest with plenty of rotten wood—simply vanished.

The last reliable report of a living huia was in December 1907. Although there have been repeated claims of sightings, none has been confirmed. Today one of the last strongholds of the huia, between Wellington and Masterton, has been taken over by farmland, housing, and light industry. It is no place for a huia, and there are none there now.

Huias *were killed by the thousand for collectors and museums. Protective legislation in 1892 came too late to save the bird, whose habitat had largely been destroyed.*

Hummingbird, Bee

Mellisuga helenae

Bee hummingbirds are found only on the island of Cuba, and the males of the species are famous for being the world's smallest living bird. Although they were once relatively common and widespread, they are now becoming increasingly rare and localized.

As its name suggests, the bee hummingbird can easily be mistaken for a large bee as it hovers to sip nectar from the blossom of a hibiscus plant or an aloe. About half of its diminutive length is taken up by its long, slender bill and short tail. Among the smallest of all vertebrate animals, it weighs about 75,000 times less than the world's largest bird, the male ostrich, and is about the same size as an ostrich eye. Bee hummingbirds are dwarfed by many of the butterflies found in their tropical forest home.

Like other hummingbirds, the bee hummingbird feeds in flight. It is a superb flyer and has wings with bones that are fused except at the shoulder joint. This wing design enables it to rotate its wings. Such prowess in the air allows it to hover in one spot, remaining almost motionless in front of a flower to feed. It can also fly sideways, straight up and down, and even backward.

When hovering, a bee hummingbird beats its wings 70 times per second. This uses up large amounts of energy—and such a tiny animal can store very little. Consequently, it must have a constant source of energy-rich food that it can convert quickly into fuel to power its proportionately large wing muscles and maintain its high metabolism. It finds this food in the form of nectar, which it sips from tubular flowers by inserting its long, slender bill and lapping up the sugary liquid with its long, grooved tongue. The bee hummingbird needs to feed every few minutes. It can only survive short periods without food, and it does so by becoming torpid, reducing its metabolic rate by 80 to 90 percent and thereby saving up to 60 percent of its energy requirements. The male bee hummingbird is fiercely territorial, driving off any intruder of the same or different species that attempts to feed from his patch of nectar-rich flowers.

Spectacular Displays

A male attracts a mate in three ways. First, he expands his gorget—a bib of feathers—and lateral plumes, which take on a glittering, jewellike appearance in sunlight and are iridescent—the colors change depending on the viewing

---

DATA PANEL

Bee hummingbird

Mellisuga helenae

Family: Trochilidae

World population: Over 10,000 birds (estimated)

Distribution: Cuba; formerly occurred on the Isla de la Juventud (Isle of Youth) to the southwest of Cuba

Habitat: Mainly coastal forests and forest margins, with thick tangles of lianas and abundant epiphytes (plants that grow on other plants); also interior forests, wooded mountain valleys, swamps, and gardens

Size: Length: 2–2.3 in (5–6 cm); male slightly smaller than female. Weight: 0.05–0.07 oz (1.6–1.9 g)

Form: Tiny bird with long, straight, black bill. Male's head, throat, lateral plumes, and gorget (bib of feathers) glitter fiery red in sunlight; rest of upperparts bluish; rest of underparts off-white. Female and immatures have green upperparts and whitish underparts

Diet: Adults eat nectar from a wide range of flowers; also small insects

Breeding: Season from March to June. Female weaves nest from dried plant fibers, camouflaged on the outside with lichens, usually partly hidden by leaves and lined with soft plant wool; 2 white eggs incubated for 21–22 days. Young fledge at 13–14 days, leaving nest at about 18 days

Related endangered species: No close relatives, but 9 hummingbird species classed as Critical, 9 as Endangered, and 9 as Vulnerable

Status: IUCN LRnt; CITES II

See also: The History of Birds **1:** 64; Firecrown, Juan Fernández **4:** 78

angle. Second, he zooms around in an aerial display. Third, he beats his wings to make a humming noise.

Pairs of birds mate in flight, after which the female builds a tiny, deep, cup-shaped nest in a forked twig or on a branch of a tree. Into it she lays two pea-sized eggs. She must keep the young supplied with a nourishing diet of nectar and partly digested insects.

Threatened Habitat

The bee hummingbird was once found throughout Cuba and the Isla de la Juventud (Isle of Youth) to the southwest of Cuba. Today it may survive only in a few sites in La Habana, Sierra de Anafe, Guanahacabibes Peninsula, Zapata Swamp, Moa, Mayarí, and the coast of Guantánamo. The bird seems to be heavily dependent on mature forest.

Much of Cuba's native vegetation has been converted for growing crops or for cattle pasture, and only 15 to 20 percent of the land remains in its natural state. Large areas of rain forest have been destroyed to make way for plantations of cacao, coffee, and tobacco, while dry forest is threatened by logging, charcoal production, and slash-and-burn cultivation. In the Zapata Swamp, burning, drainage, and agricultural expansion take their toll.

Although there are some 200 conservation areas in Cuba, making up about 12 percent of the total land area, some are probably too small to support their wildlife, and few afford sufficient protection from logging and other threats. Conservation efforts must be improved to save the bee hummingbird.

The bee hummingbird *beats its wings 70 times per second when feeding.*

Hutia, Jamaican

Geocapromys brownii

Captive breeding has helped restore numbers of the nearly extinct Jamaican hutia. In the meantime, however, the animal's natural habitat has been shrinking at an alarming rate.

Long before European settlers arrived on Jamaica, the island's hutias had been hunted by native American Indians, particularly the Arawak tribe. Archaeologists have unearthed hutia remains from ancient refuse dumps, or "middens," all over the island. Hunting increased dramatically with the arrival of Europeans. The settlers also brought with them cats, rats, dogs, and mongoose, which immediately set about attacking Jamaica's native wildlife. The island's only other endemic ground-dwelling mammal, the Jamaican rice rat, was exterminated by 1875, and most of the Jamaican hutia's relatives on other Caribbean islands met a similar fate.

By the mid-20th century Jamaican hutias were clearly becoming rare. In 1945 the Jamaican government passed the Wildlife Protection Act, which listed hutias as a protected species and made hunting them illegal. The law was not enforced, however, and the killing continued. Efforts to conserve the Jamaican hutia in the 1960s and early 1970s ran into difficulties because so little was known about the species and its habitat. Even the IUCN, when trying to categorize the hutia's conservation status, could not decide between Endangered, Vulnerable or Rare, so it was listed simply as Indeterminate.

In 1972 the Jersey Wildlife Preservation Trust took a number of hutias into captivity at the Jersey Zoo. Their captive-breeding program was so successful that within 10 years descendants of the Jersey population had been placed in zoos all over the world, and the captive population was considered stable enough to ensure the survival of the species. In 1982 an expedition went to Jamaica to study the remaining wild population and to investigate the possibilities for releasing captive-bred hutias back into the wild. What the researchers found was rather a surprise.

Secure Shelter

A detailed survey showed that the hutia's range had indeed shrunk and confirmed that hunting was still widespread. However, despite such problems, hutias appeared to be relatively abundant in some areas, even where hunting occurred. At first glance the sites appeared to have little in common—some were covered in scrub, some were dense forest, some were very dry, and others scattered with swamps. Then the researchers realized that in each place the hutias were relying on the availability of secure holes in which to shelter

DATA PANEL

Jamaican hutia (coney)

Geocapromys brownii

Family: Capromyidae

World population: Unknown

Distribution: Jamaica

Habitat: Varied forest and scrubland on highly fissured limestone from sea level to 3,300 ft (1,000 m)

Size: Length head/body: 13–18 in (33–45 cm); tail: 1–3 in (4–7 cm). Weight: 2–4 lb (1–2 kg)

Form: Large, guinea-piglike rodent with coarse, grayish-buff to dark-brown fur and short, hairy tail

Diet: Plant material

Breeding: Two litters of 1–3 young born per year after gestation of 4.5 months; able to eat solid food within 2 days. Life span up to 9 years

Related endangered species: Bahamian hutia (*Geocapromys ingrahami*) VU

Status: IUCN VU; not listed by CITES

See also: The Role of Zoos **1:** 86; Prairie Dog, Black-Tailed **7:** 92

and nest. In some parts of Jamaica, where the limestone is riddled with holes (known as rock warrens), the researchers noticed that the animals were doing particularly well. They realized that the huitas used the holes as a refuge; once they were inside, they were safe from the dogs commonly used to hunt them and could not be dug out.

Habitat Loss

Although hutias live among different types of vegetation, the animal has been losing habitat at an alarming rate. Land has been cleared for large- and small-scale agriculture and development. Some small patches of apparently ideal hutia habitat contain no hutias at all. Hutias are known to be sedentary animals—one tagged female was recaptured after five years within 20 yards (18 m) of the spot where she was originally caught. With so little tendency to disperse, it is unlikely that hutias will ever recolonize the remote sites from which they have disappeared.

While it is important that the laws forbidding hutia hunting are enforced, by far the biggest challenge is to prevent further loss of habitat. The captive-breeding program has been scaled down in the hope that conservation measures in the wild will be enough to secure the future of Jamaica's only remaining terrestrial endemic mammal.

Hutias are agile climbers, though not particularly fast-moving. They are active mostly at night and hide in rocky crevices by day.

Hyena, Brown

Hyaena brunnea

The mild-mannered cousin of the spotted and striped hyenas has been persecuted throughout much of its range for centuries. Today its survival depends largely on the protection it receives in national parks and game reserves.

The brown hyena is much less widespread than its two close cousins, the spotted and striped hyenas. Brown hyenas share the less arid parts of their range with the spotted, or laughing, hyena. Being larger, more robust, and more aggressive, the spotted hyena dominates the relationship, often harassing the brown hyena and stealing its food. Spotted hyenas are effective predators, capable of killing large animals such as wildebeest, domestic cattle, and even people. Unfortunately, the brown hyena is often wrongly assumed to have identical behavior and has been persecuted throughout much of its range as a result.

The animal's wide distribution is also increasingly broken up by areas of agricultural development and human settlement. Populations of brown hyenas rarely persist for long once an area has been settled by people. In the last 200 years brown hyenas have been forced out of most of the heavily farmed parts of South Africa and Zimbabwe. If it were not for the protection the species receives in a number of national parks and game reserves—such as the Gemsbok and Kalahari National Parks in South Africa and several other parks in Botswana—brown hyenas would almost certainly be facing extinction soon.

Lone Scavenger

The much-maligned brown hyena is, in fact, far more likely to raid a farmer's trashcans than attack his animals. There is little evidence that brown hyenas kill domestic

---

DATA PANEL

Brown hyena

Hyaena brunnea

Family: Hyaenidae

World population: Unknown, perhaps a few thousand

Distribution: Southwestern Angola, Botswana, southern Mozambique, Namibia, South Africa, southern and western Zimbabwe

Habitat: Dry scrub and grassland, semidesert and desert

Size: Length head/body: 35–54 in (90–136 cm); tail: 7–11 in (18–26.5 cm); height at shoulder: 25–34.5 in (64–88 cm). Weight: 60–104 lb (27–47 kg)

Form: Doglike animal with dark-brown body fur; gray and brown bands on the legs; front legs longer than back ones

Diet: Scavenged carcasses of large animals; also small mammals, reptiles, fruit, and fungi

Breeding: One to 5 (usually 2 or 3) pups born May–November after 3.5-month gestation; reared in den, sometimes communally; weaned at 14 months; mature at 18–36 months. Life span up to 29 years in captivity, probably no more than 15 years in wild

Related endangered species: Spotted hyena (*Crocuta crocuta*)* LRcd

Status: IUCN LRnt; not listed by CITES

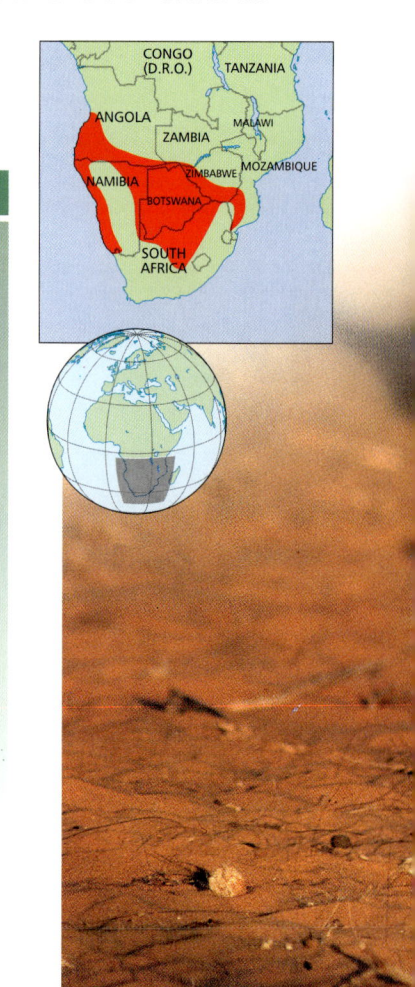

See also: National Parks 1: 92; Dog, African Wild 4: 22; Hyena, Spotted 5: 68

animals. A long-term study of a brown hyena colony living near farmland in the Transvaal recorded no attempts to kill livestock in 15 years. Individuals seen feeding on carcasses are usually just scavenging the remains of a kill made by another animal. For the most part brown hyenas tend to hunt much smaller creatures. Sometimes almost half their diet consists of ripe fruit, mushrooms, and other vegetable matter.

Spotted hyenas are not the only animals to bully brown hyenas. Lions and African hunting dogs frequently drive them away from carcasses. Because brown hyenas generally forage alone, they are rarely in a position to fight back. Instead, they usually make a quick getaway, often trying to take a portion of the kill with them to eat later if possible. If a hyena is cornered by a larger animal, it screams loudly. If that fails to have any useful effect, it may even play dead to avoid being attacked.

Survival Strategy

It seems that wherever the brown hyena shares a habitat with other large carnivores, it always comes off worst. However, the animal has one considerable advantage over other species in that it can survive quite happily in extremely dry habitats. The vegetable component of the brown hyena's diet is very important in this respect. Fruit such as wild melons and cucumbers—which have a high water content—provide the animals with a useful source of water: a precious commodity in arid areas, where they may be forced to go without drinking water for weeks or months at a time.

Brown hyenas are generally not as greedy as other species. They tend not to gorge themselves on vast meals. Any extra food is usually hidden or "cached" for later use. Their hoarding habit helps them survive in some of Africa's most hostile environments.

The brown hyena *is more doglike than its spotted cousin. It is also more sociable, less aggressive, and considerably more threatened.*

Hyena, Spotted

Crocuta crocuta

The skulking, cowardly reputation of the spotted hyena is at least partly deserved, but its behavior is all part of a deliberate and successful survival strategy.

The spotted hyena is the largest of the three hyena species living in Africa. It is also the least social. Spotted hyenas live in female-dominated clans. However, there is nowhere near the same level of cooperation as in other social carnivores. In fact, often quite the reverse is true, with individuals squabbling over food and jostling for position. The pack does not help feed the offspring of the dominant female, which may explain why the young suckle for as long as 18 months, until they are able to hold their own at a carcass.

Hyenas have a deserved reputation as brazen scavengers, but spotted hyenas are also extremely capable hunters. They will always select weak or injured prey over healthy animals, thereby minimizing effort and potential risk to themselves. They will often attack livestock; but if confronted by an angry farmer, they immediately slink off.

Skillful Scavengers

There is no doubt that scavenging is easier and less risky than hunting, so hyenas take full advantage of any opportunity. They are quick to gather at the scene of a kill, often driving away the rightful owners such as lions or cheetahs. Such apparent cowardice and laziness shows a good deal of sense, but it has done little to enhance their dishonorable image, and the hyena is an animal with few friends. Hyenas are also extremely efficient: A pack can completely demolish a zebra or antelope carcass in about 15 minutes, leaving nothing but the contents of the stomach and maybe the horn bosses and a few teeth. Bones, skin, and even small teeth are all crunched up in the hyena's powerful jaws. It is little wonder that hyenas move in on kills made by other predators: On average, a pride of lions will leave about 40 percent of a kill uneaten.

DATA PANEL

Spotted hyena (laughing hyena)

Crocuta crocuta

Family: Hyaenidae

World population: Several thousand

Distribution: Sub-Saharan Africa, excluding the Congo Basin

Habitat: Open grassland, marshy areas, and scrub up to 13,000 ft (4,000 m)

Size: Length head/body: 30–47 in (79–120 cm); tail: 10–14 in (25–36 cm); female larger than male. Weight: 105–165 lb (48–75 kg); female up to 198 lb (90 kg)

Form: Doglike animal with short muzzle, large ears, thick neck, and powerful shoulders; back legs shorter than front, creating sloping posture; fur yellowish brown and variably spotted; females have a fake penis, making it difficult to distinguish sexes

Diet: Wildebeest, gazelles, topis, buffalo, zebras, young rhinoceroses calves; carrion

Breeding: Two or 3 young born at any time of year after gestation of 3–4 months; weaned from 6 months. Average life span 12 years, but may live up to 25 years

Related endangered species: Brown hyena (*Hyaena brunnea*)* LRnt

Status: IUCN LRcd; not listed by CITES

See also: Populations 1: 20; Hyena, Brown 5: 66

Spotted hyena numbers are reasonably stable in the national parks and game reserves of southern and eastern Africa. Indeed, in areas where prey such as zebra and antelope abound, the spotted hyena is probably the most successful hunter, and perhaps the most abundant large predator in Africa. However, it inevitably comes into conflict with people wherever it threatens livestock.

The spotted hyena is an unpopular creature; outside protected areas numbers continue to decline, and the outlook for survival seems bleak. At present it has no special conservation status, and the future is

Hyenas have highly selective hunting behavior that helps maintain the overall health of prey populations by weeding out sick, weak, and elderly individuals.

even less positive for the brown and striped hyenas, both of which are in need of special protection. Smaller than the spotted hyena and less proficient hunters, they are far more dependent on scavenging and making easy kills of weak or defenseless prey. Conservationists must be careful that measures put in place to protect brown and striped hyenas do not adversely affect the spotted hyena.

Ibex, Nubian

Capra nubiana

Life is a struggle at the best of times for all desert mammals. The plight of the Nubian ibex has been made worse by trophy hunters who shoot the adult males for their horns.

Nubian ibex inhabit the rocky slopes of desert mountains in the Middle East, Arabia, and northeastern Africa. The adults are often found living alone (especially males). Females, with their young, including immature males (less than three years old), may form small groups. The ibex walks slowly among the rocks and across open slopes, searching for grasses, shoots, and leaves to eat. Like other ruminants, they will rest periodically to chew their cud before moving on in search of more food.

The Nubian is smaller than most other ibex, and the only one that is mainly adapted to life in desert conditions. Its pale, shiny coat reflects the sun's rays, helping keep the animal cool. This means that ibex can remain active even during the hottest parts of the day and wander widely in search of food.

Although there are no mammalian predators to fear in the desert, eagles and other birds of prey present a danger. Normally the ibex stay out in the open where there are plenty of escape routes and are ready to use their speed to escape attack should the need arise.

DATA PANEL

Nubian ibex

Capra nubiana

Family: Bovidae

World population: 1,200 (1986 estimate)

Distribution: Israel, Jordan, Oman, Saudi Arabia, Yemen, northeastern Sudan

Habitat: Slopes of desert mountains

Size: Length: 42–48 in (107–122 cm); height at shoulder: 24–30 in (60–75 cm). Weight: 55–150 lb (25–70 kg)

Form: A goatlike animal, sandy brown with paler hindquarters. Mature males have a dark beard and a black stripe down the back and also up the front of each foreleg. The horns sweep upward and backward in a semicircular direction, each with up to 36 prominent knobbly ridges across the outer surface of the curve. Male horns may grow to 4 ft (1.2 m); in females they are thinner and less than 14 in (35 cm) long. The young have white underparts.

Diet: Almost any type of vegetation

Breeding: Mates in late summer (or October), producing a single kid after 5-month gestation. Twins are rare. Breeds only once a year, from the age of 2–3 years onward. Life span at least 17 years

Related endangered species: Walia ibex (*Capra walie*) CR; markhor (*Capra falconeri*)* EN

Status: IUCN EN; not listed by CITES

See also: Biomes **1:** 18; War **1:** 47; Addax **2:** 4; Markhor **6:** 72; Oryx, Arabian **7:** 28

Young male Nubian ibex *like these have small horns. They remain in family groups until they are three years old.*

However, in winter it can become quite cold, especially at night, when the clear skies rapidly absorb heat from the ground, and the temperature drops. At these times the ibex may seek shelter in ravines and caves. Similarly, when it rains, the animals will try to avoid getting wet.

Threats from Hunters

The ibex is prized for its meat by local people in the countries where it is found, especially since few other animals in the desert are big enough for humans to eat. In contrast to most desert animals, the Nubian ibex likes to drink daily, so it rarely lives far from water. It can be relatively easily shot or snared as it approaches water holes, especially since these are often in clefts between rock faces and only accessible via narrow tracks. In addition, wars have frequently been fought in regions where the ibex live, and the animals would have been a welcome source of food to soldiers, who were able to kill them with their powerful rifles. Moreover, the prominent curved horns of the ibex have attracted attention from trophy hunters, who seek out big males.

Like other large desert mammals, the Nubian ibex was probably always scarce, but hunting has made it even more so. There are none left in Syria, Lebanon, or (probably) Egypt, and the few animals that remain elsewhere are scattered over a very large area and live in widely separated small groups.

The Walia ibex of Ethiopia is sometimes regarded as a separate species from the Nubian. It lives on the steep slopes of the Simien Mountains, feeding among the giant heathers. It is Critically Endangered and probably now numbers only about 100 individuals.

Ibis, Northern Bald

Geronticus eremita

With its red face and long, downcurved, red bill framed by a scruffy ruff of black feathers, the northern bald ibis has an odd charm of its own. It is one of the world's rarest birds, with a very small range and population.

The northern bald ibis was once widespread and abundant, but it is now extremely localized. Its representation in hieroglyphics dating back 5,000 years shows that it was revered as a holy bird in ancient Egypt. It bred in many places in North Africa and the Near and Middle East and until the 17th century in the mountains of Germany, Austria, Switzerland, and the former Yugoslavia. At the beginning of the 20th century the bird was rediscovered in North Africa and the Middle East to Western science. It looked very like the bird in a 16th-century Swiss drawing, but experts did not believe such an exotic species could ever have lived in Europe until a semifossilized specimen that was definitely a northern bald ibis was found there.

Decline and Persecution

The reasons for the species' decline are not known for certain. From the Middle Ages onward it was hunted for food, which may have contributed to its eventual extinction in Europe. Other factors probably included the conversion of the mountain meadows where it fed into farmland and possibly a cooling of the climate.

Following its scientific discovery, the northern bald ibis faced increased persecution as museum collectors raced to secure specimens of this rare, semimythical bird. Aided by local hunters, they wiped out whole colonies, including, by the 1930s, most of the remaining Algerian colonies and all those in Syria. The bird also faced increasing threats from the conversion of its habitat to farmland, the rising use of pesticides, and frequent droughts. By the mid-20th century the world breeding population had declined to one colony in Turkey, one in Algeria, and a few in Morocco.

Turkey

The Turkish bald ibis colony at the town of Birecik on the Euphrates River survived only because local people believed that the bird was a symbol of fertility and that it served as a guide to pilgrims to

DATA PANEL

Northern bald ibis

Geronticus eremita

Family: Threskiornithidae

World population: About 220 birds

Distribution: In Morocco breeds only at Sous-Massa National Park and nearby Tamri; captive-bred, released colony breeds at Birecik in Turkey

Habitat: Arid to semiarid, sparsely vegetated steppes on plains and rocky plateaus; cultivated fields and pastures. Wild birds breed on cliff ledges by sea

Size: Length: 27.5–31.5 in (70–80 cm); wingspan: 4.1–4.4 ft (1.3–1.4 m); male usually larger. Weight unknown

Form: Large, dark, storklike bird; iridescent black plumage shows bronze-green, copper, blue, purple, and violet gloss in sunlight; naked red face and crown; long, narrow feathers project from nape to form wispy ruff; long, red downcurved bill and relatively short reddish legs; broad wings show 3–4 separated primary feathers at tips in flight

Diet: Mainly grasshoppers, locusts, beetles, and small lizards; also woodlice, spiders, snails, scorpions, small fish, frogs, and tadpoles; occasionally nestling birds and small mammals; berries, young shoots, and other plant matter

Breeding: Breeds in colonies of 3–40 pairs; nest is loose platform of branches lined with grass, straw, and other material, including paper; female lays 2–4 brown-spotted, bluish-white eggs; incubation period lasts 3–4 weeks. Chicks fledge in 6–7 weeks

Related endangered species: Southern bald ibis (*Geronticus calvus*) VU; dwarf olive ibis (*Bostrychia bocagei*) CR; white-shouldered ibis (*Pseudibis davisoni*) CR; giant ibis (*P. gigantea*) CR; crested ibis (*Nipponia nippon*) EN

Status: IUCN CR; CITES I

See also: Pesticides 1: 51; Reintroduction 1: 92; Spoonbill, Black-Faced 9: 26

Mecca. They held an annual festival to celebrate its return each February from winter quarters in Sudan and southern Arabia. However, when Birecik grew, the newcomers did not share the local people's reverence for the ibis, and the festival was not held after 1958. As the town expanded, the bird's nesting grounds were absorbed. From an estimated 3,000 pairs in 1890 the population was reduced to 530 pairs by 1953 and 23 pairs by 1973.

The chief causes of this catastrophic decline were the use of pesticides in the surrounding habitat and the increasing human disturbance at the colonies. In 1977 a colony of captive-bred birds was created by conservationists 1.3 miles (2 km) north of Birecik, with the aim of encouraging the wild birds breeding in the town to relocate to this site. However, most of the released birds failed to integrate with the wild population, which meant that they did not migrate (the young have to learn to migrate from their parents) and so perished during the winter.

Lack of food, problems capturing wild birds, the late release of juveniles, plus the failure of the Turkish government to ban the use of pesticides resulted in a steeper decline in the population. By spring 1989 only three wild birds returned from their winter quarters, and two later died in accidents. With one bird left, the species was effectively extinct in the wild at Birecik.

Morocco

The ibis has fared better at its two surviving sites in Morocco, but has still faced severe problems, especially hunting, pesticide poisoning, and habitat loss as a result of dam building. In 1991 the Sous-Massa National Park was established specifically to protect the breeding and feeding areas of the ibis. In 1994 the Moroccan breeding population was estimated to be 300. In May 1996, 40 birds died mysteriously, possibly from botulism or unknown toxins. By 1998 numbers had declined to about 200 birds, but there has been a slight increase since then.

The northern bald ibis uses its long, downcurved bill to extract prey. It probes into crevices, among tufts of vegetation, in sand, soft soil, and under stones.

Iguana, Fijian Crested

Brachylophus vitiensis

Discovered in 1979, the Fijian crested iguana is one of the world's rarest iguanas. Regarded as sacred by some Fijians but evil by others, its main survival obstacle is disappearing habitat.

Hidden away in just a handful of the 800 small islands that make up the state of Fiji, the crested iguana was only discovered in 1979. Some islanders refer to iguanas as *saumuri,* others call them *vokai.* Attitudes toward them also differ; the animals are considered sacred to some groups but evil to others. It is taboo even to mention them on certain islands; on others they must not be mentioned in the hearing of women. Many Fijians fear the iguanas, believing that their tail has a venomous tip and that they launch themselves at intruders and can only be gotten off by using fire or saltwater. The belief may stem from the female's aggressive behavior when defending her nest.

The Fijian crested iguana is an attractive lizard, but when threatened, it turns black—another cause of islanders' superstition. The animal is thought to resemble more closely the ancestral form that had reached the islands millions of years ago, probably by "rafting" on large masses of vegetation wrenched loose in South America by fierce storms. This is now generally accepted as the means by which the islands (which were never part of the mainland) were colonized by reptiles and other land creatures.

Competition from Goats—and Other Threats

The main Fijian crested iguana population is on Yaduataba Island. When first discovered, they shared the island with a similar number of goats, which had been given to the islanders to provide a source of income from trading them. One of the main iguana foods is the vau tree, which is also enjoyed by goats. On the island of Monuriki only 12 iguanas survived: The goats had eaten most of the vegetation, apart from the high trees. The iguanas on Monuriki were all adults; youngsters had probably starved to death as a result of the goats' activities. The goats were removed and Yaduataba declared a reserve in 1981; without this action the iguanas would have died out.

Like other animals in restricted habitats, the Fijian iguanas have been affected by tree felling and predation by cats and dogs. Small islands are also vulnerable to hurricanes and further expansion of the human population.

Unlike the common green iguanas that lay up to 40 eggs per clutch, Fijian iguanas lay small clutches, and not all the eggs hatch. Reduced fertility is often the result of inbreeding and is a problem that often occurs in relatively small island

DATA PANEL

Fijian crested iguana

Brachylophus vitiensis

Family: Iguanidae

World population: About 5,500

Distribution: Yaduataba Islands, Fiji

Habitat: Shoreline forests on uninhabited islands

Size: Length: 36 in (90 cm)

Form: Dark green in color with narrow white stripes on the body, tail, and legs; a row of spines along the back; yellowish tinge around the lips and nostrils; belly mottled with green and cream. Large dewlap (loose fold of skin hanging beneath the throat)

Diet: Vau tree and other vegetation

Breeding: One clutch of 4 eggs that hatch within 6–7 months

Related endangered species: Fijian banded iguana (*Brachylophus fasciatus*) EN

Status: IUCN CR; CITES I

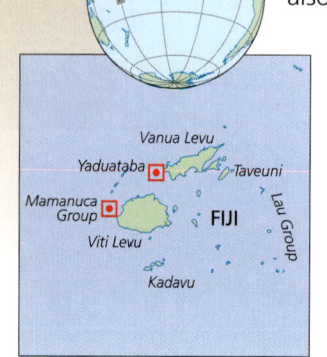

See also: Superstition 1: 47; Introductions 1: 54; iguana species 5: 76–81

IGUANA, FIJIAN CRESTED

populations. The Fijian crested iguana's eggs also take much longer to hatch than those of other iguanas.

Conservation

The Tarongo Zoo in New South Wales in Australia had already run a successful captive-management plan for the banded iguanas, and the animals had been released back into the wild; wild populations were also on the increase in Fiji and Tonga. In 1997, in view of the apparent recovery, the authorities in Fiji decided to send the captive specimens to other zoos and to concentrate efforts on the crested iguana. The International Conservation Fund for the Fijian Crested Iguana (ICFFCI) was set up to organize conservation.

According to a recent survey an estimated 5,500 crested iguanas now live on Yaduataba; the island's area is only about 173 acres (70 ha). The survey was difficult to do because Fijian iguanas are secretive and well camouflaged, so much of the research was done at night using lamps to spot the sleeping animals in the trees. Other investigations have studied the droppings of iguanas to determine the plants they eat. This is important for habitat restoration, particularly if other islands will eventually be used for releases.

Thanks to the ICFFCI a captive-breeding program for the crested iguana has been set up at Kula Eco Park in Fiji, with the Tarongo Park Zoo providing veterinary assistance and management expertise. Young crested iguanas have already been hatched and will be kept as a "reservoir population." There are also plans to restore the wild habitat.

Raising awareness and support among islanders for the conservation effort are important. Books in the Fijian language have been distributed to schools. The Kula Eco Park runs school visits in which the need for conservation is promoted, and children can see and handle the iguanas.

The Fijian crested iguana's *future looks more promising than it did when first discovered, but its small habitats are still vulnerable.*

Iguana, Galápagos Land

Conolophus subcristatus

Land iguanas were once abundant on the Galápagos Islands—a place renowned for its unusual animal life—and, like nearly all the other reptiles there, are not found anywhere else. Increasing human and animal populations have been a threat, but conservation efforts are achieving success.

The land iguana is found on six of the 19 islands that make up the Galápagos archipelago west of Ecuador. When he visited the islands in 1835, the famous English naturalist Charles Darwin commented that the huge numbers of land iguanas and their burrows left no room to pitch a tent. He also noticed their similarity to the green iguana of the mainland and the Galápagos marine iguana; the variation between them contributed to the formation of his ideas on evolution.

The land iguanas have adapted to the hot, dry climate by feeding largely on the fleshy prickly pear cactus, moving the spiny leaves around the mouth until the spines break off or breaking them off with their claws. The iguanas spend part of the day basking in the sunshine, but they later take shelter under bushes or in burrows. On some islands females travel considerable distances to find suitable nesting sites, often in the craters of dormant volcanoes.

Disturbance

Today the land iguanas on Santiago Island, where Darwin observed such large numbers, are extinct. Their numbers have also declined on other islands. The land iguanas, like the Galápagos tortoises, have suffered from habitat destruction as the human population of the islands has increased. Land for housing and cultivation has taken some of the habitat, but the animals brought by people have been extremely destructive. Cats, domestic or feral (wild), will eat young iguanas, and dogs eat even the adult lizards. Goats and donkeys compete with the iguanas for plant foods—the former can crop bare an entire area before moving on. Feral pigs enjoy iguana eggs which they root up. Feral dogs were responsible for near wipeouts of two iguana populations some 30 years ago. During the 1930s 70 land iguanas were transferred from

DATA PANEL

Galápagos land iguana

Conolophus subcristatus

Family: Iguanidae

World population: Unknown

Distribution: Galápagos Islands, Pacific Ocean

Habitat: Tropical scrub forests with open spaces for basking

Size: Length: 4 ft (1.2 m). Weight: 10–15 lb (4.5–6.8 kg)

Form: Heavy-bodied lizard with a long tail and powerful limbs. Grayish-green, yellowish, or brownish body with a crest of conical spines along the back

Diet: Prickly pear cactus and other plants

Breeding: Up to 25 eggs are laid in burrows dug by the females. Incubation period of up to 4 months

Related endangered species: Barrington Island iguana (*Conolophus pallidus*) VU

Status: IUCN VU; CITES I

See also: Island Biogeography 1: 30; Iguana, Galápagos Marine 5: 78

Baltra Island to North Seymour as an experiment. Those remaining on Baltra became extinct when the island became a military base during World War II.

Success Story

The Charles Darwin Research Station was opened in 1964 with the aim of saving the unique flora and fauna of the Galápagos Islands. Much of the early work was directed at saving the giant tortoises. In 1968 the Galápagos National Park service was set up to conserve wildlife. The two bodies cooperate in research and captive breeding. Breeding centers for tortoises on Santa Cruz Island and Isabela Island were successfully breeding tortoises when in 1980 a pair of land iguanas were installed in the Santa Cruz center.

By 1991 captive-bred iguanas were being released on Baltra after an absence of 50 years. Eradication of goats, wild dogs, and other pests was necessary and continues today. Cats and pigs still exist on some of the islands, but their numbers are controlled. Surveys have shown that the iguanas released on Baltra have started to breed. Capturing wild iguanas that are carrying eggs, housing them in the breeding center, and incubating the eggs has proved effective. The young are raised for two years to give them a better chance of survival when released. Over 800 young iguanas have been released on various islands since the program started. On Isoltes Venecia iguanas have been released into a semicaptive situation, and breeding levels there surpass those of the center.

Most of the Galápagos Islands are now protected, and some areas are out of bounds to all except scientists. Visitors are also controlled to prevent disturbing animals or spoiling the vegetation.

The Galápagos land iguana is a distinctive-looking tropical lizard. Females lay eggs in burrows; males defend the territory around it by head bobbing, posturing, biting, and tail-whipping.

Iguana, Galápagos Marine

Amblyrhynchus cristatus

The Galápagos marine iguana is a large tropical South American lizard that inhabits the Galápagos Islands west of Ecuador. It is vulnerable to changes in weather and water conditions caused by the El Niño effect.

The Galápagos marine iguana inhabits rocky seashores, diving into the sea to feed. Its adaptation to its habitat and its dependence on marine algae for food makes it unique among lizards. Its ancestors are thought to have arrived in the Galápagos Islands by rafting on floating vegetation some 10 million years ago. It is possible that the ancestral forms evolved to give rise to both the marine and the land iguana. There are about seven subspecies of marine iguana living mainly on uninhabited islands in the Galápagos. Each island's population varies slightly in color or physical appearance.

Behavioral Adaptations

Marine iguanas are ectotherms and need to achieve a certain body temperature before they can follow their normal daily activities. Once they have warmed up by basking in the sun, they dive into the sea to forage on marine algae. The sea around the islands is cold: To maintain their internal body temperature, blood is drawn into the inner organs and brain to conserve heat, and the heartbeat slows to conserve oxygen. The iguanas must bask again before they become too chilled. Young iguanas forage only on the rocks, flats, and parts exposed at low tide. A large amount of salt is ingested during feeding and expelled by being sprayed through the nostrils—often during squabbles.

Males are territorial during the three-month breeding season and can be aggressive toward humans if molested: They will hiss and bite rather than give up their basking stations. Females move inland to bury their eggs in loose soil. They guard the nest for a few days before leaving the eggs to incubate. While protecting the nest, they are vulnerable to predators.

Threats to Survival

Before humans settled on the Galápagos Islands, marine iguanas had only a few natural predators. Juveniles were at risk from certain birds, crabs, and fish, for example. However, when settlers arrived, they brought dogs and cats, and predation increased. Fortunately, people themselves did not pose a threat. The iguana's diet of marine algae did not bring it into competition with people. Moreover, the islanders did not eat the iguanas or their eggs, nor were they interested in their skins.

DATA PANEL

Galápagos marine iguana

Amblyrhynchus cristatus

Family: Iguanidae

World population: Unknown

Distribution: Galápagos Islands

Habitat: Rocky seashores

Size: Length: up to 5.6 ft (1.7 m). Weight: 20 lb (9 kg)

Form: Dark-gray to black iguana; color lightens or darkens to reflect or absorb heat. Males sometimes develop reddish spots during courtship. Long tail is flattened to function as a paddle when swimming. Spiny dorsal (back) crest; prominent granular scales on head. Strong limbs and claws provide a firm grip when climbing over rocky cliffs and ledges

Diet: Marine algae

Breeding: Female moves as far as 984 ft (300 m) inland to bury eggs in loose soil; 1–6 eggs laid

Related endangered species: Galápagos land iguana (*Conolophus subcristatus*)* VU

Status: IUCN VU; not listed by CITES

See also: Natural Disasters 1: 57; The History of Reptiles 1: 73; iguana species 5: 74–81

The Galápagos Islands are well protected because of the density of unique species there. The marine iguana benefits from such protection. There are visitor centers on several islands, but many areas are off limits to tourists. (However, scientists or film crews wanting to study Galápagos wildlife can apply for permission to visit the islands.) Collection for the pet trade has never been a problem; creating a suitable habitat in captivity would be impossible, which is why the species does not appear in zoos.

The marine iguana is not classed as Endangered within the Galápagos Islands, and the Charles Darwin Research Center—on the Galápagos island of Santa Cruz—is not currently researching the species. The marine iguana's IUCN listing is based on the vulnerability of its limited habitat, its susceptibility to introduced predators, and a recent drop in numbers.

Perhaps the most significant threat to the Galápagos marine iguana's survival is the El Niño phenomenon. El Niño is an ocean current that usually brings cold, nutrient-rich water to the Galápagos. Periodically, the current is diluted and warmer;

The Galápagos marine iguana *has strong claws to help it cling to rocks and ledges. When swimming, its long, flattened tail acts as an effective paddle.*

low-saline, nutrient-poor water replaces the normal current. The change occurred in 1982 and again in 1997. Although the flora and fauna benefited from the increased rainfall, the change in water quality affected marine creatures, including the marine iguana. A drastic reduction in green marine algae and an increase in inedible, possibly poisonous, brown algae had a severe effect on iguana numbers. On one island alone the marine iguana population fell by an estimated 90 percent, and numbers are still recovering. An oil spillage in January 2001 was another potential disaster for this fragile ecosystem.

Iguana, Grand Cayman Blue Rock

Cyclura nubila lewisi

Thought to be all but extinct 70 years ago, the Grand Cayman blue rock iguana still clings to a precarious existence in a limited territory; its future remains in the balance.

Although the Grand Cayman blue rock iguana can live between 25 and 40 years in the wild, and possibly twice as long in captivity, it is estimated that unless the program to save it is successful, the species could be extinct in 20 to 30 years. The Grand Cayman blue rock iguana belongs to the genus *Cyclura* found on many Caribbean islands. Sometimes referred to as "rock iguanas," there are eight or 10 species on different islands. Seventeen other forms are sufficiently different to be regarded as various separate subspecies.

The blue rock iguana lives on Grand Cayman, the largest of the three Cayman Islands. Its situation is typical of many island reptiles that share their habitat with people. The total area of the Cayman Islands is only 100 square miles (259 sq. km), with a human population of about 35,000. As in many countries, the population is increasing and so placing more pressure on the land for housing, food production, and fuel.

Most *Cyclura* species are a drab gray color. The blue iguana, however, is attractively marked. Its common name comes from the bluish coloration on the adults' heads and bodies, which is mainly visible when they have warmed up by basking. Before they were protected, some blue rock iguanas were taken to the United States for zoos and private breeders. It is still possible to buy captive-bred specimens if licenses are obtained. Second-generation breedings have been successful, but some specimens on sale are hybrids.

The wildlife of many Caribbean islands has suffered badly from introduced animals. Goats and pigs have destroyed vegetation, while feral (wild) and domestic cats and dogs have been responsible for heavy predation. In addition, rats and the mongoose introduced to control them have created havoc among native species on some islands.

DATA PANEL

Grand Cayman blue iguana

Cyclura nubila lewisi

Family: Iguanidae

World population: About 150

Distribution: Grand Cayman Island

Habitat: Bushy thickets; open woodland

Size: Length: 60 in (140 cm). Weight: 20 lb (42 kg)

Form: Heavy bodied with long, powerful tail; spiny dorsal crest and heavy folds of flesh under throat and around jowls (more prominent in males)

Diet: Weeds and fruit

Breeding: About 6–20 eggs laid in loose soil

Related endangered species: Little Cayman iguana (*Cyclura nubila caymanensis*) CR; Cuban ground iguana (*C. n. nubila*) VU; Jamaican iguana (*C. colleo*) CR

Status: IUCN CR; CITES I

See also: Island Biogeography 1: 30; Education 1: 94; iguana species 5: 74–79

Before the arrival of settlers the islands had been free of large mammals, and the iguanas, together with other species, had flourished throughout the Caribbean. Today the blue iguana is restricted to three or four small areas in the eastern part of Grand Cayman, much of which is jagged, volcanic rock. Although some 80 percent of the human population lives in the western half of the island, the iguana's habitat is coming under pressure from expanding agriculture. The land on Grand Cayman is poor, so new land for farming is always in demand; the iguana's habitat could be cleared at any time. Already deforestation and road building have eaten into the eastern part of the island, and this will inevitably continue. In addition, road kills are common since the iguanas like to bask on warm road surfaces.

Threatened Future for an Ancient Species
Fossil remains indicate that blue iguanas once inhabited most of the island. However, they have for many years been killed by farmers for food and because they were thought to eat their crops. A study of their diet has shown that they eat weeds and fruits from wild trees rather than domestic crops. The loss of suitable nesting sites has also had an effect on the iguana's numbers. They need loose soil in which to bury their eggs and will not use areas that have been grassed over or planted with crops.

Although they were thought to be extinct, the Grand Cayman blue rock iguanas have clung on in their shrinking habitat. The Animal Law of 1976 made them a protected species. However, unless habitat is preserved, predators controlled, and people persuaded not to kill them, they will have a bleak future.

Attempts are being made to ensure a viable population by means of a breeding program started by the National Trust for the Cayman Islands in 1990. The program aims to release captive-bred stock back into the wild. Radio tracking proved that this was feasible, and an adult pair was released in 1994. Land for reserves has been donated by various bodies, and three reserves are planned.

A series of educational initiatives has started to persuade local people that the iguanas and the islands' natural environment are worth saving. The goal of controlling encroachment and predation is highlighted every year at the National Trust Fair.

The Grand Cayman blue rock iguana *has been the subject of radio tracking, population, ecological, and behavioral studies. An ongoing program provides valuable information that could help save the lizards.*

Ikan Temoleh

Probarbus jullieni

Not widely known outside its range of Southeast Asia, the ikan temoleh has largely come to public awareness as the result of its listing as an endangered species.

The ikan temoleh is a large carplike fish of Asian origin. It was once known to occur across a wide range in Southeast Asia, but today naturally occurring wild populations can be found in only six river systems in Cambodia, Laos, and Vietnam. There is a population in Thailand, but it has developed from reintroduced stock, while in Malaysia all previously known wild populations have disappeared. However, a captive-breeding program is under way.

A Species of Many Names

The ikan temoleh is a fish of many names, which may be an indication of a former, wider distribution. The best known of the Asian names, ikan temoleh, is really Indonesian in origin; yet Indonesia is not one of the countries currently listed as having wild populations. Asian names include pla ye sok, temoleh, temelian, and trey trawsak, among many. It is not clear if the other known names represent westernized interpretations of just a few indigenous names. Among the English-language names those most frequently encountered are esok, giant river carp, Julien's golden carp, isok barb, seven-line barb, and seven-striped barb. That the species is frequently referred to as both a carp and a barb is indicative of its cyprinid characteristics. However, it is neither. It does have strong barb affinities, as its generic name *Probarbus* indicates, although it does not have the mouth barbels (whiskers) typical of barbs.

No Aquarium Demand

Unlike many other cyprinids, the ikan temoleh has never been in demand as an aquarium fish, and it is probably (at least partly) as a result of this that the species has not become better known in the West.

Undoubtedly in the past its large size of over 39 inches (100 cm) was a major factor. Today this would not present an insurmountable obstacle, since improved aquarium equipment and husbandry techniques make the keeping of large species perfectly

DATA PANEL

Ikan temoleh (seven-striped barb)

Probarbus jullieni

Family: Cyprinidae

World population: Exact numbers unknown, but population restricted to no more than 6 river systems

Distribution: Southeast Asia: Cambodia, Laos, Malaysia, Thailand, and Vietnam

Habitat: Vegetated brackish and freshwater river systems with sandy or muddy bottoms

Size: Length: up to 4 ft (1.2 m). Weight: about 46 lb (21 kg)

Form: An elongated species with well-formed fins, a downward-turned mouth that is protractile (extendible), and large eyes. The body is olive-colored on the back, shading to creamy-yellow toward the belly; head is greeny-yellow, and iris of the eye is red; 7 narrow black stripes extend from behind the gill cover toward the tail; fins are blackish with pinkish rays

Diet: Mainly aquatic vegetation, but also aquatic invertebrates and insects

Breeding: Spawns between late December and early February. Large numbers of floating eggs are released. Hatching takes place after about 32 hours under appropriate conditions

Related endangered species: From same area of Southeast Asia *Probarbus labeamajor* (no common name) DD; *P. labeaminor* (no common name) DD

Status: IUCN EN; CITES I

See also: Organizations 1: 10; Populations 1: 20; Dace, Mountain Blackside 3: 90; Danio, Barred 3: 94; Rasbora, Vateria Flower 8: 22

Two juvenile ikan temoleh. *Effective conservation management is hampered by the threat of illegal trade across national boundaries.*

feasible. Yet despite such advances, the ikan temoleh never really stood a chance of becoming one of the more sought-after species. Competition from smaller, more colorful, and easier-to-manage cyprinids is too high.

Whether this has been a good or a bad thing for the species is debatable. Heavy demand from aquarium keepers could have led to pressure on natural populations from overcollection. However, if the species had become established as a captive-bred aquarium fish, it could have have led to the creation of a "reservoir" of captive-bred stocks to assist in the conservation of the species.

Continuing Concern

Official concern about the status of the ikan temoleh in the wild was voiced in the early 1970s, leading to its listing by CITES. However, references to its status had been made in the mid-1940s, indicating that the species had been "comparatively scarce" for at least 65 years.

A review of the species was submitted to the CITES Animals Committee in 2000. The review assessed the status of the species in the wild; and although data on some of the listing criteria were unavailable for the period of the study, sufficient information was gathered to confirm that ongoing concern was indeed justified. While it does not appear that overfishing is the major cause of the decline in numbers, restricted distribution is undoubtedly a highly significant factor.

Were the ikan temoleh a sedentary species, accurate estimates could be made regarding the actual area over which it ranges. However, it migrates prior to spawning, so it is difficult to calculate the area occupied by the species overall; spawning areas are only visited for three months of the year. Questions therefore still remain regarding its exact distribution.

The migratory behavior exhibited by the species also places it at great risk from river alteration projects. Dams, for instance, present two threats: blocking of migratory routes and destruction of suitable upstream spawning sites. This can reduce the reproductive potential of the species as a whole, while local "wipeouts" through pollution or overfishing will further increase the pressure on subpopulations.

The ikan temoleh is under threat from various quarters. Data for several parameters such as population level, distribution, reproductive potential, size of spawning grounds, and habitat quality are incomplete. However, there is enough information for the species to be considered under significant risk of extinction and to warrant a total ban on trade.

Indri

Indri indri

The indri has been recognized as a special animal for hundreds of years, and it is protected by both tradition and law in its native Madagascar. However, the continuing destruction of its forest habitat is forcing it to live in ever smaller areas.

The people of Madagascar off the east coast of Africa have a story that tells how humans are descended from a mysterious manlike ancestor called Babakota. The embodiment of Babakota himself—also known as the indri—lives on in the forests of Madagascar, where he often fills the air with his strange and haunting songs.

It is easy to understand why the early human settlers on Madagascar saw human qualities in the indri. It is the largest of the lemurs and the only one with almost no tail. It holds itself more or less upright at all times, even when leaping from tree to tree. It jumps much as a human would, with arms flung out to the sides or raised above its head. However, the indri is a far more accomplished long jumper than any human athlete, capable of leaping a distance of up to 33 feet (10 m) from tree to tree.

Indris live in small family groups, dominated by the adult female, who usually takes priority over her mate when it comes to food for herself and her young. Unusually, the female leaves the responsibility of defending the family territory to the male. Meetings between rival groups do not happen often—careful scent-marking and daily sessions of singing to advertise their presence help ensure that indris from different groups usually stay well out of each other's way. The song of the indri is one of the most extraordinary and beautiful sounds in the natural world, made up of piercing but musical wails that carry up to 2 miles (3.2 km) through the forest. The indris usually sing in the morning, with others of the species joining in from miles around.

Disappearing Forest Habitat

In many areas local taboos forbid the hunting of indris. However, protection does not extend to the species' forest habitat, vast areas of which have been destroyed by generations of slash-and-burn agriculture. Trees are cut down and crops grown on the cleared ground for a year or two. The degraded land is then abandoned, and another patch of forest is cleared.

For hundreds of years the destruction was gradual enough for patches of cleared forest to regrow. In the last 50 years, however, the human population of Madagascar has boomed. An increased

---

DATA PANEL

Indri

Indri indri

Family: Indridae

World population: Fewer than 10,000

Distribution: Eastern Madagascar

Habitat: Rain forest from sea level to 6,000 ft (1,800 m)

Size: Length head/body: 24–35.5 in (61–90 cm); tail: 2–3 in (5–7 cm). Weight: 13–20 lb (6–10 kg)

Form: Large lemur with short, stumpy tail; fur variable, but usually black on back, shoulders, and arms; shades of brown and white elsewhere; hands and feet long and strong

Diet: Leaves, flowers, and fruit; occasionally earth

Breeding: Single young born after 16-month gestation, usually in May, but season varies from area to area; weaned at 6 months; stays with mother for 1–2 years; mature at 7–9 years. Life span unknown

Related endangered species: Diadem sifaka (*Propithecus diadema*) EN; golden-crowned sifaka (*P. tattersalli*)* CR; Verreaux's sifaka (*P. verreauxi*) VU; avahi (*Avahi occidentalis*) VU

Status: IUCN EN; CITES I

See also: Life Strategies 1: 24; Saving the Habitats 1: 88; Aye-Aye 2: 42; Lemur, Ruffed 6: 26; Sifaka, Golden-Crowned 8: 92

The indri is mainly a leaf-eater and spends between five and nine hours a day feeding. It occasionally comes down from the trees to eat a handful of earth, a habit that is thought to help with digestion.

demand for land has led to further encroachment into the island's forests. The rate at which the forest is felled now far outstrips any recovery that can take place. Once forests have been cleared, the area becomes uninhabitable for indris. Commercial felling of trees for the timber industry has exerted yet more pressure on the indri's habitat.

Uncertain Prospects

The indris that once occupied much of the island are now restricted to a narrow strip of fragmented forest in the east of the island. Although the species is protected by Malagasy law, only about 1 percent of Madagascar is currently designated as nature reserves. Even in the specially protected areas the forests are still being destroyed or at least disrupted by the activities of people simply trying to eke out a living for themselves and their families.

It is not known how many indris are left in the wild, but estimates put the population at just a few thousand animals. There are no indris in captivity, and captive-breeding programs are not a realistic prospect at the moment. One obstacle is the lack of suitable habitat in which to release captive-bred stock. The indri is not alone in its predicament. It is thought that well over half the lemur species that inhabited Madagascar before the arrival of people about 2,000 years ago are already extinct.

Jaguar

Panthera onca

The jaguar is the most accomplished climber of all the big cats and is almost equally at home prowling the forest floor or swimming in rivers and pools. However, its adaptability is no protection against the erosion of its forest habitat or other human activities that threaten its existence.

The jaguar is the largest cat in the Americas and the only member of the big cat genus *Panthera* to be found in this region. It bears a resemblance to the leopard and is often thought of as the South American equivalent. Its coat pattern consists of black markings on a golden-tan background. Entirely black jaguars, known as black panthers, are relatively common, the all-black or melanistic condition being caused by a single gene that overrides those for normal patterning. A cub needs to inherit only a single copy of the melanistic gene from either of its parents to be born with a jet black coat. Albino jaguars have also been recorded, but they are extremely rare.

The jaguar is more heavily built than its African cousin, the leopard. Its head and jaws are substantially larger and more powerful, an arrangement that hints at its preferred method of finishing off its prey—with a crushing bite to the skull. The jaguar is the most accomplished climber among the big cats and will often ambush prey from trees. Prey includes almost anything it can catch; over 85 different species have been recorded in its diet. Nevertheless, the jaguar prefers larger mammals such as peccaries (a kind of wild pig), tapirs, and deer, though in dense rainforest where these are hard to come by, it often turns instead to fish and reptiles. It is an excellent swimmer, and with its powerful jaw and stout canine teeth it can crack open the tough shells of turtles. Indeed, it has been suggested that this ability to attack reptilian prey is one reason the jaguar survived in the New World during the Pleistocene period, when a significant proportion of large herbivore prey became extinct. In places where human settlements spread into their territory, jaguars often take livestock. In Brazil domestic cows are the main diet of many jaguars living near cattle ranches.

The jaguar would certainly be capable of killing a human; but when people have reported being "stalked" through the forest, it is likely that the jaguar was merely making sure the trespassers were leaving its territory. If it really had intended to eat the people, they would surely not have lived to tell the tale!

Jaguars can probably breed all year round, but most births take place when prey is most abundant. The two sexes only tolerate each other when courting or mating; the male has nothing to do with the raising of offspring. Only when mating does the jaguar make much noise—a deep, throaty cry is the closest it ever gets to a roar.

Cubs are born in litters of one to four, with twins being most common. The young are blind at birth and will not leave the den until they are two weeks old. The mother moves her cubs much like other cats, grasping them by the scruff of the neck. The cubs spend a lot of time playing together, and the mother is remarkably tolerant of their boisterous games, which more often than not involve clambering all over

See also: Pasture **1:** 38; Hunting **1:** 42; Leopard, Clouded **6:** 30; Panther, Florida **7:** 54

JAGUAR

her, biting her tail, and pulling her ears! The cubs remain with the mother until she is ready to breed again, which can be as long as two years.

Threats to Survival

Jaguars were once widely hunted for their skins, which made valuable fur coats, but the trade was banned in the 1970s. Nowadays the main threat comes from cattle ranchers, who shoot jaguars that kill their livestock and may also hunt them for sport. Even more of a threat is the destruction of forests to make way for other animals. Continuous grazing by cattle and sheep prevents new trees from growing, and the vast prairies that are formed are unsuitable for the forest-dwelling jaguar.

A jaguar cub. *The animal's relatively short limbs are an adaptation for climbing; jaguars are the most arboreal of the big cats.*

DATA PANEL

Jaguar

Panthera onca

Family: Felidae

World population: Unknown, but probably in low thousands

Distribution: From Mexico to Patagonia, including Belize, Panama, Costa Rica, Guatemala, Honduras, Nicaragua, Surinam, Colombia, Ecuador, Guyana, Venezuela, French Guiana, Peru, Brazil, Bolivia, Uruguay, Paraguay, Argentina. Formerly southwestern U.S.

Habitat: Tropical forests, swamps, rivers, pools, and open country

Size: Length head/body: 44–72 in (112–185 cm); tail: 18–30 in (46–76 cm); females smaller than males. Weight: 100–250 lb (45–123 kg)

Form: Robust-looking big cat. Golden coat with black rings, rosettes, and dots; pale underside

Diet: Wild pigs, capybaras, tapirs, domestic cattle, horses, fish, frogs, turtles, tortoises, and young alligators

Breeding: Cubs born in litters of 1–4 at any time of year. Life span up to 12 years in the wild; up to 22 years recorded in captivity

Related endangered species: Other big cats, including the Asiatic lion (*Panthera leo persica*)* CR and tiger (*P. tigris*)* EN

Status: IUCN LRnt; CITES I

Kagu

Rhynochetos jubatus

The kagu hangs on in greatly reduced numbers on just one Pacific island, where local people call it the "ghost of the forest." Continued conservation efforts will be needed to ensure that the kagu does not become merely a ghostly memory.

Resembling a strange hybrid of a heron, a coot, a crane, and a pigeon, the kagu is an evolutionary relic found only on the Pacific island of New Caledonia, a French overseas territory since 1946. The sole member of the Rhynochetidae family, the knee-high kagu has several unique features, including flaps of rolled skin near the base of the bill that seal the nostrils when it digs for food.

Isolated for millions of years on its remote island home, with few natural predators, the kagu has become flightless. Although its wings are broad, and it can glide for short distances downhill, it has lost the powerful muscles needed for sustained flight.

In the past the kagu was reported as widespread in many of the island's forests, from sea level to the summits of the mountains. Today the species is restricted mainly to the least disturbed areas in the mountains inland. Here, pairs duet as the first light of day dawns, with a strange, mournful, piercing song that has been described as a cross between the barking of a puppy and the crowing of a farmyard hen. The performance can last 15 minutes, and the sound carries for up to 1.3 miles (2 km).

Dramatic Decline

Since Europeans colonized the island in the 18th century, kagus have faced increasing threats. Their major enemies are dogs, first introduced to the island by Captain Cook in 1774. The kagus' inability to fly puts them at an immediate disadvantage; and although they can run surprisingly fast on their sturdy legs, they have not developed a healthy fear of dogs and make easy prey. Dogs have been found to revisit areas where they have killed kagus until they have almost wiped them out. Other mammals introduced by the settlers also take their toll: Kagu eggs are eaten by feral pigs, which are common on the island, while kagu chicks fall prey to rats, as well as dogs.

Habitat destruction is also a serious problem. Over the years the forests have dwindled to about 20 percent of their original size. Forest fires, started by humans, have cleared large areas; the

---

DATA PANEL

Kagu

Rhynochetos jubatus

Family: Rhynochetidae

World population: Probably more than 800 individuals

Distribution: New Caledonia, an island in the southwest Pacific about 1,000 miles (1,600 km) east of Australia

Habitat: Mainly lowland rain forest and drier mountain forest; also closed-canopy scrub during the wet season

Size: Length: 22 in (55 cm); wingspan: 31 in (78 cm). Weight: 25–39 oz (700–1,100 g)

Form: Plump-bodied bird with strong, pointed orange-red bill and legs of same color. Plumage ash gray and white, darker above, with long feathers extending from nape to form crest. Broad, rounded wings have striking barred pattern on flight feathers, visible only when opened

Diet: Mainly worms, snails, and lizards; also cockroaches, beetles, spiders, centipedes, and millipedes

Breeding: Adults build a simple nest of leaves on the ground; female lays 1 creamy-brown egg with darker blotches. Incubation 4–5 weeks; young independent at about 3–4 months; parents share incubation and care of chicks, sometimes aided in latter by older offspring. Adults are monogamous, perhaps pairing for life

Related endangered species: No close relatives

Status: IUCN EN; CITES I

See also: The History of Birds 1: 64; Rail, Guam 8: 18; Takahe 9: 48; Coot, Horned 3: 62

forests are also cut down for agriculture, logging, and open-pit mining (the island contains about half of all the world's known deposits of nickel). New Caledonia also has some of the world's worst erosion problems. Road building, along with deforestation, makes it easy for dogs on the island (both strays and those used by human hunters) to enter previously undisturbed areas.

The kagu's rarity is compounded by the fact that it is a slow breeder, rarely raising more than one chick a year. As a result of their patchy distribution, and because each pair needs a large, exclusive territory, small groups of kagus have become isolated from one another, making it impossible for them to interbreed. Another consequence is the loss of diversity, both genetic and with regard to behavior that could help them in different habitats.

The kagu *still plays an important part in the tribal traditions of native New Caledonians.*

There are signs that the kagu's future survival is not a lost cause. The main source of optimism is in the example set by the island's Rivière Bleue Provincial Park, where kagu numbers increased from just 60 birds in 1980 to an estimated 300 by 1998. In addition, kagus have been found to breed readily in captivity, and a zoo in New Caledonia's capital, Noumea, provided 32 birds to restock the park.

The kagu has been adopted as the official national emblem of New Caledonia. The islanders have a vested interest in ensuring the kagu's survival, since the bird is a draw to tourists and wildlife watchers, who in turn help boost the local economy.

Kakapo

Strigops habroptilus

Conservationists saved this extraordinary parrot by translocating the few remaining birds to predator-free islands, but the population is still extremely small and inherently at risk.

The kakapo is the heaviest parrot, one of the few nocturnal species in its family, and the only one that is completely flightless. It lives mainly on the ground, where its massive legs and feet enable it to travel far and quite fast. It uses its wings to balance when running at speed and climbing up leaning trunks and branches, and to break its fall as it parachutes from branches or down steep slopes. It is incapable of gliding, let alone powered flight.

Like so much about this exceptional parrot, its social life (or lack of it) and reproductive behavior are remarkable. In contrast to other parrots, which are among the most gregarious and sociable of birds, the kakapo is solitary except during courtship, and then the interactions between males are highly aggressive; researchers who kept kakapos together found they would attack and even kill one another.

The kakapo is the only parrot species with a "lek" breeding system, in which several rival males assemble at a shared "arena" on summer nights to attract females to mate with them. This arena consists of a complex system of well-defined paths, linking a number of bowl-shaped depressions in the ground. Both paths and bowls are made by the males, and each male has a bowl of his own. He fits inside it and inflates the air sac within his chest until he swells up like a big green balloon, then releases the air to produce the loud, booming calls that act as a magnet for the waiting females. The bowl amplifies the strange sound, which is audible to humans from up to 3 miles (5 km) away.

Each male has to spend many nights booming—up to 1,000 times an hour—to secure a mate. He also carefully cleans his tracks and bowl, and defends them fiercely against rival males. After mating, a female is on her own. Having laid her eggs, she must incubate them for a month and may care for the young for a further nine months. All this activity requires a great deal of energy from both sexes. It is hardly surprising, then, that kakapos do not breed every year, but only irregularly at intervals of three to five years, triggered by the periodic abundance (known as "masting") of seeds and fruit of certain key plant species, such as the native rimu tree.

To the Brink of Extinction

Evidence from preserved bones shows that for some time after the first Maori settlers arrived in New Zealand about 1,000 years ago, the kakapo was found throughout most of the country. However, with the Maori colonization of the land the kakapo's range started contracting. The birds suffered as the settlers altered habitats, and especially as they introduced dogs and Pacific rats, which hunted down the birds—as did the Maori themselves. The Maori ate them and also valued their feathers for making cloaks.

Evolving on a group of oceanic islands that had no native mammalian predators (New Zealand lacks any native mammals apart from three species of bat), the kakapo had no need to evolve defenses against them and so was especially vulnerable. Kakapo mothers had to search for food at night, leaving their eggs and chicks unattended and so even more vulnerable.

After Europeans colonized New Zealand from the early 19th century, they introduced other carnivorous mammals such as stoats, cats, dogs, black and brown rats, and Australian brush-tailed possums. These animals caused even more devastation among kakapo

See also: Hunting **1:** 42; Introductions **1:** 54; Kea **5:** 92; Parrot, Night **7:** 58

KAKAPO

populations. By 1976 only 18 birds were known to exist in the remote mountain country of Fiordland, in the southwest corner of South Island, and all of them were males. By 1989 the Fiordland birds—the last mainland population—were gone. However, in 1977 the dramatic discovery was made of about 150 kakapos living on Stewart Island, the largest of New Zealand's offshore islands. Over half the birds were being killed each year by feral cats. Between 1980 and 1992 the 61 kakapos on Stewart Island were moved to predator-free offshore islands.

Today kakapos are tagged with miniature radio transmitters, and every nest is constantly monitored using infrared video cameras. Kakapo eggs and nestlings are kept warm with heating pads when the females leave to forage at night. Providing extra food has increased the frequency and the success of breeding attempts, and researchers are currently investigating whether rimu trees can be induced to fruit using plant hormones.

Thanks to the work of conservationists and to a run of three successful breeding seasons, the kakapo population is at last increasing. There are currently 62 kakapos, comprising 36 males and 26 females, of which 50 are capable of breeding, six are subadults, and six are juveniles. Even so, there is a long way to go before the kakapo is secure.

The kakapo *is a giant, flightless parrot that resembles an owl in its facial disks (*Strigops *means "owl face").*

DATA PANEL

Kakapo (owl parrot)

Strigops habroptilus

Family: Psittacidae

World population: 62 birds

Distribution: Translocated birds on 4 New Zealand offshore islands: Maud, Inner Chetwode, Codfish, and Pearl

Habitat: Mainly forest edges and forests in younger stages of growth

Size: Length: 23–25 in (58–64 cm); wingspan: 33–36 in (84–91 cm)

Form: Large, stout-bodied parrot with hairlike facial disk, short, broad bill with cere (bare skin at base containing nostrils) prominent and swollen; short, broad wings; scruffy, downcurved tail; massive, fleshy legs and feet with powerful claws; plumage moss-green on upperparts and greenish-yellow on underparts; mottled and barred with brown and yellowish; male has wider head and much bigger bill and is about 25% heavier than female

Diet: Leaves, stems, roots, fruit, nectar, and seeds of trees, shrubs, etc.

Breeding: Breeds every 2–5 years, coinciding with bumper crops of food plants; nests inside rotting fallen tree trunks, in hollow tree stumps, or under clumps of vegetation; 1–3 white eggs incubated by the female for 30 days; fledging period 10–12 weeks; may not attain sexual maturity until 6–9 years old

Related endangered species: There are no other members of the subgroup Strigopini, but 2 other threatened New Zealand parrots, the kaka *(Nestor meridionalis)* VU and kea *(N. notabilis)** VU, may be related; some experts think that the kakapo may be related to the night parrot *(Geopsittacus occidentalis)** CR and the ground parrot *(Pezoporus wallicus)* of Australia

Status: IUCN CR; CITES I and II

Kea

Nestor notabilis

It may be one of the most intelligent, adaptable, and enterprising of all birds, but the extraordinary kea is struggling to maintain its numbers as its mountain habitats are transformed into pasture and invaded by introduced mammals.

People normally associate parrots with the tropics, but the kea lives high in the mountains among the snowy, glacier-bound peaks that form the spine of New Zealand's South Island. It is a highly accomplished flier, able to ride the winds above the mountain ridges like a bird of prey, its ringing "keeaaaa" calls echoing through the mountain mists.

The kea spends much of its year in the temperate mountain rain forests, where there is plenty for it to eat throughout spring and summer. Unusually resourceful, it is prepared to experiment with almost any kind of food. It mainly harvests buds, seeds, and fruit, sips nectar from flowers with its brush-tipped tongue, and uses its uniquely extended and hooked upper bill to dig for succulent roots and to pry insects out of bark and rotting wood. However, it also rips into carcasses to scrape the flesh from the bones, steals the chicks of burrowing shearwaters, and often raids garbage dumps for scraps. In the fall it may venture well above the snow line to feast on berries, then move downhill to sheltered valleys to spend the winter. It often hangs around ski resorts to scavenge what it can. Sociable, inquisitive, and extremely intelligent, it is astonishingly quick at learning new foraging skills and now has a somewhat unwarranted reputation for vandalizing cars parked at mountain tourist sites. It would seem to be a born survivor.

Invasion

Like all New Zealand's native birds, the kea was able to enjoy its natural habitat for thousands of years without competition from mammals because there were no mammals on the islands. The situation was to change when human settlers arrived, along with their farm animals and an army of alien predators, including cats, stoats, and Australian brush-tailed possums.

The introduced mammals raid kea nests to kill their young or compete with them for food. Domestic grazing animals pose another threat because they rely on pasture that is often provided by clearing natural forest and scrub. Yet the kea is not the kind of creature that shrinks from a challenge; and instead of retreating to the wilderness, it has learned to exploit the invaders. Dead sheep in particular provide a good source of carrion, and by 1860 the kea had learned

---

DATA PANEL

Kea

Nestor notabilis

Family: Psittacidae

World population: About 5,000 birds

Distribution: Mainly the western side of South Island, New Zealand

Habitat: Mountain forests; subalpine scrub and grassland, often above snow line in summer. Valleys and coastal forests in winter

Size: Length: 18–19 in (46–48 cm). Weight: male 2.1 lb (960 g); female 1.7 lb (780 g)

Form: Large, stocky parrot; olive-green with scarlet underwings and rump; brown-black bill with longer upper bill. Juveniles have yellowish legs and bill bases, turning brown as birds mature (3–4 years)

Diet: Mainly nectar, berries, fruit, nuts, seeds, shoots, and buds; also insects, carrion, and scraps

Breeding: July–January. Female lays 2–4 white eggs in nest of twigs, leaves, and moss at ground level; incubates them for 20–28 days; male supplies food for female and nestlings for the next 4 weeks. Young fledge at about 3 weeks

Related endangered species: In New Zealand alone: Antipodes Island parakeet (*Cyanoramphus unicolor*) VU; kaka (*Nestor meridionalis*) VU; kakapo (*Strigops habroptilus*)* CR

Status: IUCN VU; CITES II

See also: Introductions 1: 54; Kakapo 5: 90; Parrot, Night 7: 58

to attack live sheep to steal energy-rich fat from under the skin of their backs. Such attacks are rare but can cause festering wounds that are sometimes fatal.

Inevitably, sheep farmers regard the kea as a pest, and for 100 years from about 1870 to 1970 the New Zealand government classified the bird as vermin, offering a reward for every one killed. About 150,000 were shot, poisoned, or trapped. Nearly 7,000 kea were killed in just three years from 1943 to 1946—probably more than the entire population surviving today. In 1970 the government relented, permitting farmers to kill only persistent offenders, and in 1986 even this practice was outlawed. Yet by now the kea population had dwindled to an estimated 5,000 birds, and possibly a lot fewer. Some estimates have put it as low as 1,000, although since kea are notoriously difficult to count, the figure may be pessimistic.

Some kea are still killed illegally each year by farmers, and others are accidentally poisoned by toxic materials picked up from garbage. Their habitats are fragmented and increasingly invaded by introduced mammals. According to some studies, numbers are steadily declining. So although it may be smart, the kea may not be quite smart enough to stay out of serious trouble. It needs help.

Outlook

The most pressing priority is to find out exactly how many kea there are, and whether numbers are still decreasing. A total population of only 5,000 is low enough to warrant classification by the IUCN as Vulnerable; but if numbers have dwindled to 1,000 or fewer, then the species may be judged Endangered. Researchers also need to assess the true effect of introduced predators in the wild.

In addition, the New Zealand Department of Conservation has approved a captive-management plan initiated in 1991, which aims to maintain a captive population that is self-sustaining and large enough to ensure genetic diversity. Such a population may then be used to support the conservation of the species in the wild.

The kea has an extended upper bill that it uses to probe for food, including insects and succulent roots.

Kestrel, Lesser

Falco naumanni

The lesser kestrel has suffered huge declines in recent years in its European breeding range. It also faces threats in its migratory stopover sites and wintering grounds in Africa. Changes in farming and the use of pesticides have affected insects and consequently the kestrels that depend on them.

As its common name suggests, the lesser kestrel is a smaller, more delicately proportioned relative of the common kestrel, one of the most abundant and successful of the world's birds of prey. Unlike the latter, it has a patchy distribution across Europe and in parts of North Africa and Asia, with concentrations of birds in suitable habitats and large gaps in between.

The lesser kestrel has experienced massive declines over most of its limited range in Europe during the last 50 years. In Spain, the species' European stronghold, more than 100,000 pairs are thought to have bred in the early 1960s. By 1994 numbers had declined to only 8,000 pairs (although there are signs that numbers have now stabilized).

Unusually for a bird of prey, the lesser kestrel is extremely gregarious. It usually breeds, hunts for food, roosts, migrates, and winters in groups. Nesting colonies are mainly close to human settlements, and the birds prefer holes and ledges high in tall, old buildings. By nesting high up, they try to avoid climbing mammal predators, especially rats, which can seriously affect some populations. (In one Portuguese colony, for example, rats ate 39 percent of the eggs.)

The lesser kestrel is a summer visitor to almost its entire breeding range, migrating in the fall to spend winter mainly in the drier parts of Africa south of the Sahara. The birds probably cross the Mediterranean, the Sahara, and the Middle East in fast, high-altitude, nonstop flights of a minimum of 1,500 miles (2,400 km), those from Asia making much longer journeys. In spring the birds return to their breeding grounds. The males arrive first and immediately lay claim to nest sites. The species' southerly distribution reflects the importance of insects in its diet, especially large ones such as grasshoppers, locusts, crickets, beetles, and earwigs. Generally about 80 to 90 percent of its food consists of insects and smaller numbers of other invertebrates, including large, poisonous centipedes.

Disappearing Prey

Dramatic changes in farming have had a major effect on lesser kestrel populations. The advance of intensive agriculture has swept away many of the meadows, pastures, and steppelike habitats, making it hard for the birds to find enough insect food. Areas of uncultivated grassland and cereal crops have been widely replaced by fields of sunflowers; not only does the crop contain less suitable prey, but the increased height and density of the plants mean that kestrels take much longer to find and catch the insects. Abandonment of farmland is similarly damaging to the birds, with scrub and trees being allowed to invade the open landscape.

The large-scale use of pesticides has also greatly reduced numbers of the kestrel's insect prey, as well as killing the birds themselves. Renovation and demolition of old buildings have deprived other colonies of their nest sites. It is not just in their breeding range that the birds face threats: Land-use changes and heavy pesticide use in their African winter quarters have also taken their toll.

Lesser kestrel *breeding populations of Europe and North Africa have declined by 95 percent since 1950 to an estimated 17,000 to 21,000 pairs today.*

See also: Pollution 1: 50; Kestrel, Mauritius 6: 4

KESTREL, LESSER

DATA PANEL

Lesser kestrel
Falco naumanni

Family: Falconidae

World population: Estimated at 17,000–21,000 pairs

Distribution: Scattered breeding colonies across parts of southern Europe, North Africa, Turkey, Central Asia, southern Russia, eastern Mongolia, and northern China

Habitat: Lowlands and foothills in Europe; up to 4,900 ft (1,500 m) in Asia. In open country, such as deserts, dry grassland, and low-intensity farmland

Size: Length: 11.5–12.5 in (29–32 cm)

Form: An elegant bird of prey with narrow, pointed wings and a long, slim tail, wedge-shaped at the tip; male much more colorful than barred-brown female, with gray-blue, rust-red, and whitish plumage pattern

Diet: Mainly insects; also some lizards, small mammals, and birds

Breeding: Usually 3–5 white to buff eggs with reddish spots or blotches, laid mid-April to May. Incubation 4 weeks; fledging 5–6 weeks

Related endangered species: Mauritius kestrel *(Falco punctatus)** VU; Seychelles kestrel *(F. araea)* VU; gray falcon *(F. hypoleucos)* LRnt; taita falcon *(F. fasciinucha)* LRnt; New Zealand falcon *(F. novaeseelandiae)* LRnt

Status: IUCN VU; CITES II

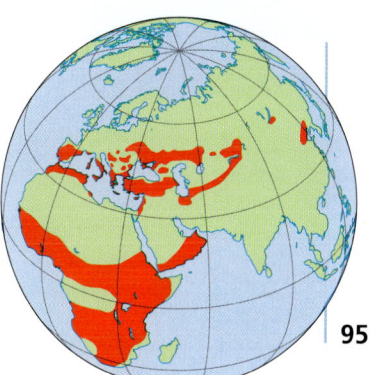

Glossary

Words in SMALL CAPITALS refer to other entries in the glossary.

Adaptation features of an animal that adjust it to its environment; may be produced by evolution—e.g., camouflage coloration
Adaptive radiation where a group of closely related animals (e.g., members of a FAMILY) have evolved differences from each other so that they can survive in different NICHES
Adhesive disks flattened disks on the tips of the fingers or toes of certain climbing AMPHIBIANS that enable them to cling to smooth, vertical surfaces
Adult a fully grown sexually mature animal; a bird in its final PLUMAGE
Algae primitive plants ranging from microscopic, single-celled forms to large forms, such as seaweeds, but lacking proper roots or leaves
Alpine living in mountainous areas, usually over 5,000 feet (1,500 m)
Ambient describing the conditions around an animal, e.g., the water temperature for a fish or the air temperature for a land animal
Amphibian any cold-blooded VERTEBRATE of the CLASS Amphibia, typically living on land but breathing in the water; e.g., frogs, toads, newts, salamanders
Amphibious able to live on both land and in water
Amphipod a type of CRUSTACEAN found on land and in both fresh and seawater
Anadromous fish that spend most of their life at sea but MIGRATE into fresh water for breeding, e.g., salmon
Annelid of the PHYLUM Annelida in which the body is made up of similar segments, e.g., earthworms, lugworms, leeches
Anterior the front part of an animal
Arachnid one of a group of ARTHROPODS of the CLASS Arachnida, characterized by simple eyes and four pairs of legs. Includes spiders and scorpions
Arboreal living in trees
Aristotle's lantern complex chewing apparatus of sea-urchins that includes five teeth
Arthropod the largest PHYLUM in the animal kingdom in terms of the number of SPECIES in it. Characterized by a hard, jointed EXOSKELETON and paired jointed legs. Includes INSECTS, spiders, crabs, etc.
Baleen horny substance commonly known as whalebone and growing as plates in the mouth of certain whales; used as a fringelike sieve for extracting plankton from seawater
Bill often called the beak: the jaws of a bird, consisting of two bony MANDIBLES, upper and lower, and their horny sheaths
Biodiversity the variety of SPECIES and the variation within them
Biome a major world landscape characterized by having similar plants and animals living in it, e.g., DESERT, jungle, forest
Biped any animal that walks on two legs. See QUADRUPED
Blowhole the nostril opening on the head of a whale through which it breathes
Breeding season the entire cycle of reproductive activity, from courtship, pair formation (and often establishment of territory) through nesting to independence of young
Bristle in birds a modified feather, with a bare or partly bare shaft, like a stiff hair; functions include protection, as with eyelashes of ostriches and hornbills, and touch sensors to help catch INSECTS, as with flycatchers
Brood the young hatching from a single CLUTCH of eggs
Browsing feeding on leaves of trees and shrubs

Cage bird A bird kept in captivity; in this set it usually refers to birds taken from the wild
Canine tooth a sharp stabbing tooth usually longer than the rest
Canopy continuous (closed) or broken (open) layer in forests produced by the intermingling of branches of trees
Carapace the upper part of a shell in a CHELONIAN
Carnivore meat-eating animal
Carrion rotting flesh of dead animals
Casque the raised portion on the head of certain REPTILES and birds
Catadromous fish that spend most of their life in fresh water but MIGRATE to the sea for SPAWNING, e.g., eels
Caudal fin the tail fin in fish
Cephalothorax a body region of CRUSTACEANS formed by the union of the head and THORAX. See PROSOMA
Chelicerae the first pair of appendages ("limbs") on the PROSOMA of spiders, scorpions, etc. Often equipped to inject venom
Chelonian any REPTILE of the ORDER Chelonia, including the tortoises and turtles, in which most of the body is enclosed in a bony capsule
Chrysalis the PUPA in moths and butterflies
Class a large TAXONOMIC group of related animals. MAMMALS, INSECTS, and REPTILES are all CLASSES of animals
Cloaca cavity in the pelvic region into which the alimentary canal, genital, and urinary ducts open
Cloud forest moist, high-altitude forest characterized by a dense UNDERSTORY and an abundance of ferns, mosses, and other plants growing on the trunks and branches of trees
Clutch a set of eggs laid by a female bird in a single breeding attempt
Cocoon the protective coat of many insect LARVAE before they develop into PUPAE or the silken covering secreted to protect the eggs
Colonial living together in a colony
Coniferous forest evergreen forests found in northern regions and mountainous areas, dominated by pines, spruce, and cedars
Costal riblike
Costal grooves grooves running around the body of some TERRESTRIAL salamanders; they conduct water from the ground to the upper parts of the body
Coverts small feathers covering the bases of a bird's main flight feathers on the wings and tail, providing a smooth, streamlined surface for flight
Crustacean member of a CLASS within the PHYLUM Arthropoda typified by five pairs of legs, two pairs of antennae, a joined head and THORAX, and calcerous deposits in the EXOSKELETON; e.g., crabs, shrimps, etc.

Deciduous forest dominated by trees that lose their leaves in winter (or in the dry season)
Deforestation the process of cutting down and removing trees for timber or to create open space for growing crops, grazing animals, etc.
Desert area of low rainfall typically with sparse scrub or grassland vegetation or lacking it altogether
Diatoms microscopic single-celled ALGAE
Dispersal the scattering of young animals going to live away from where they were born and brought up
Diurnal active during the day
DNA (deoxyribonucleic acid) the substance that makes up the main part of the chromosomes of all living things; contains the genetic code that is handed down from generation to generation
Domestication process of taming and breeding animals to provide help and useful products for humans
Dormancy a state in which—as a result of hormone action—growth is suspended and METABOLIC activity is reduced to a minimum
Dorsal relating to the back or spinal part of the body; usually the upper surface
Down soft, fluffy, insulating feathers with few or no shafts found after hatching on young birds and in ADULTS beneath the main feathers

Echolocation the process of perception based on reaction to the pattern of reflected sound waves (echos); occurs in bats
Ecology the study of plants and animals in relation to one another and to their surroundings
Ecosystem a whole system in which plants, animals, and their environment interact
Ectotherm animal that relies on external heat sources to raise body temperature; also known as "cold-blooded"
Edentate toothless; also any animals of the order Edentata, which includes anteaters, sloths, and armadillos
Endemic found only in one geographical area, nowhere else
Epitoke a form of marine ANNELID having particularly well developed swimming appendages
Estivation inactivity or greatly decreased activity during hot weather
Eutrophication an increase in the nutrient chemicals (nitrate, phosphate, etc.) in water, sometimes occurring naturally and sometimes caused by human activities, e.g., by the release of sewage or agricultural fertilizers
Exoskeleton a skeleton covering the outside of the body or situated in the skin, as found in some INVERTEBRATES
Explosive breeding in some AMPHIBIANS when breeding is completed over one or a very few days and nights
Extinction process of dying out at the end of which the very last individual dies, and the SPECIES is lost forever

Family a group of closely related SPECIES that often also look quite

GLOSSARY

similar. Zoological FAMILY names always end in -idae. Also used to describe a social group within a SPECIES comprising parents and their offspring

Feral domestic animals that have gone wild and live independently of people

Flagship species A high-profile SPECIES, which (if present) is likely to be accompanied by many others that are typical of the habitat. (If a naval flagship is present, so is the rest of the fleet of warships and support vessels)

Fledging period the period between a young bird hatching and acquiring its first full set of feathers and being able to fly

Fledgling young bird that is capable of flight; in perching birds and some others it corresponds with the time of leaving the nest

Fluke either of the two lobes of the tail of a whale or related animal; also a type of flatworm, usually parasitic

Gamebird birds in the ORDER Galliformes (megapodes, cracids, grouse, partridges, quail, pheasants, and relatives); also used for any birds that may be legally hunted by humans

Gene the basic unit of heredity, enabling one generation to pass on characteristics to its offspring

Genus (**genera**, pl.) a group of closely related SPECIES

Gestation the period of pregnancy in MAMMALS, between fertilization of the egg and birth of the baby

Gill Respiratory organ that absorbs oxygen from the water. External gills occur in tadpoles. Internal gills occur in most fish

Harem a group of females living in the same territory and consorting with a single male

Hen any female bird

Herbivore an animal that eats plants (grazers and BROWSERS are herbivores)

Hermaphrodite an animal having both male and female reproductive organs

Herpetologist ZOOLOGIST who studies REPTILES and AMPHIBIANS

Hibernation becoming inactive in winter, with lowered body temperature to save energy. Hibernation takes place in a special nest or den called a hibernaculum

Homeotherm an animal that can maintain a high and constant body temperature by means of internal processes; also called "warm-blooded"

Home range the area that an animal uses in the course of its normal activity

Hybrid offspring of two closely related SPECIES that can breed; it is sterile and so cannot produce offspring

Ichthyologist ZOOLOGIST specializing in the study of fish

Inbreeding breeding among closely related animals (e.g., cousins), leading to weakened genetic composition and reduced survival rates

Incubation the act of keeping the egg or eggs warm or the period from the laying of eggs to hatching

Indwellers ORGANISMS that live inside others, e.g., the California Bay pea crab, which lives in the tubes of some marine ANNELID worms, but do not act as PARASITES

Indigenous living naturally in a region; native (i.e., not an introduced SPECIES)

Insect any air-breathing ARTHROPOD of the CLASS Insecta, having a body divided into head, THORAX, and abdomen, three pairs of legs, and sometimes two pairs of wings

Insectivore animal that feeds on INSECTS. Also used as a group name for hedgehogs, shrews, moles, etc.

Interbreeding breeding between animals of different SPECIES, varieties, etc. within a single FAMILY or strain; Interbreeding can cause dilution of the GENE pool

Interspecific between SPECIES

Intraspecific between individuals of the same SPECIES

Invertebrates animals that have no backbone (or other bones) inside their body, e.g., mollusks, INSECTS, jellyfish, crabs

Iridescent displaying glossy colors produced (e.g., in bird PLUMAGE) not as a result of pigments but by the splitting of sunlight into light of different wavelengths; rainbows are made in the same way

Joey a young kangaroo living in its mother's pouch

Juvenile a young animal that has not yet reached breeding age

Keel a ridge along the CARAPACE of certain turtles or a ridge on the scales of some REPTILES

Keratin tough, fibrous material that forms hair, feathers, nails, and protective plates on the skin of VERTEBRATE animals

Keystone species a SPECIES on which many other SPECIES are wholly or partially dependent

Krill PLANKTONIC shrimps

Labyrinth specialized auxiliary (extra) breathing organ found in some fish

Larva an immature form of an animal that develops into an ADULT form through METAMORPHOSIS

Lateral line system a system of pores running along a fish's body. These pores lead to nerve endings that allow a fish to sense vibrations in the water and help it locate prey, detect PREDATORS, avoid obstacles, and so on. Also found in AMPHIBIANS

Lek communal display area where male birds of some SPECIES gather to attract and mate with females

Livebearer animal that gives birth to fully developed young (usually refers to REPTILES or fish)

Mammal any animal of the CLASS Mammalia—warm-blooded VERTEBRATE having mammary glands in the female that produce milk with which it nurses its young. The class includes bats, primates, rodents, and whales

Mandible upper or lower part of a bird's beak or BILL; also the jawbone in VERTEBRATES; in INSECTS and other ARTHROPODS mandibles are mouth parts mostly used for biting and chewing

Mantle cavity a space in the body of mollusks that contains the breathing organs

Marine living in the sea

Matriarch senior female member of a social group

Metabolic rate the rate at which chemical activities occur within animals, including the exchange of gasses in respiration and the liberation of energy from food

Metamorphosis the transformation of a LARVA into an ADULT

Migration movement from one place to another and back again; usually seasonal

Molt the process in which a bird sheds its feathers and replaces them with new ones; some MAMMALS, REPTILES, and ARTHROPODS regularly molt, shedding hair, skin, or outer layers

Monotreme egg-laying MAMMAL, e.g., platypus

Montane in a mountain environment

Natural selection the process whereby individuals with the most appropriate ADAPTATIONS are more successful than other individuals and therefore survive to produce more offspring. Natural selection is the main process driving evolution in which animals and plants are challenged by natural effects (such as predation and bad weather), resulting in survival of the fittest

Nematocyst the stinging part of animals such as jellyfish, usually found on the tentacles

Nestling a young bird still in the nest and dependent on its parents

New World the Americas

Niche part of a habitat occupied by an ORGANISM, defined in terms of all aspects of its lifestyle

Nocturnal active at night

Nomadic animals that have no fixed home, but wander continuously

Noseleaf fleshy structures around the face of bats; helps focus ULTRASOUNDS used for ECHOLOCATION

Ocelli markings on an animal's body that resemble eyes. Also, the tiny, simple eyes of some INSECTS, spiders, CRUSTACEANS, mollusks, etc.

Old World non-American continents

Olfaction sense of smell

Operculum a cover consisting of bony plates that covers the GILLS of fish

Omnivore an animal that eats a wide range of both animal and vegetable food

Order a subdivision of a CLASS of animals, consisting of a series of animal FAMILIES

Organism any member of the animal or plant kingdom; a body that has life

Ornithologist ZOOLOGIST specializing in the study of birds

Osteoderms bony plates beneath the scales of some REPTILES, particularly crocodilians

Oviparous producing eggs that hatch outside the body of the mother (in fish, REPTILES, birds, and MONOTREMES)

Parasite an animal or plant that lives on or within the body of another (the host) from which it obtains nourishment. The host is often harmed by the association

Passerine any bird of the ORDER Passeriformes; includes SONGBIRDS

Pedipalps small, paired leglike appendages immediately in front of the first pair of walking legs of spiders

and other ARACHNIDS. Used by males for transferring sperm to the females
Pelagic living in the upper waters of the open sea or large lakes
Pheromone scent produced by animals to enable others to find and recognize them
Photosynthesis the production of food in green plants using sunlight as an energy source and water plus carbon dioxide as raw materials
Phylum zoological term for a major grouping of animal CLASSES. The whole animal kingdom is divided into about 30 PHYLA, of which the VERTEBRATES form part of just one
Placenta the structure that links an embryo to its mother during pregnancy, allowing exchange of chemicals between them
Plankton animals and plants drifting in open water; many are minute
Plastron the lower shell of CHELONIANS
Plumage the covering of feathers on a bird's body
Plume a long feather used for display, as in a bird of paradise
Polygamous where an individual has more than one mate in one BREEDING SEASON. Monogamous animals have only a single mate
Polygynous where a male mates with several females in one BREEDING SEASON
Polyp individual ORGANISM that lives as part of a COLONY—e.g., a coral—with a saclike body opening only by the mouth that is usually surrounded by a ring of tentacles
Population a distinct group of animals of the same SPECIES or all the animals of that SPECIES
Posterior the hind end or behind another structure
Predator an animal that kills live prey
Prehensile capable of grasping
Primary forest forest that has always been forest and has not been cut down and regrown at some time
Primates a group of MAMMALS that includes monkeys, apes, and ourselves
Prosoma the joined head and THORAX of a spider, scorpion, or horseshoe crab
Pupa an INSECT in the stage of METAMORPHOSIS between a caterpillar (LARVA) and an ADULT (imago)

Quadruped any animal that walks on four legs

Range the total geographical area over which a SPECIES is distributed

Raptor bird with hooked beak and strong feet with sharp claws (talons) for seizing, killing, and dealing with prey; also known as birds of prey. The term usually refers to daytime birds of prey (eagles, hawks, falcons, and relatives) but sometimes also includes NOCTURNAL owls
Regurgitate (of a bird) to vomit partly digested food either to feed NESTLINGS or to rid itself of bones, fur, or other indigestible parts, or (in some seabirds) to scare off PREDATORS
Reptile any member of the cold-blooded CLASS Reptilia, such as crocodiles, lizards, snakes, tortoises, turtles, and tuataras; characterized by an external covering of scales or horny plates. Most are egg-layers, but some give birth to fully developed young
Roost place that a bird or bat regularly uses for sleeping
Ruminant animals that eat vegetation and later bring it back from the stomach to chew again ("chewing the cud") to assist its digestion by microbes in the stomach

Savanna open grasslands with scattered trees and low rainfall, usually in warm areas
Scapulars the feathers of a bird above its shoulders
Scent chemicals produced by animals to leave smell messages for others to find and interpret
Scrub vegetation dominated by shrubs—woody plants usually with more than one stem
Scute horny plate covering live body tissue underneath
Secondary forest trees that have been planted or grown up on cleared ground
Sedge grasslike plant
Shorebird Plovers, sandpipers, and relatives (known as waders in Britain, Australia, and some other areas)
Slash-and-burn agriculture method of farming in which the unwanted vegetation is cleared by cutting down and burning
Social behavior interactions between individuals within the same SPECIES, e.g., courtship
Songbird member of major bird group of PASSERINES
Spawning the laying and fertilizing of eggs by fish and AMPHIBIANS and some mollusks
Speciation the origin of SPECIES; the diverging of two similar ORGANISMS through reproduction down through the generations into different forms resulting in a new SPECIES
Species a group of animals that look similar and can breed with each other to produce fertile offspring
Steppe open grassland in parts of the world where the climate is too harsh for trees to grow
Subspecies a subpopulation of a single SPECIES whose members are similar to each other but differ from the typical form for that SPECIES; often called a race
Substrate a medium to which fixed animals are attached under water, such as rocks onto which barnacles and mussels are attached, or plants are anchored in, e.g., gravel, mud, or sand in which AQUATIC plants have their roots embedded
Substratum see SUBSTRATE
Swim bladder a gas or air-filled bladder in fish; by taking in or exhaling air, the fish can alter its buoyancy
Symbiosis a close relationship between members of two SPECIES from which both partners benefit

Taxonomy the branch of biology concerned with classifying ORGANISMS into groups according to similarities in their structure, origins, or behavior. The categories, in order of increasing broadness, are: SPECIES, GENUS, FAMILY, ORDER, CLASS, PHYLUM
Terrestrial living on land
Territory defended space
Test an external covering or "shell" of an INVERTEBRATE such as a sea-urchin; it is in fact an internal skeleton just below the skin
Thorax (**thoracic**, adj.) in an INSECT the middle region of the body between the head and the abdomen. It bears the wings and three pairs of walking legs
Torpor deep sleep accompanied by lowered body temperature and reduced METABOLIC RATE
Translocation transferring members of a SPECIES from one location to another
Tundra open grassy or shrub-covered lands of the far north

Underfur fine hairs forming a dense, woolly mass close to the skin and underneath the outer coat of stiff hairs in MAMMALS
Understory the layer of shrubs, herbs, and small trees found beneath the forest CANOPY
Ungulate one of a large group of hoofed animals such as pigs, deer, cattle, and horses; mostly HERBIVORES
Uterus womb in which embryos of MAMMALS develop
Ultrasounds sounds that are too high-pitched for humans to hear
UV-B radiation component of ultraviolet radiation from the sun that is harmful to living ORGANISMS because it breaks up DNA

Vane the bladelike main part of a typical bird feather extending from either side of its shaft (midrib)
Ventral of or relating to the front part or belly of an animal (see DORSAL)
Vertebrate animal with a backbone (e.g., fish, MAMMAL, REPTILE), usually with skeleton made of bones, but sometimes softer cartilage
Vestigial a characteristic with little or no use, but derived from one that was well developed in an ancestral form; e.g., the "parson's nose" (the fatty end portion of the tail when a fowl is cooked) is the compressed bones from the long tail of the reptilian ancestor of birds
Viviparous (of most MAMMALS and a few other VERTEBRATES) giving birth to active young rather than laying eggs

Waterfowl members of the bird FAMILY Anatidae, the swans, geese, and ducks; sometimes used to include other groups of wild AQUATIC birds
Wattle fleshy protuberance, usually near the base of a bird's BILL
Wingbar line of contrasting feathers on a bird's wing
Wing case one of the protective structures formed from the first pair of nonfunctional wings, which are used to protect the second pair of functional wings in INSECTS such as beetles
Wintering ground the area where a migrant spends time outside the BREEDING SEASON

Yolk part of the egg that contains nourishment for a growing embryo

Zooid individual animal in a colony; usually applied to corals or bryozoa (sea-mats)
Zoologist person who studies animals
Zoology the study of animals

Further Reading

Mammals

Macdonald, David, *The Encyclopedia of Mammals*, Barnes & Noble, New York, U.S., 2001

Payne, Roger, *Among Whales*, Bantam Press, U.S., 1996

Reeves, R. R., and Leatherwood, S., *The Sierra Club Handbook of Whales and Dolphins of the World*, Sierra Club, U.S., 1983

Sherrow, Victoria, and Cohen, Sandee, *Endangered Mammals of North America*, Twenty-First Century Books, U.S., 1995

Whitaker, J. O., *Audubon Society Field Guide to North American Mammals*, Alfred A. Knopf, New York, U.S., 1996

Birds

Attenborough, David, *The Life of Birds*, BBC Books, London, U.K., 1998

BirdLife International, *Threatened Birds of the World*, Lynx Edicions, Barcelona, Spain and BirdLife International, Cambridge, U.K., 2000

del Hoyo, J., Elliott, A., and Sargatal, J., eds., *Handbook of Birds of the World* Vols 1 to 6, Lynx Edicions, Barcelona, Spain, 1992–2001

Sayre, April Pulley, *Endangered Birds of North America*, Scientific American Sourcebooks, Twenty-First Century Books, U.S., 1977

Scott, Shirley L., ed., *A Field Guide to the Birds of North America*, National Geographic, U.S., 1999

Stattersfield, A., Crosby, M., Long, A., and Wege, D., eds., *Endemic Bird Areas of the World: Priorities for Biodiversity Conservation*, BirdLife International, Cambridge, U.K., 1998

Thomas, Peggy, *Bird Alert: Science of Saving*, Twenty-First Century Books, U.S., 2000

Fish

Bannister, Keith, and Campbell, Andrew, *The Encyclopedia of Aquatic Life*, Facts On File, New York, U.S., 1997

Buttfield, Helen, *The Secret Lives of Fishes*, Abrams, U.S., 2000

Reptiles and Amphibians

Corbett, Keith, *Conservation of European Reptiles and Amphibians*, Christopher Helm, London, U.K., 1989

Corton, Misty, *Leopard and Other South African Tortoises*, Carapace Press, London, U.K., 2000

Hofrichter, Robert, *Amphibians: The World of Frogs, Toads, Salamanders, and Newts*, Firefly Books, Canada, 2000

Stafford, Peter, *Snakes*, Natural History Museum, London, U.K., 2000

Insects

Borror, Donald J., and White, Richard E., *A Field Guide to Insects: America, North of Mexico*, Houghton Mifflin, New York, U.S., 1970

Pyle, Robert Michael, *National Audubon Society Field Guide to North American Butterflies*, Alfred A. Knopf, New York, U.S., 1995

General

Adams, Douglas, and Carwardine, Mark, *Last Chance to See*, Random House, London, U.K., 1992

Allaby, Michael, *The Concise Oxford Dictionary of Ecology*, Oxford University Press, Oxford, U.K., 1998

Douglas, Dougal, and others, *Atlas of Life on Earth*, Barnes & Noble, New York, U.S., 2001

National Wildlife Federation, *Endangered Species: Wild and Rare*, McGraw-Hill, U.S., 1996

Websites

http://www.abcbirds.org/ American Bird Conservancy. Articles, information about campaigns and bird conservation in the Americas

http://elib.cs.berkeley.edu/aw/ AmphibiaWeb information about amphibians and their conservation

http://animaldiversity.ummz.umich.edu/ University of Michigan Museum of Zoology animal diversity web. Search for pictures and information about animals by class, family, and common name. Includes glossary

www.beachside.org sea turtle preservation society

http://www.birdlife.net BirdLife International, an alliance of conservation organizations working in more than 100 countries to save birds and their habitats

http://www.surfbirds.com Articles, mystery photographs, news, book reviews, birding polls, and more

http://www.birds.cornell.edu/ Cornell University. Courses, news, nest-box cam

http://www.cites.org/ CITES and IUCN listings. Search for animals by scientific name of order, family, genus, species, or common name. Location by country and explanation of reasons for listings

www.ufl.edu/natsci/herpetology/crocs.htm crocodile site, including a chat room

www.darwinfoundation.org/ Charles Darwin Research Center

http://www.open.cc.uk/daptf DAPTF–Declining Amphibian Population Task Force. Providing information and data about amphibian declines. (International Director, Professor Tim Halliday, is co-author of this set)

http://www.ucmp.berkeley.edu/echinodermata the echinoderm phylum—starfish, sea-urchins, etc.

http://endangered.fws.gov information about endangered animals and plants from the U.S. Fish and Wildlife Service, the organization in charge of 94 million acres of wildlife refuges

http://forests.org/ includes forest conservation answers to queries

www.traffic.org/turtles freshwater turtles

www.iucn.org details of species, IUCN listings and IUCN publications

http://www.pbs.org/journeytoamazonia the Amazonian rain forest and its unrivaled biodiversity

http://www.audubon.org National Audubon Society, named after the ornithologist and wildlife artist John James Audubon (1785–1851). Sections on education, local Audubon societies, and bird identification

www.nccnsw.org.au site for threatened Australian species

http://cmc-ocean.org facts, figures, and quizzes about marine life

http://wwwl.nature.nps.gov/wv/ The U.S. National Park Service wildlife and plants site. Factsheets on all kinds of animals found in the parks

www.ewt.org.za endangered South African wildlife

http://www.panda.org World Wide Fund for Nature (WWF). Newsroom, press releases, government reports, campaigns. Themed photogallery

http://www.greenchannel.com/wwt/ Wildfowl and Wetlands Trust (U.K.). Founded by artist and naturalist Sir Peter Scott, the trust aims to preserve wetlands for rare waterbirds. Includes information on places to visit and threatened waterbird species

http://wdcs.org/ Whale and Dolphin Conservation Society site. News, projects, and campaigns. Sightings database

List of Animals by Group

Listed below are the common names of the animals featured in the A–Z part of this set grouped by their class, i.e., Mammals, Birds, Fish, Reptiles, Amphibians, and Insects and Invertebrates.

Bold numbers indicate the volume number and are followed by the first page number of the two-page illustrated main entry in the set.

Mammals
addax **2**:4
anoa, mountain **2**:20
anteater, giant **2**:24
antelope, Tibetan **2**:26
armadillo, giant **2**:30
ass
   African wild **2**:34
   Asiatic wild **2**:36
aye-aye **2**:42
babirusa **2**:44
baboon, gelada **2**:46
bandicoot, western barred **2**:48
banteng **2**:50
bat
   ghost **2**:56
   gray **2**:58
   greater horseshoe **2**:60
   greater mouse-eared **2**:62
   Kitti's hog-nosed **2**:64
   Morris's **2**:66
bear
   grizzly **2**:68
   polar **2**:70
   sloth **2**:72
   spectacled **2**:74
beaver, Eurasian **2**:76
bison
   American **2**:86
   European **2**:88
blackbuck **2**:94
camel, wild bactrian **3**:24
cat, Iriomote **3**:30
cheetah **3**:40
chimpanzee **3**:42
   pygmy **3**:44
chinchilla, short-tailed **3**:46
cow, Steller's sea **3**:70
cuscus, black-spotted **3**:86
deer
   Chinese water **4**:6
   Kuhl's **4**:8
   Père David's **4**:10
   Siberian musk **4**:12
desman, Russian **4**:14
dhole **4**:16
dog
   African wild **4**:22

bush **4**:24
dolphin
   Amazon river **4**:26
   Yangtze river **4**:28
dormouse
   common **4**:30
   garden **4**:32
   Japanese **4**:34
drill **4**:40
dugong **4**:46
duiker, Jentink's **4**:48
dunnart, Kangaroo Island **4**:50
echidna, long-beaked **4**:60
elephant
   African **4**:64
   Asian **4**:66
elephant-shrew, golden-rumped **4**:68
ferret, black-footed **4**:72
flying fox
   Rodrigues (Rodriguez) **4**:84
   Ryukyu **4**:86
fossa **4**:90
fox, swift **4**:92
gaur **5**:18
gazelle, dama **5**:20
gibbon, black **5**:26
giraffe, reticulated **5**:30
glider, mahogany **5**:32
gorilla
   mountain **5**:38
   western lowland **5**:40
gymnure, Hainan **5**:48
hare, hispid **5**:50
hippopotamus, pygmy **5**:52
horse, Przewalski's wild **5**:58
hutia, Jamaican **5**:64
hyena
   brown **5**:66
   spotted **5**:68
ibex, Nubian **5**:70
indri **5**:84
jaguar **5**:86
koala **6**:10
kouprey **6**:14
kudu, greater **6**:16
lemur
   hairy-eared dwarf **6**:22
   Philippine flying **6**:24
   ruffed **6**:26
leopard **6**:28
   clouded **6**:30
   snow **6**:32
lion, Asiatic **6**:34
loris, slender **6**:46
lynx, Iberian **6**:52
macaque
   barbary **6**:54
   Japanese **6**:56
manatee, Florida **6**:68
markhor **6**:72
marten, pine **6**:74
mink, European **6**:78

mole, marsupial **6**:80
mole-rat
   Balkans **6**:82
   giant **6**:84
monkey
   douc **6**:86
   Goeldi's **6**:88
   proboscis **6**:90
mouse, St. Kilda **6**:92
mulgara **6**:94
numbat **7**:14
nyala, mountain **7**:18
ocelot, Texas **7**:20
okapi **7**:22
orang-utan **7**:26
oryx
   Arabian **7**:28
   scimitar-horned **7**:30
otter
   European **7**:32
   giant **7**:34
   sea **7**:36
ox, Vu Quang **7**:44
panda
   giant **7**:48
   lesser **7**:50
pangolin, long-tailed **7**:52
panther, Florida **7**:54
pig, Visayan warty **7**:68
pika, steppe **7**:74
platypus **7**:82
porpoise, harbor **7**:86
possum, Leadbeater's **7**:88
potoroo, long-footed **7**:90
prairie dog, black-tailed **7**:92
pygmy-possum, mountain **8**:4
quagga **8**:8
rabbit
   Amami **8**:12
   volcano **8**:14
rat, black **8**:24
rhinoceros
   black **8**:26
   great Indian **8**:28
   Javan **8**:30
   Sumatran **8**:32
   white **8**:34
rock-wallaby, Prosperine **8**:36
saiga **8**:42
sea lion, Steller's **8**:62
seal
   Baikal **8**:70
   gray **8**:72
   Hawaiian monk **8**:74
   Mediterranean monk **8**:76
   northern fur **8**:78
sheep, barbary **8**:88
shrew, giant otter **8**:90
sifaka, golden-crowned **8**:92
sloth, maned **9**:6
solenodon, Cuban **9**:16
souslik, European **9**:18
squirrel, Eurasian red **9**:28

tahr, Nilgiri **9**:46
takin **9**:50
tamarin, golden lion **9**:52
tapir
   Central American **9**:56
   Malayan **9**:58
tenrec, aquatic **9**:64
thylacine **9**:66
tiger **9**:68
tree-kangaroo, Goodfellow's **10**:4
vicuña **10**:28
whale
   blue **10**:40
   fin **10**:42
   gray **10**:44
   humpback **10**:46
   killer **10**:48
   minke **10**:50
   northern right **10**:52
   sei **10**:54
   sperm **10**:56
   white **10**:58
wildcat **10**:62
wolf
   Ethiopian **10**:64
   Falkland Island **10**:66
   gray **10**:68
   maned **10**:70
   red **10**:72
wolverine **10**:74
wombat, northern hairy-nosed **10**:76
yak, wild **10**:90
zebra
   Grevy's **10**:92
   mountain **10**:94

Birds
akiapolaau **2**:6
albatross, wandering **2**:8
amazon, St. Vincent **2**:14
asity, yellow-bellied **2**:32
auk, great **2**:38
barbet, toucan **2**:54
bellbird, three-wattled **2**:82
bird of paradise, blue **2**:84
bittern, Eurasian **2**:90
blackbird, saffron-cowled **2**:92
bowerbird, Archbold's **3**:8
bustard, great **3**:10
cassowary, southern **3**:28
cockatoo, salmon-crested **3**:52
condor, California **3**:60
coot, horned **3**:62
cormorant, Galápagos **3**:64
corncrake **3**:66
courser, Jerdon's **3**:68
crane, whooping **3**:76
crow, Hawaiian **3**:82
curlew, Eskimo **3**:84
dipper, rufous-throated **4**:18

LIST OF ANIMALS BY GROUP

dodo **4**:20
duck
  Labrador **4**:42
  white-headed **4**:44
eagle
  harpy **4**:52
  Philippine **4**:54
  Spanish imperial **4**:56
finch
  Gouldian **4**:74
  mangrove **4**:76
firecrown, Juan Fernández **4**:78
flamingo, Andean **4**:80
flycatcher, Pacific royal **4**:82
fody, Mauritius **4**:88
grebe, Atitlán **5**:42
guan, horned **5**:44
gull, lava **5**:46
honeyeater, regent **5**:54
hornbill, writhed **5**:56
hoia **5**:60
hummingbird, bee **5**:62
ibis, northern bald **5**:72
kagu **5**:88
kakapo **5**:90
kea **5**:92
kestrel
  lesser **5**:94
  Mauritius **6**:4
kite, red **6**:6
kiwi, brown **6**:8
lark, Raso **6**:18
lovebird, black-cheeked **6**:48
macaw
  hyacinth **6**:58
  Spix's **6**:60
magpie-robin, Seychelles **6**:62
malleefowl **6**:64
manakin, black-capped **6**:66
mesite, white-breasted **6**:76
murrelet, Japanese **7**:4
nene **7**:10
nuthatch, Algerian **7**:16
owl
  Blakiston's eagle **7**:38
  Madagascar red **7**:40
  spotted **7**:42
parrot, night **7**:58
peafowl, Congo **7**:60
pelican, Dalmatian **7**:62
penguin, Galápagos **7**:64
petrel, Bermuda **7**:66
pigeon
  pink **7**:70
  Victoria crowned **7**:72
pitta, Gurney's **7**:78
plover, piping **7**:84
quetzal, resplendent **8**:10
rail, Guam **8**:18
rockfowl, white-necked **8**:38
sandpiper, spoon-billed **8**:54

scrub-bird, noisy **8**:56
sea-eagle, Steller's **8**:64
siskin, red **8**:94
spatuletail, marvelous **9**:20
spoonbill, black-faced **9**:26
starling, Bali **9**:30
stilt, black **9**:32
stork, greater adjutant **9**:34
swallow, blue **9**:42
swan, trumpeter **9**:44
takahe **9**:48
tanager, seven-colored **9**:54
teal, Baikal **9**:62
tragopan, Temminck's **9**:94
turaco, Bannerman's **10**:10
vanga, helmet **10**:26
vireo, black-capped **10**:32
vulture, Cape griffon **10**:34
warbler
  aquatic **10**:36
  Kirtland's **10**:38
woodpecker
  ivory-billed **10**:78
  red-cockaded **10**:80
wren, Zapata **10**:86

Fish
anchovy, freshwater **2**:16
angelfish, masked **2**:18
archerfish, western **2**:28
barb, bandula **2**:52
caracolera, mojarra **3**:26
catfish, giant **3**:32
cavefish, Alabama **3**:34
characin, blind cave **3**:38
cichlids, Lake Victoria
  haplochromine **3**:48
cod
  Atlantic **3**:54
  trout **3**:56
coelacanth **3**:58
dace, mountain blackside **3**:90
danio, barred **3**:94
darter, watercress **4**:4
dragon fish **4**:36
eel, lesser spiny **4**:62
galaxias, swan **5**:16
goby, dwarf pygmy **5**:34
goodeid, gold sawfin **5**:36
ikan temoleh **5**:82
lungfish, Australian **6**:50
paddlefish **7**:46
paradisefish, ornate **7**:56
pirarucu **7**:76
platy, Cuatro Ciénegas **7**:80
pupfish, Devil's Hole **7**:94
rainbowfish, Lake Wanam **8**:20
rasbora, vateria flower **8**:22
rocky, eastern province **8**:40
salmon, Danube **8**:52
seahorse, Knysna **8**:68
shark
  basking **8**:80

  great white **8**:82
  silver **8**:84
  whale **8**:86
sturgeon, common **9**:36
sucker, razorback **9**:38
sunfish, spring pygmy **9**:40
toothcarp, Valencia **9**:80
totoaba **9**:92
tuna, northern bluefin **10**:8
xenopoecilus **10**:88

Reptiles
alligator
  American **2**:10
  Chinese **2**:12
boa
  Jamaican **3**:4
  Madagascar **3**:6
chameleon, south central lesser **3**:36
crocodile, American **3**:80
dragon, southeastern lined earless **4**:38
gecko, Round Island day **5**:22
gharial **5**:24
Gila monster **5**:28
iguana
  Fijian crested **5**:74
  Galápagos land **5**:76
  Galápagos marine **5**:78
  Grand Cayman blue rock **5**:80
Komodo dragon **6**:12
lizard
  blunt-nosed leopard **6**:36
  flat-tailed horned **6**:38
  Ibiza wall **6**:40
  sand **6**:42
python, woma **8**:6
racer, Antiguan **8**:16
skink, pygmy blue-tongued **9**:4
snake
  eastern indigo **9**:10
  leopard **9**:12
  San Francisco garter **9**:14
tortoise **9**:82
  Egyptian **9**:84
  Desert **9**:82
  Galápagos giant **9**:86
  geometric **9**:88
  plowshare **9**:90
tuatara **10**:6
turtle
  Alabama red-bellied **10**:12
  bog **10**:14
  Chinese three-striped box **10**:16
  hawksbill **10**:18
  pig-nosed **10**:20
  western swamp **10**:22
  yellow-blotched sawback map **10**:24
viper, Milos **10**:30
whiptail, St. Lucia **10**:60

Amphibians
axolotl **2**:40
frog
  gastric-brooding **4**:94
  green and golden bell **5**:4
  Hamilton's **5**:6
  harlequin **5**:8
  red-legged **5**:10
  tinkling **5**:12
  tomato **5**:14
mantella, golden **6**:70
newt, great crested **7**:12
olm **7**:24
salamander
  California tiger **8**:44
  Japanese giant **8**:46
  Ouachita red-backed **8**:48
  Santa Cruz long-toed **8**:50
toad
  golden **9**:70
  Mallorcan midwife **9**:72
  natterjack **9**:74
  western **9**:76
toadlet, corroboree **9**:78

Insects and Invertebrates
ant, European red wood **2**:22
beetle
  blue ground **2**:78
  hermit **2**:80
butterfly
  Apollo **3**:12
  Avalon hairstreak **3**:14
  birdwing **3**:16
  Hermes copper **3**:18
  large blue **3**:20
  large copper **3**:22
clam, giant **3**:50
crab
  California Bay pea **3**:72
  horseshoe **3**:74
crayfish, noble **3**:78
cushion star **3**:88
damselfly, southern **3**:92
earthworm, giant gippsland **4**:58
emerald, orange-spotted **4**:70
leech, medicinal **6**:20
longicorn, cerambyx **6**:44
mussel, freshwater **7**:6
nemertine, Rodrigues **7**:8
sea anemone, starlet **8**:58
sea fan, broad **8**:60
sea-urchin, edible **8**:66
snail, *Partula* **9**:8
spider
  great raft **9**:22
  Kauai cave wolf **9**:24
  tarantula, red-kneed **9**:60
worm
  palolo **10**:82
  velvet **10**:84

Set Index

A **bold** number indicates the volume number and is followed by the relevant page number or numbers (e.g., **1**:52, 74).

Animals that are main entries in the A–Z part of the set are listed under their common names, alternative common names, and scientific names. Animals that appear in the data panels as Related endangered species are also listed under their common and scientific names.

Common names in **bold** (e.g., **addax**) indicate that the animal is a main entry in the set. Underlined page numbers (e.g., **2**:<u>12</u>) indicate the first page of the two-page main entry on that animal.

Italic volume and page references (e.g., *1:57*) indicate illustrations of animals in other parts of the set.

References to animals that are listed by the IUCN as Extinct (EX), Extinct in the Wild (EW), or Critically Endangered (CR) are found under those headings.

spp. means species.

A

Aceros spp. **5**:56
  A. leucocephalus **5**:<u>5</u>
Acestrura bombus **4**:78
Acinonyx jubatus **3**:<u>40</u>
Acipenser
  A. nudiventris **9**:36
  A. sturio **9**:<u>36</u>
Acrantophis madagascariensis **3**:<u>6</u>
Acrocephalus spp. **10**:36
  A. paludicola **10**:<u>36</u>
adaptation, reproductive strategies **1**:25
addax 2:<u>4</u>
Addax nasomaculatus **2**:<u>4</u>
Adelocosa anops **9**:<u>24</u>
Adranichthyis kruyti **10**:88
Aegialia concinna **2**:80
Aegypius monachus **10**:34
Aepypodius bruijnii **6**:64
Afropavo congensis **7**:<u>60</u>
Agapornis
  A. fischeri **6**:48
  A. nigrigenis **6**:<u>48</u>
Agelaius xanthomus **2**:92
Aglaeactis aliciae **4**:78
agricultural land use **1**:38, 61
agricultural practices **1**:52, 74; **2**:60, 63, 73, 92; **3**:10, 13, 67, 85; **4**:19, 24, 75; **5**:50, 94; **6**:6, 36, 38, 48, 82, 95; **7**:12, 19; **8**:95; **9**:4, 18; **10**:14, 34
Ailuroedus dentirostris **3**:8
Ailuropoda melanoleuca **7**:<u>48</u>
Ailurus fulgens **7**:<u>50</u>
akiapolaau 2:<u>6</u>
ala Balik **8**:52
Alabama **3**:34
alala **3**:<u>82</u>
Alauda razae **6**:<u>18</u>

albatross
  various **2**:9
  wandering 2:<u>8</u>
Algeria **7**:16
alien species **1**:71; **2**:7, 56, 77; **3**:27, 65, 83; **4**:15, 20, 50, 76, 78, 79, 88; **5**:6, 11, 17, 22, 36, 43, 46, 50, 61, 64, 74, 76, 88, 92; **6**:8, 19, 62, 65, 78, 80, 94; **7**:5, 9, 10, 14, 59, 66, 70, 82, 90; **8**:12, 19, 20, 40, 16; **9**:9, 16, 28, 32, 38, 48, 72, 81, 88; **10**:60, 87, 88
Alligator
  A. mississippiensis **2**:10
  A. sinensis **2**:12
alligator
  American 2:<u>10</u>
  Chinese 2:<u>12</u>
Allocebus trichotis **6**:<u>22</u>
Allotoca maculata **5**:36
Alsophis spp. **8**:16
  A. antiguae **8**:<u>16</u>
Alytes muletensis **9**:<u>72</u>
Amandava formosa **4**:74
amarillo **5**:36
amazon
  St. Vincent 2:<u>14</u>
  various **2**:14
Amazona spp. **2**:14
  A. guildingii **2**:<u>14</u>
Amblyopsis
  A. rosae **3**:34
  A. spelaea **3**:34
Amblyornis flavifrons **3**:8
Amblyrhynchus cristatus **5**:<u>78</u>
Ambystoma
  A. macrodactylum croceum **8**:51
  A. mexicanum **2**:<u>40</u>
Amdystoma spp. **8**:44
  A. californiense **8**:<u>44</u>
Ameca splendens **5**:36

Ammotragus lervia **8**:<u>88</u>
amphibians **1**:76
  diversity **1**:76
  risks **1**:78
  strategies **1**:76
  see also List of Animals by Group, page 100
Anas spp. **9**:62
  A. formosa **9**:<u>62</u>
  A. laysanensis **7**:10
  A. wyvilliana **7**:10
anchovy, freshwater **2**:<u>16</u>
Andes **2**:74; **3**:46; **4**:80; **10**:28
Andrias
  A. davidianus **8**:46
  A. japonicus **8**:<u>46</u>
anemone *see* sea anemone
angelfish
  masked **2**:<u>18</u>
  resplendent pygmy **2**:19
Angola **10**:94
angonoka **9**:<u>90</u>
animal products **1**:46; **3**:28, 75; **10**:42, 58
anoa
  lowland **2**:20; **6**:14
  mountain 2:<u>20</u>
Anoa mindorensis **2**:20
Anodorhynchus spp. **6**:60
  A. hyacinthus **6**:<u>58</u>
Anser erythropus **7**:10
ant, European red wood 2:<u>22</u>
anteater
  banded **7**:14
  fairy **2**:25
  giant 2:<u>24</u>
  marsupial **7**:14
  scaly **7**:<u>52</u>
antelope 2:4, <u>26</u>; 94; **4**:48; **5**:20; **6**:16; **7**:18, 28, 30; **8**:42
Anthornis melanocephala **5**:54
Anthracoceros
  A. marchei **5**:56
  A. montani **5**:56
Antigua **8**:16
Antilope cervicapra **2**:<u>94</u>
Antilophia bokermanni **6**:66
aoudad **8**:<u>88</u>
ape, barbary **6**:<u>54</u>
Aplonis spp. **9**:30
Apodemus sylvaticus hirtensis **6**:<u>92</u>
Apteryx spp. **6**:9
  A. mantelli **6**:<u>8</u>
aquaculture **8**:55
aquarium trade **1**:49; **4**:36; **8**:23, 69, 84
Aquila spp. **4**:56
  A. adalberti **4**:<u>56</u>
arapaima **7**:<u>76</u>
Arapaima gigas **7**:<u>76</u>
archerfish
  few-scaled **2**:28
  large-scaled **2**:<u>28</u>

  western **2**:<u>28</u>
Archiboldia papuensis **3**:<u>8</u>
archipelagos **1**:32
  see also islands
Arctic **2**:70
Arctic Ocean **10**:58
Arctocephalus spp. **8**:62, 78
Ardeotis nigriceps **3**:10
Argentina **3**:46; 62; **4**:18
Arizona **3**:60
armadillo
  giant 2:<u>30</u>
  various **2**:30
arowana, Asian **4**:36
artificial fertilization **1**:88
Asia **3**:10, 66; **6**:20
asity
  Schlegel's **2**:32
  yellow-bellied 2:<u>32</u>
Aspidites ramsayi **8**:<u>6</u>
ass
  African wild 2:<u>34</u>; **8**:8
  Asiatic wild 2:<u>36</u>; **8**:8
  half- **2**:36
  Syrian wild *1:37*
Astacus astacus **3**:<u>78</u>
Asterina phylactica **3**:88
Astyanax mexicanus **3**:38
Atelopus varius **5**:<u>8</u>
Atlantic Ocean **3**:54, 88; **8**:72, 76, 80; **9**:36; **10**:8, 40, 43
Atlantisia rogersi **3**:66
Atlapetes flaviceps **4**:76
Atrichornis
  A. clamosus **8**:56
  A. rufescens **8**:56
auk, great 2:<u>38</u>
aurochs *1:37*
Australia **2**:16, 28, 48, 56; **3**:16, 28; **4**:38, 46, 50, 58, 74, 94; **5**:12, 32, 54; **6**:10, 51, 64, 80, 94; **7**:14, 58, 82, 88, 90; **8**:4, 6, 36, 56; **9**:4, 66, 78; **10**:20, 22, 77
Austroglanis barnardi **3**:32
avadavat, green **4**:74
avahi **5**:84; **8**:93
Avahi occidentalis **5**:84; **8**:93
Axis kuhlii **4**:<u>8</u>
axolotl 2:<u>40</u>; **8**:44
aye-aye 2:<u>42</u>

B

babirusa 2:<u>44</u>
baboon, gelada 2:<u>46</u>
Babyrousa babyrussa **2**:<u>44</u>
baiji **4**:<u>28</u>
Balaenoptera
  B. acutorostrata **10**:<u>50</u>
  B. borealis **10**:<u>54</u>
  B. musculus **10**:<u>40</u>
  B. physalus **10**:<u>42</u>
Balantiocheilos melanopterus **8**:<u>84</u>
Balantiopteryx infusca **2**:64
Balearic Islands **6**:40; **9**:72

Bali **9**:30, 68
Baltic **8**:72; **9**:36
bandicoot
  eastern barred **2**:48
  golden **2**:48
  greater rabbit-eared *1:36*
  little barred **2**:<u>48</u>
  Shark Bay striped **2**:<u>48</u>
  western barred 2:<u>48</u>
Bangladesh **2**:72
banteng 2:<u>50</u>
barb
  bandula 2:<u>52</u>
  seven-striped **5**:82
  various **2**:52
barbet
  toucan 2:<u>54</u>
  various **2**:54
Barbus (Puntius) spp. **2**:52
  B. (P.) bandula **2**:<u>52</u>
bat
  Australian false vampire **2**:<u>56</u>
  ghost 2:<u>56</u>
  gray 2:<u>58</u>
  greater horseshoe 2:<u>60</u>
  greater mouse-eared 2:<u>62</u>
  Guatemalan **2**:62
  Indiana **2**:62
  Kitti's hog-nosed 2:<u>64</u>
  Morris's 2:<u>66</u>
  mouse-tailed **2**:64
  myotis, various **2**:66
  sheath-tailed **2**:64
  see also flying fox
Bawean Island **4**:8
bear
  Asian black **2**:68
  Asiatic black **2**:74
  brown **2**:<u>68</u>
  grizzly 2:<u>68</u>
  Mexican grizzly *1:37*; **2**:68
  polar 2:<u>70</u>
  sloth 2:<u>72</u>
  spectacled 2:<u>74</u>
beaver, Eurasian 2:<u>76</u>
beetle
  blue ground 2:<u>78</u>
  Ciervo scarab **2**:80
  delta green ground **2**:78
  Giuliani's dune scarab **2**:80
  hermit 2:<u>80</u>
  longhorn **6**:<u>44</u>
  scarab **2**:80
behavior studies **1**:85
bellbird
  bare-throated **2**:82
  Chatham Island **5**:54
  three-wattled 2:<u>82</u>
Belontia signata **7**:56
beloribitsa **8**:52
beluga **10**:58
Bering Sea **8**:62
Bermuda **7**:66
bettong, northern **7**:90
Bettongia tropica **7**:90
Bhutan **8**:28; **9**:50
big-game hunting **1**:47; **9**:68

102

SET INDEX

bilby **2**:48
bioaccumulation, toxins **1**:50, 51–52
biodiversity **1**:19
biogeographical areas **1**:19
Bioko Island **4**:40
biomes **1**:18–20
biosphere **1**:22
bird, elephant *1:37*
bird of paradise
  blue **2**:84
  McGregor's **2**:84
  Raggiana *1:46*
BirdLife International (BI) **1**:12, 67
birds **1**:64–67
  conservation organizations for **1**:12–13, 67, 88
  diversity **1**:64
  flightless **1**:28, 64
  history **1**:64–65
  risks **1**:64–67
  see also List of Animals by Group, page 100
Bison
  B. bison **2**:86
  B. bonasus **2**:88
bison
  American *1:15*; **2**:86
  European 2:88
  wood *1:37*
bittern 2:90
  Australasian **2**:90
  Eurasian 2:90
  great **2**:90
  Black Sea **8**:80; **9**:36
blackbird
  Jamaican **2**:92
  saffron-cowled 2:92
  yellow-shouldered **2**:92
blackbuck 2:94
bluebuck *1:37*
boa
  Cuban tree **3**:4
  Dumeril's **3**:6
  emerald tree *1:74*
  Jamaican 3:4
  Madagascar 3:6
  Madagascar tree **3**:6
  Mona Island **3**:4
  Puerto Rican **3**:4
  Virgin Islands **3**:4
Bolivia **2**:74; **3**:46, 62; **4**:18
bonobo **3**:44
bonytongue **4**:36
boom and bust **1**:21
Borneo **6**:30, 90; **7**:26; **8**:84
Bos
  B. frontalis **5**:18
  B. grunniens **10**:90
  B. javanicus **2**:50
  B. sauveli **6**:14
Bostrychia bocagei **5**:72
Botaurus
  B. poiciloptilus **2**:90
  B. stellaris **2**:90
Botswana **10**:34

bowerbird
  Archbold's 3:8
  various **3**:8
Brachylophus
  B. fasciatus **5**:74
  B. vitiensis **5**:74
Brachyramphus marmoratus **7**:4
Bradypus torquatus **9**:6
Branta
  B. ruficollis **7**:10
  B. sandvicensis **7**:10
Brazil **6**:58, 60, 66; **7**:76; **9**:6, 52, 54
British Columbia **5**:10
brush-turkey, Bruijin's **6**:64
Bubalus
  B. bubalis **2**:20
  B. depressicornis **2**:20; **6**:14
  B. quarlesi **2**:20
Bubo blakistoni **7**:38
Budorcas taxicolor **9**:50
buffalo **2**:87
  Indian water **2**:20
  see also bison
Bufo spp. **9**:70, 74, 76
  B. boreas **9**:76
  B. calamita **9**:74
  B. periglenes **9**:70
Bunolagus monticularis **8**:12, **8**:13
buntingi, various **10**:88
Burma see Myanmar
Burramys parvus **8**:4
bushdog **4**:93
bushmeat trade **1**:44
bustard
  great 3:10
  various **3**:10
Butan **7**:50
butterfly *1:83*
  Apollo 3:12
  Avalon hairstreak 3:14
  birdwing 3:16
  Hermes copper 3:18
  large blue 3:20
  large copper 3:22
  obi birdwing **3**:16
  Queen Alexandra's birdwing **3**:16
  Richmond birdwing **3**:16
  Rothschild's birdwing **3**:16
  swallowtail, various **3**:12

C

Cacatua spp. **3**:52
  C. moluccensis **3**:52
cachalot **10**:56
Cachorrito, various **7**:94
cage-bird trade **1**:49; **2**:14, 55; **3**:52; **4**:55, 74; **5**:44; **6**:48, 58; **7**:72, 78; **8**:94; **9**:30, 54
cahow **7**:66
Caimen, black **2**:10, 12
Calicalicus rufocarpalis **10**:27
California **3**:14, 18, 60; **9**:14

Callaeas cinerea **5**:60
catbird, tooth-billed **3**:8
callimico **6**:88
Callimico goeldii **6**:88
Callithrix
  C. flaviceps **6**:88
  C. nigriceps **6**:88
Callorhinus ursinus **8**:78
Calotes liocephalus **4**:38
Camarhynchus heliobates **4**:76
Cambodia **2**:50; **5**:26, 82; **6**:14, 86; **9**:34
camel, wild bactrian **3**:24
Camelus
  C. bactrianus **3**:24
  C. dromedarius **3**:25
Cameroon **4**:40; **10**:10
Campephilus
  C. imperialis **10**:78
  C. principalis **10**:78
Camptorhynchus labradorius **4**:42
Canada **2**:70, 86; **3**:74, 76, 84; **4**:42; **5**:10; **7**:36, 42, 84; **9**:44, 76; **10**:74
canine distemper **1**:56
Canis
  C. lupus **10**:68
  C. rufus **10**:72
  C. simensis **10**:64
Cape Verde Islands **6**:18
Capito spp. **2**:54
Capra
  C. falconeri **6**:72
  C. nubiana **5**:70
  C. walia **5**:71; **6**:73
Caprolagus
  C. hispidus **5**:50
Capromys brownii **5**:64
captive breeding **1**:22, 57, 87; **2**:12, 15, 19, 34, 43, 53, 86, 88, 94; **3**:4, 7, 13, 27, 33, 42, 47, 49, 53, 56, 60, 77, 81, 83, 95; **4**:6, 10, 12, 24, 28, 31, 36, 45, 53, 55, 60, 66, 85, 88, 92; **5**:5, 15, 22, 24, 28, 37, 38, 41, 52, 58, 64, 75, 77, 80, 82, 88, 93; **6**:5, 12, 26; 31, 47, 61, 65, 70, 78, 87, 89; **7**:11, 28, 46, 56, 70, 77, 81, 90; **8**:6, 14, 16, 19, 23, 53, 69, 85, 88, 95; **9**:9, 10, 15, 30, 33, 37, 41, 49, 52, 58, 68, 72, 79, 81, 85, 87, 91; **10**:7, 9, 14, 17, 21, 23, 25, 60, 70, 72, 88
captivity **10**:49
Carabus
  C. intricatus **2**:78
  C. olympiae **2**:78
caracolera, mojarra 3:26
Carcharhinus spp. **8**:86
Carcharias spp. **8**:86
Carcharodon carcharias **8**:82
Carcinoscorpius rotundicoruda **3**:74

Carduelis spp. **8**:94
  C. cucullata **8**:94
Carettochelys insculpta **10**:20
Caribbean **5**:80; **7**:84; **8**:16, 80; **10**:60
carp *1:52*
carpione del Garda **8**:52
Carpodectes antoniae **2**:82
cassowary
  Australian **3**:28
  common **3**:28
  double-wattled **3**:28
  dwarf **3**:28
  northern **3**:28
  southern 3:28
  two-wattled **3**:28
Castor fiber **2**:76
Casuarius
  C. bennetti **3**:28
  C. casuarius **3**:28
  C. unappendiculatus **3**:28
cat
  African wild **3**:31
  Asiatic golden **3**:32
  bay **3**:30
  black-footed **3**:31
  European wild **3**:31
  fishing **3**:32
  flat-headed **3**:30
  Iriomote 3:30
  jungle **3**:32
  leopard **3**:32
  margay **3**:31
  sand **3**:32
  tiger **3**:31
catfish
  Barnard's rock **3**:32
  giant 3:32
  Mekong **3**:32
  Thailand giant **3**:32
Catopuma badia **3**:30
cavefish
  Alabama **3**:34
  various **3**:34
Centropyge resplendens **2**:19
Cephalophus
  C. adersi **4**:49
  C. jentinki **4**:48–49
  C. nigrifrons **4**:49
Cephalopterus glabricollis **2**:82
Cephalorhynchus hectori **10**:48
Cerambyx cerdo **6**:44
Ceratophora tennentii **4**:38
Ceratotherium simum **8**:34
Cercartetus macrurus **8**:4
cetaceans see dolphin; porpoise; whale
Cetorhinus maximus **8**:80
Chad **7**:30
Chaetophractus retusus **2**:30
chameleon
  Labord's **3**:36
  Madagascar forest **3**:36
  Senegal *1:72*
  south central lesser 3:36
chamois cattle **9**:50

characin
  blind cave 3:38
  naked **3**:38
characodon, black prince **5**:36
Characodon spp. **5**:36
Charadrius spp. **7**:84
  C. melodus **7**:84
cheetah *1:57*; **3**:40
Chile **3**:46, 62; **4**:78
chimpanzee 3:42
  common **3**:42
  dwarf **3**:44
  pygmy 3:44
China **2**:12, 26, 36; **3**:12, 24, 32; **4**:6, 10, 12, 16, 28; **5**:26, 58, 94; **6**:30, 32; **7**:32, 38, 48, 50; **9**:50, 62, 94; **10**:16, 90
chinchilla
  long-tailed **3**:46
  short-tailed 3:46
Chinchilla breviacaudata **3**:46
chiru **2**:26
Chlamydogobius squamigenus **5**:34
Chlamydotis undulata **3**:10
Chlamyphorus truncatus **2**:30
Chlorochrysa nitidissima **4**:76
Chloropipo flavicapilla **6**:66
Chocó Endemic Bird Area **2**:54
Choeropsis liberiensis **5**:52
Choloepus
  C. didactylus **9**:6
  C. hoffmanni **9**:6
Chondrohierax wilsoni **6**:7
Chrysocyon brachyurus **10**:70
Cichlasoma spp. **3**:26
  C. bartoni **3**:26
cichlid
  Barton's **3**:26
  Lake Victoria haplochromine 3:48
  Steindachner's **3**:26
Ciconia
  C. boyciana **9**:34
  C. stormi **9**:34
Cinclus schulzi **4**:18
Cistothorus apolinari **10**:86
CITES see Convention on International Trade in Endangered Species of Wild Fauna and Flora
clam, giant 3:50
class, taxonomic group **1**:58–59
classification
  animal kingdom **1**:58
  species **1**:26
  taxonomic **1**:58–59
Clemmys spp. **10**:14
  C. muhlebergii **10**:14
climate change **1**:8, 53, 78; **2**:56; **3**:13; **6**:48; **7**:30, 48, 66, 88; **8**:36; **9**:70
cloning **5**:19
Cnemidophorus
  C. hyperythrus **10**:61

103

C. vanzoi **10**:60
cochin **6**:86
cockatoo
  salmon-crested 3:52
  various **3**:52
cod
  Atlantic 3:54
  blue-nosed **3**:56
  Clarence River **3**:56
  Mary River **3**:56
  northern **3**:54
  rock **3**:56
  trout 3:56
coelacanth 3:58
  Sulawesi **3**:58
Coelingena prunellei **9**:20
Coenagrion
  C. hylas freyi **3**:92
  C. mercuriale **3**:92
Coleura seychellensis **2**:64
collecting **2**:80; **3**:13, 63, 82; **6**:21; **7**:24; **8**:23; **10**:78
Colombia **2**:54
colugo **6**:24–25
  Malayan **6**:22
Columba spp. **7**:71
  C. mayeri **7**:70
Columbia **2**:74
combtail **7**:56
Commander Islands **8**:78
commensalism **3**:34
communities **1**:22
Comoro Islands **3**:58
competition **2**:7, 34, 48, 55, 56, 77; **3**:13, 24, 27, 29, 31, 44; **4**:15, 19, 24, 32, 45, 79, 89; **5**:6, 11, 19, 31, 36, 43, 66, 74, 76, 92; **6**:62, 72, 78, 84; **7**:30, 59, 65, 66, 88; **8**:21, 25, 34, 36, 63, 88; **9**:9, 28, 49, 66, 72, 86; **10**:55, 72, 77, 90, 95
computer modeling **1**:8
condor
  Andean **3**:60
  California *1*:86; **3**:60
coney **5**:64
Congo **7**:60
Conolophus
  C. pallidus **5**:76
  C. subcristatus **5**:76
conservation **1**:10–13, 67, 84–95
Conservation Dependent *see* Lower Risk, Conservation Dependent
Conservation International (CI) **1**:12
conservation research **1**:84–86
Convention on International Trade in Endangered Species of Wild Fauna and Flora (CITES) **1**:11, 16–17
coot
  Caribbean **3**:62
  Hawaiian **3**:62
  horned 3:62
  Mascarene **3**:62
cooter, Rio Grande **10**:12

Copsychus
  C. cebuensis **6**:62
  C. sechellarum **6**:62
coral
  red **3**:51
  reef *1*:82
  see also sea fan
Corallium rubrum **3**:51; **8**:60, 61
cormorant
  Galápagos 3:64
  Pallas's *1*:36
  various **3**:64
corncrake 3:66
Corvus spp. **3**:82
  C. hawaiiensis **3**:82
Costa Rica **8**:10; **9**:70
costs, conservation **1**:87–89
cotinga
  turquoise **2**:82
  yellow-billed **2**:82
Cotinga ridgwayi **2**:82
courser, Jerdon's 3:68
cow
  golden fleeced **9**:50
  sea **4**:46
  Steller's sea *1*:36; **3**:70
crab
  California Bay pea 3:72
  California fiddler *3*:73
  horseshoe 3:74
  king **3**:74
crane
  various **3**:76
  whooping 3:76
Craseonycteris thonglongyai **2**:64
crawfish, noble **3**:78
crayfish
  noble 3:78
  Tennessee cave **3**:78
creeper, Hawaii **2**:6
Crex crex **3**:66
crimson-wing, Shelley's **4**:74
Critically Endangered (CR), IUCN category, definition, **1**:14; **2**:4, 12, 34, 52, 80; **3**:34, 46, 58, 60, 68, 82, 84, 94; **4**:10, 28, 54, 76, 78, 84, 88, 94; **5**:12, 16, 34, 71, 72, 74, 80; **6**:14, 18, 34, 60, 62; **7**:6, 54, 58, 68, 78; **8**:20, 26, 30, 32, 76, 92; **9**:30, 32, 36, 52, 70, 72, 92; **10**:16, 18, 22, 30, 64, 72, 76, 78
crocodile *1*:75
  American 3:80
  various **3**:80
Crocodile Specialist Group (CSG) **3**:81
Crocodylus spp. **3**:80
  C. acutus **3**:80
Crocuta crocuta **5**:68
crossbreeding **1**:26
  see also interbreeding
crow
  Hawaiian 3:82
  various **3**:82
Cryptoprocta ferox **4**:90
Cryptospiza shelleyi **4**:74

Ctenophorus yinnietharra **4**:38
Cuba **5**:62; **10**:78, 86
culling **8**:72; 79
Cuon alpinus **4**:16
Cuora spp. **10**:16
  C. trifasciata **10**:16
curlew
  Eskimo 3:84
  slender-billed **8**:54
  various **3**:84
cuscus
  black-spotted 3:86
  various **3**:86
cushion star 3:88
Cyanopsitta spixii **6**:60
Cyanoramphus unicolor **5**:92
Cyclades Islands **10**:30
cyclones **7**:70
Cyclopes spp. **2**:25
Cyclura
  C. colleo **5**:80
  C. nubila lewisi **5**:80
  C. n. spp. **5**:80
Cygnus buccinator **9**:44
Cynocephalus
  C. varigatus **6**:22
  C. volans **6**:22
Cynomys spp. **7**:92
  C. ludovicianus **7**:92
Cynoscion macdonaldi **9**:92
cypriniformes **9**:80
Cyprinodon spp **7**:94
  C. diabolis **7**:94
cyprinodontiformes **9**:80

D

dace
  mountain blackside 3:90
  Tennessee **3**:90
Dactilopsila tatei **5**:32; **7**:88
Dalatias licha **8**:86
dam building **1**:40; **2**:92; **4**:19, 26, 29; **5**:83; **7**:82; **8**:47, 53; **9**:37; **10**:37
damselfly
  Frey's **3**:92
  southern 3:92
danio, barred 3:94
Danio pathirana **3**:94
darter
  Maryland **4**:4
  watercress 4:4
Darwin, Charles **1**:28; **5**:76
Dasycercus cristicauda **6**:94
Data Deficient (DD), IUCN category, definition **1**:16
Daubentonia madagascariensis **2**:42
DDT **1**:50, 51–52
deer
  Bawean **4**:8
  black musk **4**:12
  Chinese water 4:6
  forest musk **4**:12
  Kuhl's 4:8
  Père David's 4:10
  Schomburgk's *1*:36
  Siberian musk 4:12

deforestation **1**:38, 41, 73; **2**:7, 22, 31, 42, 44, 65, 72, 75, 83, 85; **3**:8, 29, 44, 87; **4**:34, 40, 48, 52, 55, 60, 61, 66, 84, 86, 88, 91; **5**:26, 38, 40, 44, 45, 49, 52, 57, 63, 83, 84, 86, 88; **6**:4, 8, 14, 22, 24, 26, 31, 46, 58, 63, 66, 70, 76, 86, 88, 91; **7**:26, 35, 38, 41, 51, 68, 70, 78, 89; **8**:11, 12, 23, 32, 38, 41, 47, 49, 65, 91; **9**:7, 31, 34, 52, 54, 76; **10**:4, 21, 24, 26, 72, 78, 85
Delphinapterus leucas **10**:58
Democratic Republic of Congo **3**:42; **5**:38, 40; **7**:22; **8**:34
Dendrocopus dorae **10**:80
Dendroica spp. **10**:38
  D. kirtlandii **10**:38
Dendrolagus spp. **10**:4
  D. goodfellowi **10**:4
desertification **1**:38–40; **5**:20
desman
  Pyrenean **4**:14
  Russian 4:14
Desmana moschata **4**:14
developing countries, conservation **1**:89, 95
devilfish **10**:44
dhole 4:16
Dicerorhinus sumatrensis **8**:32
Diceros bicornis **8**:26
dinosaurs **1**:34–35
Diomedea spp. **2**:9
  D. amsterdamensis **2**:9
  D. antipodensis **2**:9
  D. dabbenena **2**:9
  D. exulans **2**:8
dipper, rufous-throated 4:18
disease **1**:40, 55–56, 65, 79; **2**:7, 50, 89; **3**:29, 42, 57, 78, 83; **4**:5, 22, 26, 57, 94; **5**:12, 38; **6**:10, 14, 46, 48, 56; **8**:28, 36; **9**:56, 66, 76, 82; **10**:64, 72
dispersal corridors *see* habitat corridors
dodo *1*:28–29, *31*, *37*; **4**:20
dog
  African wild 4:22
  Asian wild **4**:16
  bush 4:24
  red **4**:16
Dolomedes plantarius **9**:22
dolphin
  Amazon river 4:26
  boto **4**:26–27
  Chinese river 4:28
  Ganges river **4**:26, 28
  Hector's **10**:48
  Indus river **4**:26, 28
  pantropical spotted **10**:48
  pink **4**:26
  striped **10**:48
  whitefin **4**:28
  Yangtze river 4:28
  see also porpoise
domestic animals **1**:38–40, 56

see also alien species; grazing
dormouse
  common 4:30
  garden 4:32
  hazel *1*:53; **4**:30
  Japanese 4:34
  various **4**:30, 32, 34
dotterel, New Zealand **7**:84
dragon
  southeastern lined earless 4:38
  Yinnietharra rock **4**:38
  see also Komodo dragon
dragon fish 4:36
dragonfly
  orange-spotted emerald **4**:70
  various **4**:70
drainage *see* wetland drainage
drift nets *see* fishing nets
drill 4:40
Driloleirus americanus **4**:58; **10**:82
Driloleirus macelfreshi **4**:58
drought *1*:52; **3**:38; **8**:51
Drymarchon corais couperi **9**:10
Dryomys nitedula **4**:30
Dryomys sichuanensis **4**:32, 34
duck
  Labrador 4:42
  pink-headed **4**:44
  various **7**:10
  white-headed 4:44
dugong 4:46; **6**:69
Dugong dugon **4**:46
duiker
  Ader's **4**:49
  Jentink's 4:48
  Ruwenzori black-fronted **4**:49
  squirrel **4**:48
dunnart
  Kangaroo Island **1**:24, 50
  sooty **4**:50
  various **4**:50
Durrell Wildlife Conservation Trust (DWCT) **1**:12
Dusicyon australis **10**:66
Dyscophus antongilii **5**:14

E

eagle
  Adalbert's **4**:56
  bald *1*:94
  greater spotted **4**:56
  harpy 4:52
  Imperial **4**:56
  monkey-eating 4:54
  New Guinea harpy **4**:53, 54
  Philippine 4:54
  Spanish imperial 4:56
  white-tailed sea *1*:94; **8**:64
earthworm
  giant gippsland 4:58
  Oregon giant **4**:58
  Washington giant **4**:58; **10**:82
echidna
  long-beaked 4:60**

SET INDEX

short-beaked **4**:60
Echinus esculentus **8**:66
ecology **1**:18–37
ecosystems **1**:22–24
ecotourism **1**:90–92; **5**:38; **6**:27; **10**:39
Ecuador **2**:54, 74; **4**:82
education **1**:94
Edwardsia ivelli **8**:58
eel, lesser spiny 4:62
egg collectors **2**:38, 91
El Niño **3**:64; **5**:79; **7**:65; **8**:10
Elaphe situla **9**:12
Elaphrus
  E. viridis **2**:78
  E. davidianus **4**:10
Elassoma
  E. alabamae **9**:40
  E. boehlkei **9**:40
  E. okatie **9**:40
elephant
  African 4:64
  Asian *1*:95; **4**:66
  Indian 4:66
elephant-shrew
  golden-rumped 4:68
  various **4**:68
Elephantulus revoili **4**:68
Elephas maximus **4**:66
Eliomys
  E. elanurus **4**:30, 32
  E. quercinus **4**:32
Elusor macrurus **10**:22
Emballonura semicaudata **2**:64
emerald, orange-spotted 4:70
emperor fish **4**:36
Endangered (EN), IUCN category, definition **1**:15
endemic species, definition **1**:30
energy flow **1**:23–24
Enhydra lutris **7**:36
Ephippiorhynchus asiaticus **9**:34
Epicrates
  E. angulifer **3**:4
  E. inornatus **3**:4
  E. monensis grati **3**:4
  E. monensis monensis **3**:4
  E. subflavus **3**:4
Epimachus fastuosus **2**:84
Equus
  E. africanus **2**:34; **8**:8
  E. grevyi **10**:92
  E. hemionus **2**:36
  E. przewalskii **5**:58
  E. quagga **8**:8
  E. zebra **10**:94
  E. z. hartmannii **10**:94
  E. z. zebra **10**:94
Eretmochelys imbricata **10**:18
Eriocnemis mirabilis **4**:78
  E. nigrivestis **9**:20
Erythrura
  E. gouldiae **4**:74
  E. viridifacies **4**:74
Eschrichtius robustus **10**:44
Estrilda poliopareia **4**:74
Etheostoma
  E. nuchale **4**:4
  E. sellore **4**:4
ethics, conservation **1**:88, 94–95
Ethiopia **2**:34, 46, 66; **6**:84; **7**:18; **10**:64, 92
Euathlus smithi **9**:60
Eubalaena
  E. australis **10**:52
  E. glacialis **10**:52
Eudyptes
  E. pachyrhynchus **7**:64
  E. robustus **7**:64
Eulidia yarrellii **4**:78
Eumetopias jubatus **8**:62
Eunice viridis **10**:82
Eunicella verrucosa **8**:60
Eupleres goudotii **4**:91
European Habitats Directive **6**:52
Euryceros prevostii **10**:26
Eurynorhynchus pygmeus **8**:54
evolution, speciation **1**:26–28
exploitation **1**:49, 62, 75
Extinct (EX), IUCN category, definition **1**:14; **2**:38; **3**:70; **4**:20, 42; **5**:42, 60; **8**:8; **9**:66; **10**:66
Extinct in the Wild (EW), IUCN category, definition, **1**:14; **4**:72; **5**:36, 58; **7**:30; **8**:19
extinction **1**:34, 36
see also natural extinction

F

falanoka **4**:91
falanouc **4**:91
Falco spp. **5**:95
  F. araea **6**:5
  F. naumanni **5**:94
  F. punctatus **6**:4
falcon, various **5**:95
Falkland Island **10**:66
family, taxonomic group **1**:58–59
Fauna & Flora International (FFI) **1**:12, 88
feather products **1**:46; **2**:85; **5**:50
Federal Bureau of Land Management **9**:83
Felis
  F. iriomotensis **3**:30
  F. pardinis **7**:20
  F. silvestris **10**:62
Ferminia cerverai **10**:86
ferreret **9**:72
ferret, black-footed 4:72
field studies **1**:84
Fiji **5**:74; **10**:82
finback **10**:42
finch
  Cochabamba **4**:76
  Galápagos *1*:28
  Gouldian 4:74
  Hawaiian *1*:27
  mangrove 4:76
  olive-headed brush **4**:76
painted **4**:74
purple-breasted **4**:74
rainbow **4**:74
finner **10**:42
  Japan **10**:54
firecrown, Juan Fernández 4:78
fires **1**:57, 73; **2**:25, 33, 59, 62, 92; **3**:19, 83; **4**:24, 68, 75; **5**:50; **6**:10, 42, 46, 65, 76, 81, 86; **7**:14, 17, 55, 88; **8**:14, 56; **9**:82, 89, 90; **10**:32, 38, 86
fish **1**:68–71
  definition **1**:68–69
  diversity **1**:68
  history **1**:69–70
  risks **1**:70–71
  see also List of Animals by Group, page 100
fish-eagle, various **8**:64
fishing **1**:45; **3**:33, 55, 65; **4**:26, 28, 44; **7**:38; **8**:53, 62, 72, 75, 76, 79, 80, 82, 85; **10**:9, 45, 48, 52
  see also overfishing; sports fishing
fishing controls **3**:55
fishing nets **4**:15; **5**:42; **6**:68; **7**:5, 86; **10**:46
fishing techniques **2**:8
fishing-owl, rufous **7**:42
flagship species *1*:9
flamingo
  Andean **4**:80
  various **4**:81
flightless birds **1**:28, 64
flooding **1**:40; **6**:38; **7**:66; **9**:56
florican
  Bengal **3**:10
  lesser **3**:10
flycatcher
  Atlantic royal **4**:82
  Pacific royal 4:82
  royal **4**:82
  tyrant **4**:82
flying fox
  Rodrigues (Rodriguez) **4**:84
  Ryukyu 4:86
fody
  Mauritius 4:88
  Rodrigues **4**:88
  Seychelles **4**:88
food chains/webs **1**:23–24
food shortage **4**:75; **7**:65
forest management **4**:30
Formica
  F. aquilonia **2**:22
  F. lugubris **2**:22
  F. polyctena **2**:22
fossa 4:90
Fossa fossa **4**:91
Foudia
  F. flavicans **4**:88
  F. rubra **4**:88
  F. seychellarum **4**:88
fox
  Simien **10**:64
  South American **10**:66
swift **4**:92
fragmented distribution **1**:8
  see also habitat fragmentation
French Polynesia **9**:8
friarbird, dusty **5**:54
Friends of the Earth **1**:13
frog
  Archey's **5**:6
  corroboree **9**:78
  gastric-brooding 4:94
  golden mantella 6:70
  green and golden bell 5:4
  green and golden swamp **5**:4
  Hamilton's 5:6
  harlequin 5:8
  Maud Island **5**:6
  New England swamp **5**:4, 5
  northern timber **5**:12
  northern tinker **5**:12
  Palestinian painted *1*:37
  platypus **4**:94
  red-legged 5:10
  sharp-snouted day **5**:12
  tinkling 5:12
  tomato 5:14
  various **5**:10
fruit bat *see* flying fox
Fulica spp. **3**:62
  F. cornuta **3**:62
fund raising, conservation **1**:90
fur trade **1**:46; **2**:46, 74, 76; **3**:46; **4**:14, 92; **5**:86; **6**:28, 31, 33, 75; **7**:20, 34, 36, 82; **8**:70, 72, 78, 90; **10**:28, 74
Furcifer
  F. campani **3**:36
  F. labordi **3**:36
  F. minor **3**:36

G

Gadus morhua **3**:54
Galápagos Islands **3**:64; **4**:76; **5**:46, 76, 78; **7**:64; **9**:80, 86
galaxias
  swan 5:16
  various **5**:16
Galaxias spp. **5**:16
  F. fontanus **5**:16
Galemys pyrenaicus **4**:14
Gallinula
  G. pacifica **9**:48
  G. sylvestris **9**:48
Gallirallus spp. **8**:18
  G. owstoni **8**:18
Gambelia silus **6**:36
gamekeeping **6**:74
garefowl **2**:38
gaur 5:18
gavial **5**:24
Gavialis gangeticus **5**:24
Gazella
  G. arabica **5**:20
  G. cuvieri **5**:20
  G. dama **5**:20
  G. leptoceros **5**:20
gazelle
  Arabian **5**:20
  Cuvier's **5**:20
  dama 5:20
  sand **5**:20
gecko
  fat-tailed *1*:74
  Namaqua day **5**:22
  Rodrigues day **5**:22
  Round Island day 5:22
  Standing's day **5**:22
genera, taxonomic **1**:58
generalist species **1**:29
genetics **1**:56
Genicanthus personatus **2**:18
Geocapromys
  G. brownii **5**:64
  G. ingrahami **5**:64
Geochelone spp. **9**:86, 89
  G. radiata **9**:90
  G. nigra **9**:86
  G. yniphora **9**:90
Geonemertes roderica **7**:8
Geopsittacus occidentalis **7**:58
Geronticus
  G. calvus **5**:72
  G. eremita **5**:72
Ghana **8**:38
gharial 5:24
gibbon
  black 5:26
  concolor **5**:26
  crested 5:26
  silvery **5**:26
Gibraltar **6**:54
Gila monster 5:28
Giraffa camelopardalis reticulata **5**:30
giraffe, reticulated 5:30
Girardinichthys spp. **5**:36
Glareola nordmanni **3**:68
glider, mahogany 5:32
Glirulus japonicus **4**:32, 34
Glis glis **4**:30
Globicephala macrorhynchus **10**:48
Glossolepis spp. **8**:20
  G. wanamensis **8**:20
glutton **10**:74
Glyphis gangeticus **8**:86
gnu-goat **9**:50
goat **9**:46
goby
  dwarf pygmy 5:34
  Edgbaston **5**:34
Goodea spp. **5**:36
goodeid
  gold sawfin 5:36
  various **5**:36
goose
  Hawaiian *1*:87; **7**:10
  various **7**:10
Gopherus
  G. agassizii **9**:82
  G. flavomarginatus **9**:82
  G. polyphemus **9**:82
Gorilla
  G. gorilla beringei **5**:38
  G. g. gorilla **5**:40

105

G. g. graveri **5**:39, 40
gorilla **1**:*45*
  eastern lowland **5**:39, 40
  mountain **1**:*91*; **5**:38
  western lowland 5:40
Goura
  G. cristata **7**:72
  G. scheepmaker **7**:72
  G. victoria **7**:72
Grantiella picta **5**:54
Graphiurus ocularis **4**:34
Graptemys spp. **10**:24
  G. flavimaculata **10**:24
grassland destruction **2**:92
grayling, New Zealand **1**:*36*
grazing animals **1**:38–40; **7**:17
grebe
  Atitlán 5:42
    giant pied-billed **5**:42
    various **5**:42
  Greece **9**:12; **10**:30
  greenhouse gases **1**:53
  Greenland **2**:70
  Greenpeace **1**:13
  greenshank, spotted **8**:54
  griffon, Cape 10:34
  ground squirrel
    European **9**:18
    various **9**:18
Grus spp. **3**:76
  G. americana **3**:76
Guam **8**:18
guan
  horned 5:44
  various **5**:44
guanaco **3**:25; **10**:28
Guatemala **5**:42; 44; **8**:10
Guinea **8**:38
gull
  black-billed **5**:46
  lava 5:46
  Olrog's **5**:46
  relict **5**:46
  Saunder's **5**:46
Gulo gulo **10**:74
Guyana, pirarucu **7**:76
Gymnobelideus leadbeateri **7**:88
Gymnocharacinus bergii **3**:38
Gymnogyps californianus **3**:60
Gymnomyza aubryana **5**:54
gymnure
  Hainan 5:48
  various **5**:48
Gyps spp. **10**:34
  G. coprotheres **10**:34

H

habitat conservation **1**:10, 88–92
habitat corridors **4**:67; **6**:36, 65; **7**:55; **10**:23
habitat creation **3**:13; **9**:53; **10**:38
habitat fragmentation **2**:69; **3**:18, 22, 29, 42; **4**:31, 34; **5**:32, 55; **6**:10, 42, 66, 82; **7**:48, 78; **8**:10, 12, 45; **9**:54; **10**:15, 26
habitat management **3**:61, 67; **4**:19; **8**:69
habitat restoration **3**:13, 93; **4**:79; **6**:65; **9**:15; **10**:23
Habroptila wallacii **9**:48
haddock **3**:54
Hainan Island **4**:10; **5**:26, 48
Haliaeetus spp. **8**:64
  H. pelagicus **8**:64
Halichoerus grypus **8**:70, 72
Hapalemur
  H. aureus **6**:26
  H. simus **6**:26
Haplochromis spp. **3**:48
hare
  Amami **8**:12
  bristly **5**:50
  bushman **8**:12, *8*:*13*
  harsh-furred **5**:50
  hispid 5:50, *8*:*13*
  mouse **7**:74
  Sumatran **8**:12, *8*:*13*
Harpia harpyja **4**:52
Harpyopsis novaeguineae **4**:53, 54
harvesting **10**:83
Hawaiian Islands **1**:36; **2**:6, 18; **3**:82; **7**:10; **8**:74; **9**:24
heat pollution **1**:52
Heliangelus spp. **9**:20
  H. zusii **4**:78
Heloderma
  H. horridum **5**:28
  H. suspectum **5**:28
Hemignathus munroi **2**:6
Hemitragus
  H. hylocrius **9**:46
  H. jayakari **9**:46
  H. jemlahicus **9**:46
Herichthys spp. **3**:26
  H. bartoni **3**:26
Heteralocha acutirostris **5**:60
Heteromirafra ruddi **6**:18
Hexanchus griseus **8**:86
Hexaprotodon liberiensis **5**:52
hibernation **1**:53
hide trade *see* fur trade; skin trade
Himalayas **5**:50; **6**:32, 73; **7**:50; **9**:94
Himantopus novaezelandiae **9**:32
Hippocampus capensis **8**:68
hippopotamus
  common **5**:53
  pygmy 5:52
Hippopotamus amphibius tschadensis **5**:53
Hirudo medicinalis **6**:20
Hirundo
  H. atrocaerulea **9**:42
  H. megaensis **9**:42
hog
  pygmy **2**:45
  see also pig
Honduras **8**:10
honeycreeper, Hawaiian **2**:6

honeyeater
  crow **5**:54
  painted **5**:54
  regent 5:54
hornbill
  Mindanao wrinkled **5**:56
  various **5**:56
  writhed 5:56
horns **6**:16, 72; **8**:26, 28, 32, 34
horse, Przewalski's wild 5:58
Houbaropsis bengalensis **3**:10
Hubbsina turneri **5**:36
Hucho hucho **8**:52
huia 5:60
human competition **1**:61–62
human disturbance **2**:4, 59, 63; **3**:41, 75; **4**:28, 56; **5**:43; **6**:42, 84; **7**:63, 84; **8**:38, 74, 76; **10**:34, 46
hummingbird
  bee 5:62
  sapphire-bellied **4**:78
hunting **1**:42–49
  see also big-game hunting; fur trade; persecution; skin trade; traditional medicine
hutia
  Bahamian **5**:64
  Jamaican 5:64
Hyaena brunnea **5**:66
Hydrodamalis gigas **3**:70
Hydropotes inermis **4**:6
hyena
  brown 5:66, 69
  laughing **5**:68
  spotted 5:68
  striped **5**:69
Hylobates
  H. concolor **5**:26
  H. moloch **5**:26
Hylomys
  H. hainanensis **5**:48
  H. parvus **5**:48

I

ibex
  Nubian 5:70
  Portuguese **1**:*37*
  walia **5**:71; **6**:73
ibis
  crested **9**:26
  northern bald 5:72
  scarlet **1**:*21*
  various **5**:72
Iceland **8**:72
Ichthyophaga
  I. humilis **8**:64
  I. ichthyaetus **8**:64
iguana
  Barrington Island **5**:76
  Cuban ground **5**:80
  Fijian banded **5**:74
  Fijian crested 5:74
  Galápagos land 5:76
  Galápagos marine 1:*28*; **5**:78
  Grand Cayman blue rock 5:80

  Jamaican **5**:80
  Little Cayman **5**:80
ikan temoleh 5:82
inbreeding **1**:56, 87; **2**:75, 89; **3**:41, 42, 89; **4**:26, 34, 72; **5**:6, 19, 37, 58, 74; **6**:46, 92; **7**:28; **8**:88; **9**:68, 79; **10**:77
inca, black **9**:20
India **2**:72, 94; **3**:68; **4**:16, 44, 62; **5**:18, 24; **6**:30, 34, 46; **8**:28; **9**:34, 46, 50, 68; **10**:90
Indian Ocean **3**:58; **4**:47; **8**:80
Indian Ocean islands **4**:84
Indochina **5**:18; **6**:86
Indonesia **2**:16, 20, 28, 44, 50; **3**:8, 28, 52; **4**:8, 36, 67; **5**:34; **6**:12, 30; **7**:26, 72; **8**:30, 32, 84; **9**:30, 58; **10**:88
indri 5:84
Indri indri **5**:84
industrial development **1**:40; **5**:11; **8**:55, 65; **9**:27; **10**:22, 31
  see also mining; quarrying
Inia geoffrensis **4**:26
insects *see* invertebrates
interbreeding **1**:26, 40, 57; **2**:50, 88; **3**:27, 38; **4**:45; **5**:37, 58; **6**:79; **7**:69; **9**:33, 38, 79; **10**:62, 64, 68, 72, 90
International Union for the Conservation of Nature (IUCN) **1**:11, 88–89
  categories **1**:14
internet trade **2**:80
introductions **1**:54–55
  see also alien species
invertebrates
  diversity **1**:80
  history **1**:81–83
  risks **1**:83
  see also List of Animals by Group, page 100
Iran **2**:36
Irian Jaya **10**:20
irrigation **1**:40; **2**:36; **3**:11; **4**:19, 26; **7**:55, 81; **8**:53; **9**:84
islands **1**:20
islands *see* individual island names
isolation **1**:26–28; **6**:92; **10**:94
Isoodon auratus **2**:48
IUCN *see* International Union for the Conservation of Nature
ivory **1**:*16*; **4**:64, 67
Ivory Coast **4**:48; **8**:38

J

jackal, Simien **10**:64
jaguar 5:86
jaguarundi **3**:*31*
Jamaica **3**:4; **5**:64; **10**:85
Japan **3**:30; **4**:34, 86; **6**:56; **7**:4, 38; **8**:12, 46, 64
Java **4**:16; **6**:30; **9**:68

Jamaican **5**:80
Jersey Zoo **1**:86
Juan Fernández archipelago **4**:78
junco, Guadalupe **4**:76
Junco insularis **4**:76

K

"K" reproductive strategy **1**:25
kagu 5:88
kaka **5**:51, 92
kakapo 5:90
Kalmykia, saiga **8**:42
Kazakhstan **2**:36; **8**:42
kea 5:92
Kenya **4**:68; **10**:92
kestrel
  lesser 5:94
  Mauritius 6:4
  Seychelles **5**:95; **6**:5
kite
  Cuban **6**:7
  red 1:56; **6**:6
  white-collared **6**:7
kittiwake, red-legged **5**:46
kiwi
  brown 1:*66*; **6**:8
  various **6**:9
koala 6:10
kokako **5**:60
Komodo dragon 6:12
Korea **4**:6, 12
kouprey 6:14
kudu, greater 6:16

L

Labrador **8**:72
Lacerta spp. **6**:42
  L. agilis **6**:42
Lake Wanam rainbowfish 8:20
Lama
  L. guanaco **10**:28
  L. guanicöe **3**:25
Lamma nasus **8**:86
land reclamation *see* wetland drainage
langur, douc **6**:86
Laos **5**:82; **6**:86; **7**:44; **10**:16
lark
  Raso 6:18
  Razo **6**:18
  various **6**:18
Larus spp. **5**:46
  L. fuliginosus **5**:46
Lasiorhinus krefftii **10**:77
Lathamus discolor **7**:58
Latimeria
  L. chalumnae **3**:58
  L. menadoensis **3**:58
Latin names **1**:59
Least Concern *see* Lower Risk, Least Concern (LRlc)
leech, medicinal 6:20
Leeward Islands **8**:74
Leiopelma
  L. archeyi **5**:6

SET INDEX

L. hamiltoni **5**:6
L. pakeka **5**:6
Leipoa ocellata **6**:64
lemming **1**:21
lemur
  broad-nosed gentle **6**:26
  Coquerel's mouse **6**:22
  golden bamboo **6**:26
  hairy-eared dwarf 6:22
  Philippine flying 6:24
  red-fronted *1*:33
  ruffed 6:26
  variegated **6**:26
  see also indri; sifaka
Leontopithecus spp. **9**:52
  L. chrysopygus **6**:88
  L. rosalia **9**:52
leopard 6:28
  clouded 6:30
  snow 6:32
Leopardus pardalis albescens **7**:20
Lepidopyga lilliae **4**:78
Leptodon forbesi **6**:7
Leptoptilos
  L. dubius **9**:34
  L. javanicus **9**:34
Lesotho **10**:34
Leucopsar rothschildi **9**:30
Liberia **4**:48; **8**:38
life strategies **1**:24–26
light pollution **1**:43, 53
Limnogale mergulus **9**:64
Limulus polyphemus **3**:74
Linnaeus **1**:58
linnet, Warsangli **8**:94
lion *1*:23; **9**:69
  Asiatic 6:34
  Barbary *1*:37
Lipotes vexillifer **4**:28
Litoria
  L. aurea **5**:4
  L. castanea **5**:4
live animal trade **1**:49; **3**:58; **7**:46
  see also aquarium trade; cage-bird trade; medical research; pet trade; scientific research; zoos
lizard
  blunt-nosed leopard 6:36
  flat-tailed horned 6:38
  Gila monster 5:28
  Ibiza wall 6:40
  Komodo dragon 6:12
  Lilford's wall **6**:40
  Mexican beaded **5**:28
  Miles wall **6**:40
  ocellated green *1*:74
  sand 6:42
  Schreiber's green **6**:42
  Soutpansberg rock **6**:42
  spineless forest **4**:38
  Tennent's leaf-nosed **4**:38
locust, desert *1*:81
Loddigesia mirabilis **9**:20
longicorn
  cerambyx 6:44
  rosalia **6**:44

loris
  pygmy **6**:46
  slender 6:46
Loris tardigradus **6**:46
lovebird
  black-cheeked 6:48–49
  Fischer's **6**:48
Lower Risk (LR) IUCN category, definition **1**:16
Lower Risk, Conservation Dependent (LRcd), IUCN category, definition **1**:16
Lower Risk, Least Concern (LRlc), IUCN category, definition **1**:16
Lower Risk, Near Threatened (LRnt), IUCN category, definition **1**:16
Laxities bailout **2**:6
Loxodonta africana **4**:64
lungfish, Australian 6:50
Lutra spp. **7**:35
  L. lutra **7**:32
luxury products **1**:46; **7**:53; **8**:81
Lycaena
  L. dispar **3**:22
  L. hermes **3**:18
Lycaon pictus **4**:22
Lycosa ericeticola **9**:24
lynx, Iberian 6:52
Lynx pardinus **6**:52

M

Macaca spp. **6**:54, 57
  L. fuscata **6**:56
  L. sylvanus **6**:54
macaque
  barbary 6:54
  Japanese 6:56
  various **6**:54, 56
macaw
  black 6:58
  blue 6:58
  hyacinth 6:58
  hyacinthine **6**:58
  Jamaican green and yellow *1*:37
  little blue **6**:60
  Spix's 6:60
  various **6**:60
Maccullochella spp. **3**:56
  M. macquariensis **3**:56
Macgregoria pulchra **2**:84
mackerel, Spanish **10**:8
Macrocephalon maleo **6**:64
Macroderma gigas **2**:56
Macrognathus aral **4**:62
Macrotis lagotis **2**:48
Macrovipera schweizeri **10**:30
Macruromys elegans **6**:92
Maculinea arion **3**:20
Madagascar **1**:33; **2**:32, 42; **3**:6, 36; **4**:90; **5**:14, 84; **6**:22, 26, 70, 76; **7**:40; **8**:92; **9**:64, 90; **10**:26
magpie-robin, Seychelles 6:62

Malaysia **2**:50; **4**:16, 36; **5**:18, 82; **6**:30; **7**:26; **8**:32, 84; **9**:58
maleo **6**:64
malleefowl 6:64
Malpulutta kretseri **7**:56
mammals **1**:60–63
  definition **1**:60
  diversity **1**:60
  history **1**:60–61
  risks **1**:61–63
  see also List of Animals by Group, page 100
manakin
  black-capped 6:66
  various **6**:66
manatee
  African **3**:70
  Amazon **3**:70
  American **3**:70
  Florida 1:42; **6**:68
  various **4**:47; **6**:69
Manchuria **4**:12
mandrill **4**:40
Mandrillus
  M. leucophaeus **4**:40
  M. sphinx **4**:40
Manis spp. **7**:52
  M. tetradactyla **7**:52
Manorina melanotis **5**:54
mantella, golden 6:70
Mantella aurantiaca **6**:70
Margaritifera spp. **7**:6
  M. auricularia **7**:6
  M. margaritifera **7**:6, 7
Mariana Islands **8**:18
markhor 6:72
marl **2**:48
Marmaronetta augustirostris **9**:62
marmoset
  black-headed **6**:88
  Goeldi's **6**:88
  golden-white tassel-ear **6**:88
marten, pine 6:74
Martes martes **6**:74
mass extinctions **1**:34
Mauritania **8**:76
Mauritius **1**:30–31; **4**:20, 88; **5**:22; **6**:4; **7**:8, 70
maxclapique **5**:36
Mayailurus iriomotensis **3**:30
medical research **2**:31, 41; **3**:42, 44; **6**:56
medical use, medicinal leech **6**:21
medicinal products **2**:12, 73, 75; **3**:42, 54; **4**:6, 12, 46, 80; **5**:24, 26; **6**:31, 46, 72; **7**:53; **8**:12, 26, 28, 30, 32, 42, 69, 81; **9**:21, 68; **10**:16, 21
Mediterranean **3**:88; **4**:44; **8**:76, 80; **9**:36
Megapodius spp. **6**:64
Megaptera novaeangliae **10**:46
Megascolides australis **4**:58
Melanogrammus aeglefinus **3**:54
Melanosuchus niger **2**:10, 12
melidectes, long-bearded **5**:54

Melidectes princeps **5**:54
Mellisuga helenae **5**:62
Melursus ursinus **2**:72
mesite
  brown **6**:77
  subdesert **6**:77
  white-breasted 6:76
Mesitornis
  M. unicolor **6**:77
  M. variegata **6**:76
Metallura
  M. baroni **4**:78
  M. iracunda **4**:78
metaltail
  Perijá **4**:78
  violet-throated **4**:78
metamorphosis **1**:76
Mexico **2**:40; **3**:26, 38, 74; **4**:53; **5**:10, 36, 44; **7**:42, 80, 84; **8**:10, 14; **9**:56, 60, 82, 92; **10**:32
Microgale spp. **9**:64
Micronesia **9**:8
Micropotamogale spp. **9**:64
  M. lamottei **8**:90
  M. ruwenzorii **8**:90
millerbird **10**:36
Milvus milvus **6**:6
Minimum Viable Population (MVP) **1**:21
mining **1**:40; **2**:56; **3**:25, 91; **4**:52, 55, 81; **7**:43, 61; **10**:4, **10**:21
mink
  American *1*:54, 55
  European 4:72; **6**:78
minnow, Sarasin's **10**:88
minor, black-eared **5**:54
Mirafra ashi **6**:18
Mirza coquereli **6**:22
moa, giant **1**: 36, *1*:36
mole
  marsupial 6:80
  northern marsupial **6**:80
  southern marsupial **6**:80
mole-rat
  Balkans 6:82
  giant 6:84
  various **6**:84
Monachus
  M. monachus **8**:76
  M. schauinslandi **8**:74
  M. tropicalis **8**:74, 76
Mongolia **2**:36; **3**:12, 24; **5**:58, 94; **8**:42
Monias benschi **6**:77
monkey
  China **6**:86
  douc 6:86
  Goeldi's 6:88
  grizzled leaf **6**:86
  Guizhou snub-nosed **6**:86
  pig-tailed snub-nosed **6**:86
  proboscis 1:40; **6**:90
Monodon monoceros **10**:58
montane biotype **1**:20
moonrat
  dinagat **5**:48
  Hainan **5**:48

moorhen
  Makira **9**:48
  Samoan **9**:48
Morocco **5**:72
Moschus
  M. berezovskii **4**:12
  M. chrysogaster **4**:12
  M. fuscus **4**:12
  M. moschiferus **4**:12
mountains, ecology **1**:20
mouse
  crest-tailed marsupial **6**:94
  Florida **6**:92
  St. Kilda 6:92
Mozambique **10**:34
mulgara 6:94
murrelet
  Japanese 7:4
  various **7**:4
Muscardinus avellanarius **4**:30
mussel
  freshwater 7:6
  freshwater pearl **7**:6
  Spengler's freshwater **7**:6
Mustela spp. **4**:72
  M. lutreola **6**:78
  M. nigripens **4**:72
MVP *see* Minimum Viable Population
Myanmar **4**:36; **6**:30; **7**:50; **8**:32; **9**:50, 94
Mycteria
  M. cinerea **9**:34
  M. leucocephala **9**:34
myna
  Bali **9**:30
  helmeted **9**:30
  Rothschild's **9**:30
Myomimus spp. **4**:34
Myotis spp. **2**:62
  M. cobanensis **2**:66
  M. grisescens **2**:58
  M. morrisi **2**:66
  M. myotis **2**:62
Myrmecobius fasciatus **7**:14
Myrmecophaga tridactyla **2**:24
myxomitosis **1**:55
myzomela, white-chinned **5**:54
Myzomela albigula **5**:54

N

Namibia **10**:94
Nandopsis
  N. bartoni **3**:26
  N. labridens **3**:26, 27
  N. steindachneri **3**:26
Nannoperca oxleyana **3**:56
narwhal **10**:58
Nasalis larvatus **6**:90
National Association of Audubon Societies for the Protection of Wild Birds and Animals **1**:12–13, 88
national parks **1**:13, 92; **2**:24, 46, 64, 69, 83, 89; **3**:4, 16, 25, 69, 76; **4**:16, 19, 24, 40, 48, 55, 60, 67, 68, 79; **5**:41, 46, 66, 69, 72, 77; **6**:30, 34,

47, 52, 94; **7**:17, 19, 26, 41, 61; **8**:14, 28, 31; **9**:7, 53, 64, 78, 87; **10**:21, 28, 64, 77, 87
national wildlife refuges **2**:7; **7**:94; **8**:75; **9**:15, 45
natural disasters **1**:57; **2**:15; **3**:63, 76; **4**:46, 55, 85; **5**:22, 35, 42, 46, 79; **6**:19; **7**:65, 75; **8**:77; **9**:88; **10**:94
natural extinction **4**:32; **7**:88
Natural Resources Conservation Service **9**:10
nature reserves *see* reserves
Near Threatened *see* Lower Risk, Near Threatened (LRnt)
Nematostella vectensis **8**:58
nemertine
  Rodrigues (Rodriguez) **7**:8
nene *1*:87; **7**:10
Neoceratodus forsteri **6**:50
Neodrepanis hypoxanthus **2**:32
Neofelis nebulosa **6**:30
Neopelma aurifrons **6**:66
Neophema chrysogaster **7**:58
Neotoma anthonyi **6**:92
Nepal **2**:72, 94; **5**:24; **6**:30; **7**:50; **8**:28
Nesolagus netscheri **8**:12, **8**:13
Nestor
  N. meridionalis **5**:51, 92
  N. notabilis **5**:92
New Caledonia **5**:88
New Guinea **3**:28, 86; **4**:60; **10**:20
New Mexico **3**:76
New Zealand **1**:89; **5**:6, 50, 60, 92; **6**:8; **9**:32, 48; **10**:6
newt
  Danube **7**:12
  great crested **7**:12
  warty **7**:12
Nicaragua **8**:10
Nigeria **4**:40
Nipponia nippon **5**:72; **9**:26
noise pollution **1**:52
Norway **2**:70
Nosy Mangabe **2**:43; **6**:26
Not Evaluated (NE), IUCN category, definition **1**:16
Notiomystis cincta **5**:54
notornis **9**:48
Nova Scotia **8**:72
numbat **7**:14
Numenius spp. **3**:84
  N. borealis **3**:84
  N. tenuirostris **8**:54
nuthatch
  Algerian **7**:16
  various **7**:16
nyala, mountain **7**:18
Nycticebus pygmaeus **6**:46

O

ocelot *3*:31
  Texas **7**:20
Ochotona
  O. helanshanenesis **7**:74
  O. kolsowi **7**:74
  O. pusilla **7**:74
off-road vehicles **5**:29; **6**:38; **7**:84; **10**:12, 18
oil products **3**:33; **4**:27, 46; **8**:70, 81; **10**:56
oil spills **7**:5
okapi **7**:22
Okapia johnstoni **7**:22
olm **7**:24
Oncorhynchus ishikawai **8**:52
Onychorhynchus
  O. occidentalis **4**:82
  O. swainsoni **4**:82
oo, Kauai *1*:36
orang-utan **7**:26
orca **10**:48
Orcinus orca **10**:48
Orconectes incomtus **3**:78
orders, taxonomic **1**:58
Oreomystis mana **2**:6
Oreophasis derbianus **5**:44
organizations **1**:11–13, 88
Oriolia bernieri **10**:27
Ornithoptera
  O. aesacus **3**:16
  O. alexandrae **3**:16
  O. richmondia **3**:16
  O. rothschildi **3**:16
Ornithorhynchus anatinus **7**:82
oryx, Arabian **7**:28
Oryx
  O. dammah **7**:30
  O. leucoryx **7**:28
oryx
  scimitar-horned **7**:30
  white **7**:28
Osmoderma eremita **2**:80
Other (O), category, definition **1**:16
Otis tarda **3**:10
otter
  European *1*:50; **7**:32
  giant **7**:34
  sea **1**:24; **7**:36
  various **7**:35
otter shrew, various **9**:64
Otus
  O. hartlaubi **7**:42
  O. ireneae **7**:42
ou **2**:6
overfishing **1**:71; **3**:55, 56; **7**:46, 63; **8**:63, 65, 79; **9**:37, 93; **10**:41, 43
owl
  Blakiston's eagle **7**:38
  Blakiston's fish **7**:38
  Madagascar grass **7**:40
  Madagascar red **7**:40
  Rodrigues little *1*:37
  rufous fishing- **7**:42
  São Tomé scops- **7**:42
  Sokoke scops- **7**:42
  spotted *1*:85; **7**:42
  various **7**:40
owlet, long-whiskered **7**:42
ox
  Cambodian forest **6**:14
  Vu Quang **7**:44
Oxygastra curtisii **4**:70

Oxyura leucocephala **4**:44
ozone layer depletion **1**:53–54, 79; **8**:51

P

Pacific islands **2**:6; **5**:76, 88; **8**:78
Pacific Ocean **3**:50; **4**:47; **8**:62, 78, 80; **9**:8, 86; **10**:40, 43, 44, 82
paddlefish *1*:88; **7**:46
  Chinese **7**:46
paiche **7**:76
Pakistan **2**:94
palila **2**:6
Pan
  P. paniscus **3**:44
  P. troglodytes **3**:42
Panama **8**:10
panda
  giant *1*:9; **7**:48
  lesser **7**:50
  red **7**:50
Pandaka pygmaea **5**:34
Pangasianodon gigas **3**:32
pangolin
  long-tailed **7**:52
  various **7**:52
panther
  eastern **7**:54
  Florida **7**:54
Panthera
  P. leo **9**:69
  P. l. persica **6**:34
  P. onca **5**:86
  P. pardus **6**:28
  P. tigris **9**:68
Pantholops hodgsoni **2**:26
Papilio
  P. jordani **3**:12
  P. leucotaenia **3**:12
Papua New Guinea **2**:16, 28, 84; **3**:8, 16; **7**:72; **8**:20; **10**:4
Paracentrotus lividus **8**:66
Paradisaea rudolphi **2**:84
paradisefish, ornate **7**:56
parakeet
  Antipodes **5**:92
  Carolina *1*:37
  Guadeloupe *1*:37
Parapinnixa affinis **3**:72
parasites **3**:13; **4**:75, 94; **10**:33, 38, 72
Pardosa diuturna **9**:24
Parnassius
  P. apollo **3**:12
  P. autocrator **3**:12
parrot
  broad-billed *1*:31
  ground **5**:51
  night **7**:58
  owl **5**:50
  St. Vincent **2**:14
  various **7**:58
  see also lovebird
parrotfinch, greenfaced **4**:74
Partula spp. **9**:8
Pavo muticus **7**:60

peacock, Congo **7**:60
peafowl
  Congo **7**:60
  green **7**:60
pearl trade **7**:6
pearlshell
  Alabama **7**:6
  Louisiana **7**:6
peat extraction **10**:37
pedomorphism **2**:40; **8**:46
pelican
  Dalmatian **7**:62
  spot-billed **7**:62
Pelicanus
  P. crispus **7**:62
  P. philippensis **7**:62
Penelope spp. **5**:44
Penelopides
  P. mindorensis **5**:56
  P. panini **5**:56
penguin
  Galápagos **7**:64
  various **7**:64
Pentalagus furnessi **8**:12
Perameles
  P. bourgainville **2**:48
  P. gunnii **2**:48
perch, oxleyan pygmy **3**:56
perfume **4**:12
perfume trade **10**:56
Peripatus spp. **10**:84
persecution **1**:40, 47; **2**:10, 42, 68, 72, 90; **3**:42; **4**:6, 16, 24, 40, 66; **5**:24, 28, 66, 93; **6**:4, 6, 24, 28, 33, 52, 54, 56, 74, 82; **7**:20, 38, 54, 75; **8**:7, 14, 25, 28, 77, 82; **9**:12, 34, 62, 66; **10**:31, 34, 48, 59, 64, 67, 70, 72, 74, 77
Peru **2**:74; **3**:46; **4**:82; **7**:76; **9**:20
pesticides **1**:50, 51–52; **2**:60; **3**:10, 19, 93; **4**:55; **5**:94; **6**:4, 6, 63; **8**:23, 65; **9**:24; **10**:49
pet trade **2**:22; **3**:42; **5**:15, 28, 38, 41; **6**:24, 26, 38, 70, 87; **7**:26, 53; **9**:14, 52, 60, 82, 84, 88, 91; **10**:12, 14, 16, 21, 24, 31
  see also aquarium trade; cage-bird trade
Petaurus gracilis **5**:32
petrel
  Bermuda *1*:55; **7**:66
  various **7**:66
Petrogale persephone **8**:36
Pezophaps solitaria **4**:20
Pezoporus wallicus **5**:51
Phalacrocorax spp. **3**:64
  P. harrisi **3**:64
Phalanger spp. **3**:86
  P. atrimaculatus **3**:86
  P. maculatus rufoniger **3**:86
Pharomachrus mocinno **8**:10
Phascolarctos cinereus **6**:10
pheasant **9**:94
Phelsuma spp. **5**:22
  P. guentheri **5**:22
Philemon fuscicapillus **5**:54

Philepitta schlegeli **2**:32
Philesturnus carunculatus **5**:60
Philippines **1**:23; **4**:36, 54; **5**:34, 56; **6**:24; **7**:68
Phoca
  P. caspica **8**:70, 72
  P. sibirica **8**:70
Phocarctos hookeri **8**:62
Phocoena
  P. phocoena **7**:86
  P. sinus **7**:86; **10**:56
  P. spinipinnis **7**:86
Phodilus prigoginei **7**:40
Phoeniconaias
  P. andinus **4**:80
  P. jamesi **4**:81
Phoenicopterus
  P. chilensis **4**:81
  P. minor **4**:81
Phoxinus
  P. cumberlandensis **3**:90
  P. tennesseensis **3**:90
Phrynops
  P. dahli **10**:22
  P. hogei **10**:22
Phrynosoma m'callii **6**:38
phylum **1**:58–59
Physeter macrocephalus **10**:56
Picathartes
  P. gymnocephalus **8**:38
  P. oreas **8**:38
picathartes, white-necked **8**:38
Picoides
  P. borealis **10**:80
  P. ramsayi **10**:80
pig
  Javan warty **2**:45
  Visyan warty **7**:68
  see also babirusa; hog
pigeon
  blue *1*:31
  chestnut-tailed **7**:70
  Mauritius pink **7**:70
  passenger *1*:22, 37
  pink **7**:70
  southern crowned **7**:72
  various **7**:71
  Victoria crowned **7**:72
  western crowned **7**:72
pika
  Helan Shan **7**:74
  Koslov's **7**:74
  steppe **7**:74
Pinguinus impennis **2**:38
pintail, Eaton's **9**:62
Pipile spp. **5**:44
Pipra vilasboasi **6**:66
Piprites pileatus **6**:66
pirarucu **7**:76
Pithecophaga jefferyi **4**:54
pitta
  black-breasted **7**:78
  Gurney's **7**:78
  various **7**:78
Pitta spp. **7**:78
  P. gurneyi **7**:78
plants, nonnative invasions **9**:40, 42
Platalea minor **9**:26

108

SET INDEX

Platanista
  P. gangetica **4**:26, 28
  P. minor **4**:26, 28
platy
  Cuatro Ciénegas 7:80
  Monterrey **7**:80
  Muzquiz **7**:80
  northern **7**:80
  red **5**:36
platypus 7:82
Plethodon spp. **8**:48
  P. serratus **8**:48
plover
  piping 7:84
  various **7**:84
Podarcis
  P. lilfordi **6**:40
  P. milensis **6**:40
  P. pityusensis **6**:40
Podiceps spp. **5**:42
Podilymbus gigas **5**:42
Podogymnura
  P. aureospinula **5**:48
  P. truei **5**:48
Podomys floridanus **6**:92
poisoning **4**:57, 92; **5**:93; **6**:63, 86; **7**:93; **8**:25, 65, 75; **9**:45; **10**:34
Poliocephalus rufopectus **5**:42
pollution **1**:40, 42, 50–53; **2**:10, 22, 40, 52, 77, 91; **3**:13, 35, 38, 49, 65, 76, 89, 95; **4**:5, 15, 19, 27, 29, 44, 70, 80; **5**:11, 15, 35, 43, 79; **6**:68, 78; **7**:24, 32, 35, 36, 46, 55, 63, 66, 77, 81, 82, 84; **8**:23, 41, 53, 55, 59, 62, 65, 69, 70, 75, 85, 91; **9**:14, 27, 34, 37, 38, 41, 45, 65, 75; **10**:12, 15, 21, 25, 41, 43, 45, 49, 52, 59
  see also light pollution; noise pollution; oil spills; pesticides
Polyodon spathula **7**:46
Pongo pygmaeus **7**:26
Poospiza garleppi **4**:76
population modeling **1**:8
populations **1**:20–22
porbeagle **8**:86
Porphyrio mantelli **9**:48
porpoise
  Burmeister's **7**:86
  Gulf of California **7**:86
  harbor 7:86
  vaquita **10**:56
Portugal **6**:52
possum, Leadbeater's 7:88
Potamogale velox **8**:90
potoroo
  Gilbert's **7**:90
  long-footed 7:90
Potorous
  P. gilbertii **7**:90
  P. longipes **7**:90
poverty **1**:89, 95; **3**:7, 37, 45; **8**:29, 34
power cables **4**:57; **7**:63; **10**:34

prairie dog
  black-tailed 7:92
  various **7**:92
pratincole, black-winged **3**:68
Presbytis comata **6**:86
pressure groups **1**:13
Prioailurus planiceps **3**:30
Priodontes maximus **2**:30
Prionailurus iriomotensis **3**:30
Probarbus spp. **5**:82
  P. jullieni **5**:82
Procnias
  P. nudicollis **2**:82
  P. tricarunculata **2**:82
Propithecus
  P. diadema **5**:84; **8**:93
  P. tattersalli **8**:92
  P. verreauxi **5**:84; **8**:93
Prosobonia cancellata **8**:54
Proteus anguinus **7**:24
Psammobates geometricus **9**:88
Psephotus chrysopterygius **7**:58
Psephurus gladius **7**:46
Pseudemydura umbrina **10**:22
Pseudemys
  P. alabamensis **10**:12
  P. gorzugi **10**:12
  P. rubriventris **10**:12
Pseudibis
  P. davisoni **5**:72
  P. gigantea **5**:72
Pseudocotalpa giulianii **2**:80
Pseudophryne spp. **9**:78
  P. corroboree **9**:78
Pseudoryx nghetinhensis **7**:44
Psittirostra psittacez **2**:6
Pterodroma spp. **7**:66
  P. cahow **7**:66
Pteronura brasiliensis **7**:34
Pteropus
  P. dasymallus **4**:86
  P. rodricensis **4**:84
puffleg
  black-breasted **9**:20
  colorful **4**:78
Puma concolor
  P. c. coryi **7**:54
  P. c. cougar **7**:54
pupfish
  Devil's Hole 7:94
  various **7**:94
Pygathrix nemaeus **6**:86
pygmy-possum
  long-tailed **8**:4
  mountain 8:4
Pygopididae **1**:74
python
  Ramsay's **8**:6
  woma 8:6

Q

quagga **1**:37; **8**:8
  Bonte **8**:8
quarrying **1**:40; **2**:58; **3**:69; **6**:42; **10**:30
quetzal, resplendent 8:10

R

"r" reproductive strategy **1**:25
rabbit
  Amami **8**:12
  Assam **5**:50
  Ryukyu **8**:12
  volcano 8:13, 14
racer
  Antiguan **8**:16
  various **8**:16
racerunner **10**:60
rail **1**:31
  Guam **8**:18
  invisible **9**:48
  Owston's **8**:18
  various **3**:66; **8**:18
rainbowfish
  Lake Wanam **8**:20
  various **8**:20
Rallus antarcticus **3**:66
Rana spp. **5**:10
  R. aurora **5**:10
Ranthanbore National Park **1**:92
Raphus cucullatus **4**:20
Rare Animal Relief Effort (RARE) **2**:15
rasbora
  fire **8**:22
  golden **8**:22
  pearly **8**:22
  vateria flower 8:22
Rasbora vaterifloris **8**:22
rat
  Alexandrine **8**:24
  Asian black **1**:55
  black 8:24
  climbing **8**:24
  gray **8**:24
  roof **8**:24
  ship **8**:24
  various **6**:92
  see also mole-rat
rat kangaroo **7**:90
Rattus rattus **8**:24
razorback **10**:42
Red Data Book (IUCN) **1**:10–11, 14
reintroduction **1**:22, 56, 87, 92; **2**:69, 76, 79; **3**:33, 56, 60, 76, 83; **4**:15, 31, 53, 72, 92; **5**:58; **6**:5, 26, 61; **7**:11; **8**:19, 53; **9**:9, 38, 41, 49, 52, 87, 91; **10**:7, 23, 68, 73
relocation *see* translocation
reproductive strategies **1**:25–26
reptiles
  diversity **1**:72
  history **1**:73
  risks **1**:73–75
  see also List of Animals by Group, page 100
research *see* conservation research; medical research; scientific research
reserves **1**:33, 92; **2**:37, 43, 55, 59; **3**:69; **4**:16, 39; **5**:57; **6**:19, 26, 42, 47, 89; **7**:11,
41, 55, 73, 81, 89; **8**:41; **9**:7, 9, 53, 67, 85, 88, 89, 91; **10**:22, 25, 33, 37, 95
  see also national parks; wildlife refuges
reservoir building **2**:31; **7**:43; **9**:41; **10**:34
restricted distribution **1**:8
Rheobatrachus silus **4**:94
Rhincodon typus **8**:86
Rhinoceros
  R. sondaicus **8**:30
  R. unicornis **8**:28
rhinoceros
  black 8:26
  great Indian 8:28
  Javan 8:30
  Sumatran 8:32
  white 8:34
Rhinolophus ferrumequinum **2**:60
Rhinopithecus brelichi **6**:86
Rhinopoma macinnesi **2**:64
Rhinoptilus bitorquatus **3**:68
Rhodonessa caryophyllacea **4**:44
Rhynchocyon
  R. chrysopygus **4**:68
  R. petersi **4**:68
Rhynochetos jubatus **5**:88
Rissa brevirostris **5**:46
ritual objects **2**:85; **3**:29; **5**:5
road building **2**:55; **3**:19; **4**:52, 67; **7**:54, 73, 90; **8**:5; **9**:84, 88; **10**:85
road kills **2**:77; **3**:29, 31; **4**:22, 92; **5**:80; **6**:10, 38, 52, 75; **7**:55; **8**:7, 36; **9**:10, 82; **10**:31
roatelo, white-breasted **6**:76
Robinson Crusoe Island **4**:78
rock-wallaby, prosperine 8:36
rockfowl
  bare-headed **8**:38
  gray-necked **8**:38
  white-necked 8:38
rocky, eastern province 8:40
Rodrigues (Rodriguez) Island **7**:8
Romania **6**:82
Romerolagus diazi **8**:13, 14
rorqual
  common **10**:42
  great northern **10**:40
Rosalia alpina **6**:44
Round Island **5**:22
Royal Society for the Protection of Birds (RSPB) **1**:13, 88
Russia **2**:70; **4**:32; **5**:94; **6**:78; **7**:32, 36, 38, 74; **8**:42, 54, 64; **10**:74
Rwanda **5**:38

S

saddleback **5**:60
Saguinus leucopus **6**:88
Sahara **2**:4
Sahel **5**:20

saiga **8**:42
Saiga tatarica **8**:42
St. Lucia **10**:60
salamander
  California tiger **8**:44
  Chinese giant **8**:46
  flatwood **8**:44
  Japanese giant **8**:46
  Lake Lerma **8**:44
  Ouachita red-backed **8**:48
  Santa-Cruz long-toed **8**:51
  southern red-backed **8**:48
  various **8**:48
  see also axolotl
Salmo spp. **8**:52
salmon
  Adriatic **8**:52
  Danube **8**:52
  European **8**:52
  Satsukimasa **8**:52
  various **1**:68
Salmothymus obtusirostris **8**:52
samaruc **9**:80
Samoa **10**:82
Sandelia bainsii **8**:40
sandpiper
  spoon-billed **8**:54
  Tuamotu **8**:54
Sanzinia madagascariensis **3**:6
sao la **7**:44
Sapheopipo noguchii **10**:78
Sapo Dorado **9**:70
saratoga
  southern **7**:77
  spotted **4**:36
Sarcogyps calvus **10**:34
sardina ciega **3**:38
Scandinavia **3**:12; **8**:72
scientific research **2**:46; **4**:62; **10**:50
Sciurus vulgaris **9**:28
Scleropages
  S. formosus **4**:36
  S. leichardi **7**:77
  S. leichardti **4**:36
Scomberomorus concolor **10**:8
scops-owl **7**:42
Scotopelia ussheri **7**:42
scrub-bird
  noisy 8:56
  rufous **8**:56
scrubfowl, various **6**:64
sea anemone
  Ivell's **8**:58
  starlet **8**:58
sea cow 4:46
  Steller's **3**:70
sea fan, broad 8:60
sea lion
  Hooker's **8**:62
  northern **8**:62
  Steller's **8**:62
sea-eagle
  Pallas's **8**:64
  Steller's **8**:64
sea-urchin 1:24
  edible **8**:66
seahorse 1:69
  Cape **8**:68

109

Knysna **8**:68
seal
  Baikal 8:70
  Baltic gray **8**:70
  Caribbean monk **1**:*37*; **8**:74, 76
  Caspian **8**:70, 72
  fur, various **8**:62
  Galápagos fur **8**:78
  gray 8:72
  Guadaloupe fur **8**:78
  Hawaiian monk 8:74
  Juan Fernandez fur **8**:78
  Mediterranean monk 1:43; **8**:76
  northern fur 8:78
seminatural habitats **1**:38
Semnornis ramphastinus **2**:54
Sephanoides fernandensis **4**:78
Sepilok Rehabilitation Center **1**:*95*
Sericulus bakeri **3**:8
Seychelles **6**:62
shama, black **6**:62
shark
  basking 8:80
  great white 8:82
  silver 8:84
  various **8**:86
  whale 8:86
shatoosh trade **2**:26
sheep, barbary 8:88
shrew
  giant African water **8**:90
  giant otter 8:90
  Nimba otter **8**:90
  pygmy otter **8**:90
  Siberia **4**:12; **8**:54, 70; **9**:62, 68; **10**:74
sicklebill, black **2**:84
Sierra Club **1**:13
Sierra Leone **4**:48; **8**:38
sifaka
  Diadem **5**:84; **8**:93
  golden-crowned 8:92
  Verreaux's **5**:84; **8**:93
Simias concolor **6**:86
sirenians **3**:70; **4**:46; **6**:68
siskin
  red 8:94
  saffron **8**:94
  yellow-faced **8**:94
Sites of Special Scientific Interest **6**:42
Sitta spp. **7**:16
  S. ledanti **7**:16
Skiffia francesae **5**:36
skin trade **2**:11, 36; **3**:7, 70, 80; **4**:46; **7**:53; **8**:9, 62, 74, 81, 88; **9**:56; **10**:58, 94
skink
  pygmy blue-tongued 9:4
  Réunion **1**:*37*
  western **1**:*74*
slash-and-burn agriculture **6**:76
sloth
  Hoffmann's two-toed **9**:6
  Linné's two-toed **9**:6
  maned 9:6

slow reproduction **1**:8, 25
Sminthopsis spp. **4**:50
  S. aitkeni **4**:50
snail, *Partula* **9**:8
snake
  Cuban tree boa **3**:4
  Cyclades blunt-nosed viper **10**:30
  Dumeril's boa **3**:6
  eastern indigo 9:10
  emerald tree boa **1**:*74*
  Jamaican boa 3:4
  leopard 9:12
  Madagascar boa 3:6
  Madagascar tree boa **3**:6
  Milos viper 10:30
  Mona Island boa **3**:4
  Puerto Rican boa **3**:4
  racer, Antiguan **8**:16
  Ramsay's python **8**:6
  San Francisco garter 9:14
  sharp-snouted **1**:*74*
  two-striped garter **9**:14
  Virgin Islands boa **3**:4
  woma python 8:6
solenodon
  Cuban 9:16
  Haitian **9**:16
Solenodon
  S. cubanus **9**:16
  S. paradoxus **9**:16
solitaire
  Réunion **1**:*37*
  Rodrigues (Rodriguez) **4**:20
Solomys ponceleti **6**:92
Somalia **2**:34
Somatochlora
  S. calverti **4**:70
  S. hineana **4**:70
Sosippus placidus **9**:24
souslik
  European 9:18
  European spotted **9**:18
South Africa **3**:40; **8**:8, 40, 68; **9**:89; **10**:34, 94
South America **2**:24, 30, 54, 74, 92; **3**:46, 62, 80, 84; **4**:18, 24, 26, 53, 78, 82; **5**:86; **6**:58, 66, 88; **7**:35, 76; **8**:94; **9**:6, 20, 52, 54; **10**:28, 70
Southern Ocean **2**:8; **10**:40, 43
souvenir trade **2**:46; **3**:6, 50, 75, 80; **4**:67; **5**:38, 41; **8**:60, 66, 69, 82; **10**:18
Spain **1**:*42–43*; **4**:56; **6**:52; **9**:80
Spalax spp. **6**:82
  S. graecus **6**:82
sparrow
  house **1**:*64*
  Zapata **4**:76
spatuletail, marvelous 9:20
specialization **1**:28–30
speciation **1**:26–28
species
  definition **1**:26
  taxonomic groupings **1**:58–59

Species Survival Commission (SSC) **1**:10
specimen collectors **2**:38; **5**:60, 72
Speoplatyrhinus poulsoni **3**:34
Speothos venaticus **4**:24, 93
Spermophilus spp. **9**:18
  S. citellus **9**:18
Spheniscus
  S. demersus **7**:64
  S. humboldti **7**:64
  S. mendiculus **7**:64
Sphenodon
  S. guntheri **10**:6
  S. punctatus **10**:6
spider
  great raft 9:22
  Kauai cave wolf 9:24
  red-kneed tarantula 9:60
  wolf, various **9**:24
Spilocuscus rufoniger **3**:86
Spizocorys fringillaris **6**:18
spoonbill
  black-faced 9:26
  lesser **9**:26
sport, exploitation of animals for **1**:47–48
sports fishing **10**:8
squirrel
  Arctic ground **1**:*24*
  Eurasian red 9:28
  European red **9**:28
  see also ground squirrel
Sri Lanka **2**:52, 72; **3**:94; **4**:62, 67; **6**:46; **7**:56; **8**:22
starling
  Bali 9:30
  various **9**:30
steamerduck, Chubut **4**:42
Stenella
  S. attenuata **10**:48
  S. coeruleoalba **10**:48
Stenodus leucichthys leucichthys **8**:52
stilt, black 9:32
stitchbird **5**:54
stork
  greater adjutant 9:34
  various **9**:34
Strigops habroptilus **5**:50
Strix occidentalis **7**:42
Strymon avalona **3**:14
sturgeon
  Baltic **9**:36
  common 9:36
  ship **9**:36
Sturnella defilippii **2**:92
Sturnus spp. **9**:30
sub-Antarctic islands **2**:8
sucker
  harelip **9**:38
  razorback 9:38
sulphur-bottom **10**:40
Sumatra **4**:16; **6**:30; **7**:26
sunangel
  Bogotá **4**:78
  various **9**:20
sunbeam, purple-backed **4**:78

sunfish
  blue-barred pygmy **9**:40
  Carolina pygmy **9**:40
  oceanic **1**:*68*
  spring pygmy 9:40
  superstition **1**:47; **3**:86
see also ritual objects; traditional medicine
Sus
  S. cebifrons **7**:68
  S. salvanius **2**:45
  S. verrucosus **2**:45
swallow
  blue 9:42
  white-tailed **9**:42
swan, trumpeter 9:44
Synthliboramphus spp. **7**:4
  S. wumizusume **7**:4
Sypheotides indica **3**:10

T

Tachybaptus spp. **5**:42
Tachyeres leucocephalus **4**:42
Tachyglossus aculeatus multiaculeatus **4**:60
Tachyoryctes spp. **6**:84
  T. macrocephalus **6**:84
Tachypleus
  T. gigas **3**:74
  T. tridentatus **3**:74
tagging *see* tracking and tagging
Tahr
  Arabian **9**:46
  Himalayan **9**:46
  Nilgiri 9:46
Taiwan **6**:30
takahe 9:48
Takin 9:50
tamaraw **2**:20
tamarin
  golden lion 9:52
  golden-rumped **6**:88
  various **9**:52
  white-footed **6**:88
Tanagara spp. **9**:54
  T. fastuosa **9**:54
tanager
  multicolored **4**:76
  seven-colored 9:54
  various **9**:54
Taphozous troughtoni **2**:64
tapir
  Central American 9:56
  Malayan 9:58
  mountain **9**:56, 58
Tapirus
  T. bairdii **9**:56
  T. pinchaque **9**:56, 58
tarantula, red-kneed 9:60
tarictic
  Mindoro **5**:56
  Visayan **5**:56
tarpan **1**:*37*
Tasmania **5**:16; **9**:66
Taudactylus
  T. acutirostris **5**:12
  T. rheophilus **5**:12

Tauraco spp. **10**:11
  T. bannermani **10**:10
  T. fischeri **10**:11
  T. ruspolii **10**:11
taxonomic classification **1**:26, 58
teal
  Baikal 9:62
  various **9**:62
tenrec
  aquatic 9:64
  long-tailed **9**:64
  web-footed **9**:64
teporingo **8**:14
Testudo spp. **9**:84
  T. kleinmanni **9**:84
tetra, Mexican **3**:38
Tetrax tetrax **3**:10
Texas **7**:20; **10**:32
Thailand **2**:50, 64; **4**:36; **5**:82; **6**:30; **7**:78; **8**:32, 84
Thamnophis
  T. gigas **9**:14
  T. hammondi **9**:14
  T. sirtalis tetrataenia **9**:14
Theropithecus gelada **2**:46
threat
  IUCN, categories of **1**:14–17
threats, general **1**: 38–57
Thryothorus nicefori **10**:86
thryssa, New Guinea **2**:16
Thryssa scratchleyi **2**:16
Thunnus spp. **10**:8
  T. thynnus **10**:8
thylacine 1:*36*; **9**:66
Thylacinus cynocephalus **9**:66
Tibet **2**:26; **9**:50; **10**:90
tiger 1:*9, 95*; **9**:68
  Bali **1**:*36*
  Tasmanian **9**:66
Tiliqua adelaidensis **9**:4
timber treatment chemicals **2**:61, 62
toad
  boreal **9**:76
  cane **1**:*54*
  golden 9:70
  Mallorcan midwife 1:*77*; **9**:72
  natterjack 9:74
  running **9**:74
  Surinam **1**:*77*
  various **9**:70, 74, 76
  western 9:76
toadlet
  corroboree 9:78
  various **9**:78
tokoeka **6**:9
Tolypeutes tricinctus **2**:30
toothcarp
  Corfu **9**:80
  valencia 9:80
torgos tracheliotus **10**:34
Torreornis inexpectata **4**:76
tortoise
  Abingdon Island **1**:*37*
  bolson **9**:82
  Charles Island **1**:*37*
  desert 9:82

SET INDEX

domed **1**:31
Egyptian 9:84
Galápagos giant 9:86
geometric 9:88
gopher **9**:82
Mauritian giant **1**:37
plowshare 9:90
radiated **9**:90
various **9**:84, 86, 89
tortoiseshell trade **10**:18
totoaba 9:92
Totoaba macdonaldi **9**:92
tourism **1**:42–43; **2**:4; **3**:41, 52, 65; **5**:38, 88; **6**:41; **7**:65; **8**:5, 14, 69, 76; **9**:12, 46, 56, 81, 84; **10**:18, 25, 31
see also ecotourism
toxins, bioaccumulation **1**:50, 51
Toxotes oligolepis **2**:28
tracking and tagging **1**:14–15, 85
traditional land management **1**:38
traditional medicine **1**:46; **10**:34
Tragelaphus
  T. buxtoni **7**:18
  T. strepsiceros **6**:16
tragopan
  Temminck's 9:94
  various **9**:94
Tragopan spp. **9**:94
  T. temminckii **9**:94
translocation **5**:17; **10**:60
tree-kangaroo
  Goodfellow's 10:4
  various **10**:4
Tremarctos ornatus **2**:74
Trichechus spp. **3**:70; **4**:47; **6**:69
  T. manatus latirostris **6**:68
Tridacna gigas **3**:50
Tringa guttifer **8**:54
triok, Tate's **5**:32; **7**:88
Triturus
  T. cristatus **7**:12
  T. dobrogicus **7**:12
trogon, resplendent **8**:10
trout
  Danube **8**:52
  European river **8**:52
  Ohrid **8**:52
  rainbow **1**:71
tuatara 10:6
  Cook Strait **10**:6
Tubulanus superbus 7.9
tuna
  Atlantic bluefin **10**:8
  northern bluefin 10:8
  various **10**:8
Tunisia **7**:30
turaco
  Bannerman's 10:10
  Fischer's **10**:11
  Prince Ruspoli's **10**:11
  various **10**:11
turtle **1**:43
  Alabama red-bellied 10:12
  American red-bellied **10**:12

bog 10:14
box, various **10**:16
Chinese three-striped box 10:16
Fly River **10**:20
green **1**:72
hawksbill 10:18
map, various **10**:24
New Guinea softshell **10**:20
pig-nosed 10:20
various **10**:14, **10**:22
western swamp 10:22
yellow-blotched sawback map 10:24
Tympanocryptis lineata pnguicolla **4**:38
Typhlichthys subterraneus **3**:34
Tyto
  T. inexspectata **7**:40
  T. nigrobrunnea **7**:40
  T. soumagnei **7**:40

U

Uganda **5**:38
ultraviolet (UV) radiation damage **8**:51; **9**:76
umbrellabird, bare-necked **2**:82
Uncia uncia **6**:32
United States **2**:10, 58, 68, 70, 86; **3**:14, 15, 18, 34, 60, 72, 74, 76, 80, 90, 84; **4**:4, 42, 72, 93; **5**:10, 28; **6**:36, 38, 68; **7**:20, 36, 42, 46, 54, 84, 92, 94; **8**:45, 48, 51, 58; **9**:10, 14, 38, 40, 44, 60, 76, 82; **10**:12, 14, 24, 32, 38, 72, 74, 80
United States Fish and Wildlife Service **3**:81
urban development **3**:16, 19, 21, 31; **4**:38; **5**:11, 49; **6**:31, 42, 72, 86; **7**:35, 43; **8**:45, 59, 65, 76; **9**:14, 84, 88; **10**:12, 22, 24, 31, 33, 62
Ursus
  U. arctos **2**:68
  U. a. nelsoni **2**:68
  U. maritimus **2**:70
  U. thibetanus **2**:68, 74
UV radiation *see* ultraviolet radiation

V

Valencia
  V. hispanica **9**:80
  V. letourneuxi **9**:80
vanga
  helmet 10:26
  various **10**:27
Varanus komodoensis **6**:12
Varecia variegata **6**:26
Venezuela **2**:74; **8**:94
Vicugna vicugna **10**:28
vicuña 10:28
Vietnam **2**:50; **4**:36; **5**:26, 82; **6**:14, 30, 86; **7**:44; **8**:30, 32; **9**:94; **10**:16

viper
  Cyclades blunt-nosed **10**:30
  Milos **10**:30
  various **10**:30
Vipera spp. **10**:30
vireo
  black-capped 10:32
  Chocó **10**:32
  St. Andrew **10**:32
  San Andrès **10**:32
Vireo
  V. atricapillus **10**:32
  V. caribaeus **10**:32
  V. masteri **10**:32
Viverridae **4**:90
Vulnerable, definition **1**:15–16
Vulpes velox **4**:92
Vultur gryphus **3**:60
vulture
  Cape **10**:34
  Cape griffon 10:34
  various **10**:34

W

wallaby
  prosperine rock 8:36
  Toolache **1**:36
walpurti **7**:14
war **1**:47; **4**:48, 55, 67; **5**:38, 41, 52; **6**:16, 86; **7**:22, 44; **8**:31, 34
warbler
  aquatic 10:36
  Kirtland's 10:38
  Manchurian reed **10**:36
  streaked reed **10**:36
  various **10**:38
Washington Convention *see* Convention on International Trade in Endangered Species of Wild Fauna and Flora
water balance **1**:40
water buffalo, Indian **2**:20
water extraction **8**:53; **10**:21, 22
water shortages **2**:34, 36; **8**:34; **10**:92
waxbill, Anambra **4**:74
weasel
  black-striped **4**:72
  Colombian **4**:72
  Indonesian mountain **4**:72
weaverbirds **4**:88
West Indies **2**:14
wetland drainage **1**:40, 74; **2**:11, 40, 90; **3**:11, 22, 63, 92; **4**:26, 44, 70; **5**:5, 35; **6**:21, 91; **7**:63; **8**:30, 53, 55, 59; **9**:14, 22, 27, 33, 34, 63; **10**:14, 22, 25, 37, 86
whale
  blue **10**:40
  California gray **10**:44
  coalfish **10**:54
  fin 10:42
  gray **1**:62, 90; **10**:44
  herring **10**:42
  humpback **10**:46

killer **10**:48
  minke **1**:44; **10**:50
  northern right 1:25; **10**:52
  pollack **10**:54
  right **1**:25
  Rudolphi's **10**:54
  sardine **10**:54
  scrag **10**:44
  sei **10**:54
  short-finned pilot **10**:48
  southern right **10**:52
  sperm **10**:56
  spermaceti **10**:56
  white **10**:58
whaling **1**:45
whiptail
  Colorado checkered **1**:74
  orange-throated **10**:61
  St. Lucia, **1**:86, **10**:60
white eye, Lord Howe Island **1**:36
wildcat 10:62
wildlife refuge **3**:76; **10**:33, 73
wildlife surveys **1**:84
Williamsonia lintneri **4**:70
Windward Islands **10**:60
wolf **1**:47
  Antarctic **10**:66
  Ethiopian 10:64
  Falkland Island 1:37; **10**:66
  gray **10**:68
  maned **10**:70
  marsupial **9**:66
  red **1**:93; **10**:72
  Simien **10**:64
  Tasmanian **9**:66
  timber **10**:68
wolverine 10:74
wombat
  northern hairy-nosed 10:77
  Queensland hairy-nosed **10**:76
  soft-furred **10**:76
woodpecker
  Arabian **10**:80
  imperial **10**:78
  ivory-billed 10:78
  Okinawa **10**:78
  red-cockaded 10:80
  Sulu **10**:80
woodstar
  Chilean **4**:78
  little **4**:78
wool trade **2**:26
World Bank **1**:89
World Conservation Union *see* International Union for the Conservation of Nature
World Parrot Trust **2**:15
World Wide Fund for Nature (WWF) **1**:13
World Wildlife Fund *see* World Wide Fund for Nature
worm
  Palolo **10**:82
  ribbon **7**:8
  velvet **10**:84
see also earthworm

wren
  Apolinar's **10**:86
  Fermina **10**:86
  Niceforo's **10**:86
  Stephen Island **1**:37
  Zapata **10**:86

X

Xanthomyza phrygia **5**:54
Xanthopsar flavus **2**:92
Xenoglaux loweryi **7**:42
Xenoophorus captivus **5**:36
Xenopirostris damii **10**:27
xenopoecilus 10:88
Xenopoecilus spp. **10**:88
  X. saranisorum **10**:88
Xiphophorus spp.
  X. couchianus **7**:80
  X. gordoni **7**:80
  X. meyeri **7**:80
Xyrauchen texanus **9**:38

Y

yak, wild **10**:90
yamane **4**:34
yamion **10**:76
Yellowstone National Park **1**:10
Yugoslavia **7**:24

Z

zacatuche **8**:14
Zaglossus bruijni **4**:60
Zaire *see* Democratic Republic of Congo
Zambia **6**:48
zebra
  Burchell's **8**:8
  Cape mountain **10**:94
  Grevy's 10:92
  Hartmann's **10**:94
  mountain 10:94
zebu cattle **1**:38
Zimbabwe **4**:22
zoogeographic regions **1**:19, 20
zoos **1**:86; **5**:41; **8**:38
see also captive breeding

Acknowledgments

The authors and publishers would like to thank the following people and organizations:
Aquamarines International Pvt. Ltd., Sri Lanka, especially Ananda Pathirana; Aquarist & Pond keeper Magazine, U.K.; BirdLife International (the global partnership of conservation organizations working together in over 100 countries to save birds and their habitats). Special thanks to David Capper; also to Guy Dutson and Alison Stattersfield; Sylvia Clarke (Threatened Wildlife, South Australia); Mark Cocker (writer and birder); David Curran (aquarist specializing in spiny eels, U.K.); Marydele Donnelly (IUCN sea turtle specialist); Svein Fossa (aquatic consultant, Norway); Richard Gibson (Jersey Wildlife Preservation Trust, Channel Islands); Paul Hoskisson (Liverpool John Moores University); Derek Lambert; Pat Lambert (aquarists specializing in freshwater livebearers); Lumbini Aquaria Wayamba Ltd., Sri Lanka, especially Jayantha Ramasinghe and Vibhu Perera; Isolda McGeorge (Chester Zoological Gardens); Dr. James Peron Ross (IUCN crocodile specialist); Zoological Society of London, especially Michael Palmer, Ann Sylph, and the other library staff.

Picture Credits

Abbreviations
AL   Ardea London
BBC   BBC Natural History Unit
BCC   Bruce Coleman Collection
FLPA Frank Lane Photographic Agency
NHPA Natural History Photographic Agency
OSF   Oxford Scientific Films
PEP   Planet Earth Pictures
b = bottom; **c** = center; **t** = top; **l** = left; **r** = right

Jacket
Ibiza wall lizard, illustration by Denys Ovenden from *Collins Field Guide: Reptiles and Amphibians of Britain and Europe*; Grevy's zebra, Stan Osolinski/Oxford Scientific Films; Florida panther, Lynn M. Stone/BBC Natural History Unit; silver shark, Max Gibbs/Photomax; blue whale, Tui de Roy/Oxford Scientific Films

4–5 Pavel German/NHPA; **7** Robin Bush/OSF; **9** Ken Preston-Mafham/Premaphotos Wildlife; **11** David M. Dennis/OSF; **13** Hans & Judy Beste/AL; **15** Pete Oxford/PEP; **18–19** Richard Packwood/OSF; **21** Animals Animals/Margot Conte/OSF; **23** P. Morris/AL; **24–25** Animals Animals/Zig Leszczynski/OSF; **27** Dave Watts; **28–29** Michael Fogden/OSF; **31** Steve Turner/OSF; **37** Aquarian Fish Foods; **39** Daniel J. Cox/OSF; **41** Stan Osolinski/OSF; **44–45** R. Van Nostrand/FLPA; **47** W. Pfunder/OSF; **51** Joanna van Gruisen/AL; **53** Rafi Ben-Shahar/OSF; **58–59** Survival Anglia/William Paton/OSF; **61** P. Morris; **63** Robert A. Tyrrell/OSF; **65** F.W. Lane/FLPA; **66–67** Richard Goss/Partridge Productions Ltd./OSF; **68–69** Wendy Dennis/PEP; **70–71** Eyal Bartov/OSF; **73** Phil Savoie/BBC; **75** Jean-Paul Ferrero/AL; **76–77** Tui de Roy/OSF; **78–79** Mike Hill/OSF; **80–81** M. Gore/FLPA; **83** F.W. Lane/FLPA; **84–85** Daniel J. Cox/OSF; **86–87** Nick Gordon/OSF; **89** Daniel Heuclin/NHPA; **91** Robin Bush/OSF; **93** Tom Ulrich/OSF; **95** Carlos Sanchez/OSF.

Artists

Graham Allen, Norman Arlott, Priscilla Barrett, Trevor Boyer, Ad Cameron, David Dennis, Karen Hiscock, Chloe Talbot Kelly, Mick Loates, Michael Long, Malcolm McGregor, Denys Ovenden, Oxford Illustrators, John Sibbick, Joseph Tomelleri, Dick Twinney, Ian Willis

While every effort has been made to trace the copyright holders of illustrations reproduced in this book, the publishers will be pleased to rectify any omissions or inaccuracies.